March

To Julie —
welcome to, and
best wishes in, the
wonderful world of
Adolescent Psychiatry!

Dick Marohn

JUVENILE DELINQUENTS: PSYCHODYNAMIC ASSESSMENT AND HOSPITAL TREATMENT

Juvenile Delinquents: Psychodynamic Assessment and Hospital Treatment

by

RICHARD C. MAROHN, M.D.

Director, Adolescent Program
Illinois State Psychiatric Institute
Attending Psychiatrist
Psychosomatic and Psychiatric Institute
Michael Reese Hospital
Associate Professor, Department of Psychiatry
Abraham Lincoln School of Medicine
University of Illinois

DIANE DALLE-MOLLE, M.S.C., R.N., M.S.

Formerly Milieu Supervisor
Delinquent Adolescent Unit
Illinois State Psychiatric Institute

ELAINE McCARTER, O.T.R.

Supervisor, Activity Therapy Services
Delinquent Adolescent Unit
Illinois State Psychiatric Institute

and

DORIS LINN, M.A., A.C.S.W.

Supervisor, Social Service
Delinquent Adolescent Unit
Illinois State Psychiatric Institute

BRUNNER/MAZEL, *Publishers* • New York

Library of Congress Cataloging in Publication Data

Main entry under title:
Juvenile delinquents.

   Bibliography: p.
Includes index.

   1. Juvenile delinquency. 2. Adolescent psychiatry. 3. Psychiatric hospital care. I. Marohn, Richard C. [DNLM: 1. Juvenile delinquency—Psychology. 2. Juvenile delinquency—Rehabilitation. 3. Hospitalization. WS463 J97]
RJ506.J88J88   616.89'022   80-18398
ISBN 0-87630-239-8

Published by
BRUNNER/MAZEL, INC.
19 Union Square
New York, New York 10003

To the patients and staff of the Juvenile Delinquency Research and Treatment Unit at the Illinois State Psychiatric Institute, 1969-1979.

People are freaking me out. I feel like my head is spinning around and around very fast. I am going to fall. I hope someone will talk to me, anyone at all. . . . As I sit I feel like no one even knows I am alive. . . . I was thinking how much I like you. I miss sitting down and talking to you. . . . I feel sad right now like I am the only one up here. I want to talk to someone. . . . I think of what you will say to me if I show you this or not. . . . If I get busted I don't know what I will do. You may have a difficult time reading this but that's tuf shit.

Barry's Marijuana Journal for his therapist, 1972

It's about time, it's about space.
It's about leaving this place.
It's about time, it's about space
I should have hit you in the face.

Theresa, 1973

There's more of my behavior than there is me.

Ursula, 1976

Foreword

Adolescents have always perplexed their elders, whether due to jealousy ("Too bad youth is wasted on the young") or to deep suspicions and concerns ("Twenty years ago young people knew their place —they treated their elders with respect"). It is surprising, therefore, to note that most young people grow up relatively unscathed. If anything, the problem is that they turn out to be very much like their parents and hence perpetuate whatever their human frailty is for many, many generations, without an end in sight.

The normal adolescent does have his growing pains, but he can sail through his teenage years to the surprise of many, including himself. Later looking back on his high school years, he finds that they were full of pleasure and excitement.

The disturbed adolescent and his family obviously have a different problem. Not only is the teenager disturbed and in need of treatment, but he also belongs to that age group that until recently has been left unattended. In our society we have had good therapeutic programs for adults and children for over a century. These therapeutic programs were not necessarily curative, but they encompassed the best that was available in any particular generation. It has only been for the past 25 years that these programs also paid special attention to adolescents (ages 13-18).

Our psychiatric experience with disturbed adolescents (be they schizophrenic, depressed or delinquent, to use only a few examples) is minimal. The mental health profession, in general, and the psychiatric profession, in particular, have had difficulty in correctly diagnosing disturbed adolescents. Research in adolescent development (normal as well as deviant) has been scant. We are, for example, still awaiting the first comprehensive study of adolescent females. Most of the literature on adolescence is filled with statements about teenagers which are based solely on few case studies. The psychiatric assessment of treatment, its process and its outcome, is rare indeed. Usually, the reader has to take the author's word on what actually went on in the treatment situation.

Dr. Marohn, Ms. Dalle-Molle, Ms. McCarter and Ms. Linn have presented us with much-needed data. They have had the stamina required to work with seriously disturbed adolescents. Their work has been integrated with a carefully documented empirical study of these same adolescents at the Illinois State Psychiatric Institute. The latter study has served as a foundation for diagnostic assessment, careful study of behavior and the overall success (or failure) of the treatment process. Rather than writing on the treatment for all acting-out adolescents or all seriously disturbed teenagers, they explicitly define and limit their population, so that the reader can place the treatment approach in perspective.

The authors clearly state their treatment philosophy: "Virtually any adolescent, regardless of socioeconomic status or race, is capable of participating in meaningful insight oriented psychotherapy." Some mental health professionals may want to argue with the authors, believing that the authors have overstated their case. However, in my opinion, this clear statement makes it easier to critically evaluate the findings presented in this volume. The strength of this book stems from just this kind of open approach to their own psychiatric "Weltanschauung." Throughout the monograph, the reader is presented time and again with a careful analysis of a situational problem, its psychological antecedents and how it was handled by the staff. Results of an intervention are also often presented. The reader can, then, think of alternative ways of solving a problem; at the same time he is helped to learn how disturbed adolescents can be helped psychotherapeutically.

Further he might not be as scared of the raw aggression which disturbed adolescents cary within them.

We have now entered a new decade. There is much criticism of the mental health field. Our psychological treatment approaches are often described as outdated, outmoded and even worthless. This book clearly demonstrates that, in order to help seriously disturbed individuals (in this case adolescents), we need time, patience and skill. The authors had all three. They are to be congratulated on having shared with us these most remarkable experiences. The book should interest all those who are trying to help the seriously disturbed adolescent.

DANIEL OFFER, M.D.
Chairman, Department of Psychiatry,
Michael Reese Hospital and Medical Center.
Professor of Psychiatry, University of
Chicago.

Chicago, Illinois
June, 1980

Contents

Introduction

At age seven, Nancy began to steal. She was a disciplinary problem in school, defied teachers and fought with students. She challenged her mother's efforts to discipline her with threats of violence aimed at both her mother and sister. Nancy's delinquent acts accelerated and her behavior became more disturbing until at age 10 she was hospitalized for threatening to kill her mother. This hospitalization marked the first in a series of various placements, each initiated or terminated because of runaways, suicidal gestures, explosive episodes, or violent attacks. On admission to our delinquency treatment and research unit, Nancy was a volatile, emotionally labile 13-year-old who was quick to react with rage and anger. Her controls were tenuous. She was argumentative, verbally abusive, impulsive and would have what seemed to be unprecipitated fits of temper and crying spells. While not diagnosed as psychotic, she often appeared uncomprehending and would, during a violent episode, seem overwhelmed by an opposing environment she could neither understand nor control. She showed virtually no remorse about her aggressive acts, did not seem beset by conflict, and resisted change, stating that she liked the way she was. It was during Nancy's first therapy session that she stated she felt she was being treated like "a piece of paper." Only later did the significance of this statement become apparent. To be a piece of paper is to be less than human, two-dimensional, empty and worthless—to be shuffled around, manipulated, used, abused, and discarded at whim. Her verbalizations, while reactive rather than insightful, far from camouflaged her feelings, but to the sensitive listener, revealed concisely the reasons for her rage.

Nancy is not typical, as no individual can be regarded as typical, but what she shares with an increasing number of adolescents is the externalization through delinquent behavior of stress, turmoil, and inner chaos. That Nancy's problems may differ in severity from the problems of other delinquents is relatively unimportant. That when she is troubled, she acts, thoughtlessly, and in ways not sanctioned by society, *is* significant and links her to the countless other adolescents called delinquents.

Delinquency is age-specific. Adolescents who run away, are truant, vandalize, abuse alcohol and drugs, steal, or engage in disruptive or violent acts are regarded as delinquent. These same adolescents, if ignored or left untreated, may shed the delinquent label as they become adults and be viewed instead as criminals, drunks, undesirables, misfits, or psychotics. At best they may drift out of sight but lead lives of personal impoverishment. Statistics underscore the seriousness of the problem.

In 1974, there were over 6,100,000 arrests in the United States for serious crimes such as criminal homicide, forcible rape, robbery, aggravated assault, and arson; of these, 1,700,000, or just over 27% were committed by persons under 18 years of age (Mann, 1976). Juveniles commit 10% of all the murders, 19% of all the forcible rapes, 32% of all the robberies, 17% of all the aggravated assaults, and 58% of all the arsons. When burglary, larceny, and motor vehicle thefts are added to this list, more than half of all the serious crimes in the United States are found to be committed by youths from 10 to 17 years of age (*Time*, 1977).

An exhaustive survey of youth in Illinois, conducted by the Institute for Juvenile Research in 1972, demonstrated that from 25% to 94% of Illinois Youth (varying with gender, race, age, socioeconomic status, and community size) were involved in violent acts (Schwartz and Puntil, 1972).

Parents, teachers, and others who live and work with teenagers know that when teenagers are troubled, they act. These acts, however random or meaningless they might appear, are repetitions of things past, and the promise of things to come.

What goes wrong with these children? Why do they become delinquent? No singular phenomenon can sufficiently explain the reasons an individual acts in a particular way. Genetic endowment, the social, educational, and economic milieu into which the child is born, the historical and cultural context into which the child is placed, the mother-child relationship, relationships with peers, social upheavals— these forces and more, intricately interwoven, influence and direct the course of development. Simple and definitive answers to complex questions are inevitably short-sighted, but one must establish a way of thinking about the multiple forces that eventually come together to form a pattern. To think about a child psychodynamically is to unravel the thread that binds and gives shape to the pattern. A psychodynamic approach to the understanding of delinquency is a delicate and difficult process, but it means that it is the individual who incorporates, rejects, interprets, and embodies the innumerable forces that exist in himself and the world. A psychological understanding of him can make sense of the whole and guide the hand of teachers, parents, psychiatrists, or child care workers who try to reshape his troubled life.

Adolescence is a developmental stage marked by great vulnerability, a transitional stage, during which the youngster reworks psychologically earlier childhood conflicts, separates from the omnipotent parental figures of his past, and engages in sexual experimentation, and from which he emerges when successful, capable of assuming the adult role economically, socially, and personally.

If the adult role lacks definition or is shrouded by the ambiguities of change, then the assumption of that role becomes problematic. If, in addition, the economic state is such that opportunities for employment and full participation in the economic system are limited or doubtful, then the problem of becoming adult is compounded. Both such conditions exist from time to time. Many of the adolescents we see regard their futures pessimistically and cannot anticipate a future role in society. In the psychodynamic present, these same adolescents cannot find themselves in relation to time, space, or other individuals.

While changing attitudes, adult roles, and economic conditions are bound to affect this already tumultuous developmental stage, can these forces be isolated as causing delinquency? Some adolescents, after all, do manage to grow into autonomous, well-functioning adults. Are these just the fortunate ones whose social and economic privileges have allowed them to escape society's ills and upheavals? Middle-class delinquency does exist, although differential ways of acknowledging, cataloging, and treating the offenders may disguise its presence and apparent increase. In the Offer (1969, 1975) study of modal teenage boys, chosen for their satisfactory adjustment and their being viewed by themselves and others as "average," 25% of the subjects, from white, middle-class suburbs, were involved in significant delinquency.

Delinquency can and does occur in all social classes, urban and suburban, in small and large communities. It is not inextricably tied to race or sex. Society's injustices and cultural trends affect each individual, and in some may act as the catalyzing agent that triggers the overt misbehavior of delinquency or other personal problems. But what happens to the adolescent that provides a key to understanding delinquency?

Adolescents separate from and deidealize parents, and invest in friends and the pervasive peer culture, which may include gangs, alcohol and drugs, sexual experimentation, TV violence, and rock stars. In this deluge of stimuli surface innumerable reasons for delinquency. Invariably, advocates point to too much of this or too little of that. TV violence causes delinquency. The availability of hand guns causes delinquency. Sexual permissiveness or moral degeneracy causes delinquency. Theories abound and with them come proposed solutions to the problem of delinquency. Legislative change, more often dictated by the condition of the treasury than by ideology, and diffuse recommendations with regard to "planning and training" proliferate. Occasionally someone suggests that psychological attitudes and ways of dealing with delinquents are at fault, but too often these notions are reduced to a formula as simplistic as labeling: if you don't call children troublemakers, they won't make trouble.

In a complex society such as ours, there are indeed many ugly and destructive elements which need to be corrected, and the adolescent is bombarded by overwhelming stimuli daily. Even the healthiest adolescent has difficulty sorting out, assimilating, and making sense of his environment. The adolescents we treat find their environment to be overwhelming and confusing because they experience an equally real, devastating inner chaos. Confronting a particularly weakened psychic structure, any stimulus of sufficient intensity can trigger disturbing or delinquent behavior. To stop or censor TV violence, for example, might remove a specific stimulus and perhaps eliminate certain delinquent behavior. Without psychological restructuring, however, the delinquency-prone adolescent will misbehave again, propelled by a different impetus.

On the threshold of adolescence, the internal psychological world of a child has already been formed. Its unique shape, be it characterized by disorganization, rigidity, or strength, has in turn been molded by dynamic and interacting forces. In some children, severe psychological disorganization has already taken its toll in diagnosable childhood psychopathology. In others, however, loosely bound psychological structures begin to fall apart at the seams during the onslaught of adolescence. Some adolescents flounder, lose perspective and proper orientation, and begin to act up. This behavior, however, is psychologically motivated and can and should be understood psychodynamically.

If one accepts this premise, then new problems arise, for it follows that delinquency will be alleviated only as a consequence of internal psychological change and character restructuring. This statement and its implications spur resistances in all of us. How much easier it would be if delinquency could be reduced to simple cause and effect. If poverty is the villain, clear out the slums. If it is TV violence, censor television. If it is judicial leniency, incarcerate delinquents for definitive sentences. Indeed, the attractiveness of many of these hypotheses, without discarding the truth in each of them, is that they allow one to circumvent frustration, complexity, and introspection by paving the way for concrete, specific, and immediate action. But the problem is not a simple one, nor is there a ready or easy solution.

In order to understand the delinquent psychodynamically, we must look inside the individual and attempt to discover the psychological motivations that underlie behavior. We must also, however, be willing to look inside ourselves, because countertransference, frustrations, and resistances may appear in many disguises and hamper our search. The process of understanding the adolescent is in itself dynamic. But the knowledge gained can illuminate and make sense of complicated phenomena and inform and direct those who care for and treat the emotionally disturbed teenager.

Our treatment goal at the Illinois State Psychiatric Institute is to achieve internal psychological change and character restructuring. This takes time and is costly. But the cost of long-term treatment intervention is minimal compared to the future costs in tax dollars and human suffering if these teenagers are left unaided, or incarcerated, or supported on welfare. Most costly is the emergence in adulthood of a crippled, limited, deficient, and disturbed adult, perhaps criminal, perhaps not, but nonetheless damaged.

Our research orientation helps us to maintain an atmosphere of continuous self-criticism and self-reflection while, at the same time, it pushes us to conceptualize the fate and proper treatment of delinquents.

We have demonstrated that some adolescents act out when they are overstimulated, not necessarily by angry or hostile feelings, but conversely by strong affectionate longings and emotions. We have discovered that contagion or riot in a group has many causes and results from the participation of many systems, including the psychological and intrapsychic. We have learned through bitter experience that violence can escalate from verbal threats, to damage to property, to personal assault. We have also learned that we can predict the likelihood of violent behavior from psychological test data. Moreover, our research has helped us to identify four psychologically meaningful subtypes of delinquents: the impulsive delinquent, the narcissistic delinquent, the depressed borderline, and the empty borderline (Marohn et al., 1979; Offer et al., 1979).

This book chronicles the work of four professionals from different mental health disciplines: psychiatry, nursing, occupational therapy, and social service. We initiated a program together, worked, struggled, fought, and learned. We discovered that behaviorally disordered teenagers could be understood and helped and that our various points of view could be integrated into a cohesive milieu. Our laboratory was a hospital. The advantage of this setting is that we could, more or less, control the environment. In so doing, the forces that impinge upon the adolescent and drain his already depleted psychological resources can be minimized. Treatment, an integration of individual psychotherapy and milieu therapy, can then proceed.

This book focuses independently upon what we believe to be the critical issues for the adolescent, namely his* relation to time, space, and things, and his experience with psychotherapy. This design is for the purpose of clarity, however, for no such differentiated experience exists. We hope to show, rather, how a thoughtfully designed, well-structured environment can facilitate individual psychotherapy. It is the very interdependence of milieu and psychotherapy that is crucial, for if an adolescent is able to understand and manage the very real demands of daily living, he is in turn freer to engage in a therapeutic alliance. Ultimately, the success of treatment depends on the establishment of an interpersonal relationship in which the adolescent can rework conflicts that beset him, learn, grow, and heal, and from which he can eventually separate.

We will return, in the last chapter of the book, to take an in-depth look at Nancy. We hope to reveal, through the unfolding of her story, that adolescent behavioral problems are complex but understandable. We hope, as well, to demonstrate how we work with a disturbed teenager. Nancy's is not a success story, and at the time of discharge from the hospital, she showed persisting limitations and deficits. However, her story is significant and, while we can offer no magical solutions, we are convinced that a psychodynamic approach to the understanding and treatment of adolescent delinquents can and does make a difference.

What we say here about the hospitalized adolescent is equally true of the adolescent at home, in school, on the streets, or in detention centers, whose behavior is unacceptable, disturbed, and disturbing. That treatment is denied or not made available to many of them is regrettable. For the delinquent is not "wicked." Paradoxically, his excess activity reveals both his despair and his hope. We know that the delinquent is still searching, has not given up hope, and may indeed, if permitted, include one of us in his search.

---

* The pronouns "he," "his," and "himself" are used to refer to the individual adolescent, whether male or female, throughout this volume for convenience and readability.

Acknowledgments

We wish to acknowledge the encouragement and support of many of our friends and colleagues.

The Illinois Department of Mental Health provided very tangible support, and continues to do so, by staffing our treatment unit, and providing for us a degree of freedom and flexibility to pursue our goals. Specifically, Lester Rudy, M.D., the Director of the Illinois State Psychiatric Institute (ISPI) at the inception of this project, and Jack Weinberg, M.D., at that time Clinical Director and now the Director of ISPI, made suggestions about staffing the unit, encouraged our work, and annually allocated the funds and personnel for the unit. Roy R. Grinker, Sr., M.D., and Daniel Offer, M.D. encouraged the establishment of this unit. Dr. Offer continues to collaborate with us as both a researcher and a consultant.

The llinois Law Enforcement Commission provided partial support for the research work that paralleled our treatment efforts, and the Judith Baskin Offer Fund supported in part the final revisions and rewritings of the manuscript.

Several people assisted in writing this volume. Herbert Weinstein wrote much of the chapter on time and collaborated with us in preparing the initial draft. Lita Simpson Sabonis assisted in preparing the case report of the last chapter. Sally Phelps McCaughan provided invaluable editorial assistance, suggestions, and rewriting throughout the text, and Judith Kahn Marohn and Mary E. Doheny, Ph.D. reviewed the manuscript several times and offered helpful suggestions.

We appreciate the fact that Jaime Trujillo-Gomez, M.D. and his staff continue to develop and refine this program and its policies. We trust that this unique unit will continue to thrive.

We acknowledge, with great indebtedness, the conscientiousness, dedication, talent, and hard work of Jean Melton, Secretary to the Program Director, without whom this book and many other enterprises would never be possible.

RICHARD C. MAROHN
DIANE DALLE-MOLLE
ELAINE MCCARTER
DORIS LINN

Chicago
June, 1980

JUVENILE DELINQUENTS: PSYCHODYNAMIC ASSESSMENT AND HOSPITAL TREATMENT

1

Adolescence and Behavior

Adolescence is a unique maturational and developmental phase of life. For a long time, many believed that adolescence was simply a recapitulation of childhood, a psychological reworking of earlier childhood conflicts and solutions. That this resurgence occurs is true, but adolescence is more than this. Adolescence presents phase specific problems and challenges, as well as the maturation of phase specific strengths and skills. To understand adolescent behavior more completely, we must look at developmental lines, the assessment of normality in adolescence, and delinquency as a symptom of pathology.

DEVELOPMENTAL LINES IN ADOLESCENCE

We can describe adolescence from the points of view of psychosexual development, ego development and defenses, separation/individuation, narcissism and the self, identity formation, and cognitive development.

In "Three Essays on the Theory of Sexuality," Freud (1905) characterized adolescence as a phase distinguished by the genitalization of the libidinal drives. By this he meant that all earlier infantile sexuality with various aims and objects becomes organized under the primacy of a heterosexual, genital experience. Freud indicated that, as a result of this genitalization, adolescents needed to separate from their parents. Prior to adolescence, because of the incest barrier, earlier oedipal fantasies had simply been repressed. Now, because the

3

adolescent has the genital apparatus to do something about his sexual wishes, he can no longer experience them, even unconsciously, toward the parent of the opposite sex. These sexual drives are displaced onto peers of the opposite sex, and psychological separation results. Freud maintained that this was simply a reworking of earlier preoedipal and oedipal issues.

Anna Freud (1946, 1958) described adolescence as a phase of significant ego development, distinguished by explorations and trials with various new psychological defenses and ways of adapting and coping. She expanded on her father's concepts of genitalization and incest barrier leading to psychological separation, and described six ways in which teenagers achieve psychological separation from their parents. Such psychological separation does not require physical separation but means that the adolescent experiences his parents not as the omnipotent, perfect, and all-knowing parents of childhood, but rather as people who have a special place in one's life, but may have failings and weaknesses. They are neither overidealized nor over-depreciated.

Some adolescents displace their intense affectionate feelings for the parent onto others; often this may be the first "crush" of adolescence, frequently an attachment to an older adult of the opposite sex, a teacher, a rock star, a movie star, a therapist, or a neighbor. This displacement indicates that the adolescent is attempting to achieve psychological separation. Eventually, these attachments are experienced with teenagers of the opposite sex. Initially, they are fleeting, but intense, so that a boy or girl may be going steady and planning marriage one week, and may be infatuated with someone else the next.

Another common way a teenager deals with intense affectionate feelings is by reversing them into the opposite feelings; consequently, teenagers are frequently angry, hostile, belligerent, stubborn, and rebellious. Every teenager does a bit of this, but the teenager who uses this mechanism extensively finds himself in considerable difficulty because, in essence, he cannot relate to anyone. As soon as the adolescent experiences affectionate feelings, he needs to convert them into something hostile. Usually the teenager is not satisfied with this transformation and feels guilty and depressed about hating the very people he cares about. Some teenagers deal with their wishes to cling to their parents in a paranoid manner, by accusing parents and other authority figures of attempting to dominate and control their lives. Others regress to a more infantile level of development; ascetics permit themselves no pleasurable gratifications at all; others seek absolute self-perfection. For example, a boy may deprive himself of a favorite food or TV show whenever he experiences a sexual thought or wish. Because such a personality structure is too limited and brittle to face the unpredictable challenges of adolescent and adult living, this adolescent is equivalently psychotic or pre-psychotic and requires intense psychiatric attention.

Anna Freud developed a classification of adolescent psychology based on this separation process and the defenses utilized. She stresses that the healthy adolescent uses a variety of defenses and experiments a good deal; he may rebel one day and regress the next. The sicker adolescent has one mechanism in his repertoire; he can only rebel, or regress, or whatever. In the process of separating from his parents, the adolescent deprives himself of their psychological support; no matter how helpful parents want to be, the adolescent cannot accept some of their support because it is too much like being a "baby." Furthermore, giving up the parents of childhood involves some mourning and grief. Consequently, even normal adolescents are frequently depressed.

Anna Freud held that the hallmark of health in adolescence is not only the variety of psychological maneuvers the teenager uses, but also the gradual, rather than precipitous, manner in which separation is achieved. This differs somewhat from the findings of Daniel and Judith Offer (1975) who demonstrated that modal teenagers who cope well may achieve separation in surges and even in progressive and regressive swings rather than in a consistently progressive manner.

What is part of a healthy adolescent's separation repertoire may, in another adolescent, be exaggerated and lead to delinquency. For example, a healthy girl may argue openly and vehemently with her mother about clothing, curfews, or choice of friends, but she maintains a basic attachment and sees herself as part of the family. However, another girl runs away from home because she is unable to deal consciously with the inner forces that are propelling her to separate. She is torn between intense wishes to cling to her mother and pressure to break off an infantile attachment. Such tension is discharged in running away and expressed concretely in physical separation. It is amazing to hear certain runaways talk very positively about their parents, oblivious to their wishes to separate, while other runaways talk bitterly about their mother's attempts to infantilize them, projecting externally their own longings to cling to the omnipotent parent.

Peter Blos (1967) has described adolescence as a second separation/individuation phase in which the adolescent builds on the earlier process of separating and individuating from a symbiotic tie to his mother. He sees much of the psychopathology of adolescence resulting from difficulties in resolving these issues. For example, promiscuous sexual behavior or premature curtailment of sexual experimentation is indicative of an inadequate resolution. The promiscuous adolescent may be attempting to defend desperately against feelings of loss while the adolescent who rushes into marriage may be attempting to replace the infantile ties to a parent with a strong dependent attachment to a spouse. In either case, difficulties will arise. The failure to resolve crucial separation issues is evident in many young adults who drift, failing to make career choices or personal commitments. This is what Blos calls prolonged adolescence (1962). Such a young adult fails to assume personal, financial, or vocational responsibility and functions virtually like an eternal teenager.

Masterson and Rinsley (1975) have examined crucial difficulties in the child's early attempts to navigate the rapprochement subphase of separation/individuation, resulting in borderline pathology in adolescence. Mahler (1975) has described the process of moving away from mother and returning to touch home base, so crucial to the toddler's successful separation. In Masterson's view (1972), the borderline feels good when connected to and part of a symbiotic relationship with a mothering figure, but empty and devastated when separated; his disturbed behavior expresses his pain but fills the void left by the separation. Rinsley (1971) explores the difficulties in working with the borderline adolescent and notes a tremendous resistance to separating from the original symbiosis and propensity for testing behavior as he struggles to engage in treatment.

Kohut (1971) describes the changes that occur in the maturation of narcissism or self-love. The narcissistic line of development traces the movement from a primitive narcissism of the grandiose self and the idealized parental imago to secondary or mature transformations of narcissism such as slf-esteem, enthusiasm, ambition, respect and admiration for others, ideals, and goals. Adolescence, as a developmental stage, represents a significant way station in the course of such transformations, wherein adolescents test out their grandiosity and ambitions against the demands and constraints of reality. At the same time they deidealize those previously omnipotent parents and idealize other adult figures, heroes, ideas, or movements, gradually modifying their overly idealistic view of the world into an outlook that cherishes certain values and respects certain people. Wolf, Gedo, and Terman (1972) emphasized that "a change in the self emerges as the pivotal focus during adolescent development." They describe deidealization of archaic parental imagos and the acquisition of new idealizations as being facilitated by group membership. This deidealization process is usually quiescent, but for some, the struggle is considerably more tumultuous, and disillusionment may lead to significant rebellion, criminal activity, gang behavior, drug abuse, runaway, or premature heterosexual commitment. Some search for the perfect and omnipotent parent in the intense infatuation of a love affair. When the internal idealized parent is externalized to the outside world, a youth shows a fanaticism to achieve a perfect world—when society is found to be imperfect, he experiences disillusionment, rage, or irrational violence (Blos, 1972).

It is the excitement and the enthusiasm of adolescence that tell us that love of self is resurgent, only too soon to wane. The unmodified grandiosity of the teenager—who deceives and steals from his parents, who looks upon others with disdain and contempt, who boasts of his aggressive and sexual prowess, and who strives to defeat authority and flaunts his violation of rules—derives from the adolescent's failure to modify primitive narcissistic structures. All adolescents struggle with resurgent grandiosity. Kohut (1978) suggests that the major task of adolescence in the narcissistic line of development is "reforming the self" which "may evoke in us, temporarily, old fragmentation fear until a new self is again firmly established" (p. 662).

Closely related to adolescent shifts in self-esteem regulation and idealization is the transformation of the self. Early on, the infant experiences himself and the outside world, particularly his mother, as fragments, without cohesion or constancy. He gradually becomes one with mother, and a cohesion, a union, or symbiosis develops. Eventually, the child experiences himself as separate and distinct from mother, yet he turns to self-objects, people who are parts of him, yet separate, in order to maintain self-esteem or cohesion, and to ward off fragmentation. Self-cohesion is threatened in adolescence as the individual moves away from the stable supports of childhood, particularly the relationship with parents and parental values, and tries to develop his own internal supports as well as new relationships.

What Blos has called "pseudoheterosexuality," heterosexual behavior to achieve individuation from mother (1967), may also serve to prevent fragmentation, insofar as sexual stimulation provides the adolescent with a sense of self and cohesion. Similarly, the grandiosity of many delinquents is an attempt to cling to those relatively stable structures of a cohesive self and defend against fragmentation. Such grandiosity may represent a relatively stable primitive and archaic self, despite temporary states of fragmentation and constant struggle against fusion and merger with others.

Some grandiosity is not experienced consciously, but rather as a nagging sense of failure and low self-esteem, as the child's performance in reality fails to live up to his repressed grandiose perfect self; this accounts for many adolescent depressions. Slavson (1965) has described a "doom motif" in which delinquents characterize their futures very pessimistically. While some attribute this hopelessness to unfortunate experiences with school and authorities, Slavson believes that this is due to an internalization of a punitive parental superego with chronic and severe self-condemnation. Many delinquents are chronically depressed and act up in order to relieve themselves of such feelings of depression. Some are burdened by a "doom motif," but others find that their performances never live up to their repressed grandiose fantasies of greatness and perfection, and life is experienced as one chronic failure after another. Other delinquents are pessimistic about their futures because they are aware of their inability to control their behavior and to predict from one moment to the next what they may do (Marohn, Offer, and Ostrov, 1971).

Erikson (1950, 1959) has attempted to correlate adolescent psychological development with sociocultural factors and sees adolescence as the stage of identity formation. Identity diffusion results when persons achieve no clear-cut sense of themselves or of the goals in their lives. This is similar, but not identical, to Blos' "prolonged adolescence" (1962) or the lack of identity integration that Kernberg (1975) describes in the psychotic and the borderline. Many adolescents develop negative or counter-identities to distinguish themselves from others, particularly their parents, and do so in a negativistic way through rebellion or antisocial behavior. Adolescents who attempt to separate this way never really free themselves, because they are constantly plagued by an attachment to parents, parental values, and childhood against which they must constantly and vigilantly defend themselves.

Piaget (1969) has described significant adolescent cognitive transformations, specifically a capacity for abstract and formal thinking. Much therapeutic work with the adolescent can be a verbal psychotherapy, something that is not always possible in working with children. Again, the adolescent is in the "in between" phase. Although he can talk about feelings and ideas, he is also action prone and may prefer to express inner tensions through deviant behavior, rather than to speak about them. Some adolescents apparently do not achieve formal thinking (Dulit, 1972), and may have difficulty understanding the language of some therapists.

To recapitulate, adolescence as a developmental and maturational phase may be described from various vantage points: psychosexual development, ego development, defensive operations, separation and individuation, narcissism and the self, identity formation, and cognitive development. From an understanding of these schemata, our understanding of both normal adolescent adjustment and adolescent psychopathology flows. Delinquency, too, has its roots in these formulations.

NORMALITY IN ADOLESCENCE

Anna Freud (1958) held that adolescence is a time of tumultuous behavior, reflecting internal psychological reorganizations. She went so far as to suggest that the adolescent who does not experience mood swings or periods of turmoil might be quite abnormal. "Adolescence is by its nature an interruption of peaceful growth . . . the upholding of a steady equilibrium during the adolescent process is in itself abnormal." The "good" child who shows no "outer evidence of inner unrest" is experiencing a "delay of normal development." For example, a well functioning 14-year-old girl described her thirteenth year as "terrible," noting that she was always unhappy and always confused, and was glad that the year was over, even though her school work and her relationships with her peers and parents never really suffered. According to Anna Freud, such unrest is expectable. The Offers (1969, 1975) have shown that although some normal adolescents do experience turmoil, others mature quietly and without disruption.

Some adults, on the other hand, dismiss too quickly the turmoil of the adolescent as a "phase" that he will "outgrow" unscathed. Masterson (1967) noted that many adolescents evaluated at a treatment center were not provided therapy because they seemed to be experiencing "adjustment reactions." Later on, they demonstrated significant and disabling pathology, often of a delinquent nature. Thus, there is a danger in dismissing turmoil as an expectable phase of adolescence because many adolescents in turmoil need and would benefit from therapeutic intervention.

Consequently, assessing the adolescent and his behavior is a most difficult task. Most teenagers do not exhibit their psychiatric problems in flagrant psychoses or in serious depressions or suicide attempts. In fact, of the adolescents in psychiatric hospitals, only about 25% are psychotic. Most adolescents referred for treatment exhibit behavior disorders; that is, behavior which gets them into trouble with the law, authorities, school, or parents. Delinquent, deviant, disturbed, and disruptive behaviors are the final common pathways for most adolescent psychopathology. The sick adolescent is usually not depressed and immobilized or delusional and hallucinating, but tends, instead, to externalize his difficulties onto the environment and onto other people. To minimize these difficulties as "phases," to moralize over corrupt youth, or to debate the kinds of laws or police work needed to cope with burgeoning youth crime is to miss the point. Beneath the delinquency is an adolescent in pain, whose very activity is an attempt to heal the self and to establish contact with a potentially helpful person.

UNDERSTANDING ADOLESCENT BEHAVIOR
DISORDERS PSYCHODYNAMICALLY

Freud (1905) found that certain character disorders and perversions are the reverse of the psychoneuroses; that is, the psychological conflict, instead of being felt internally or resulting in neurotic symptoms, is externalized via an alloplastic solution. The problem becomes not one of internal pain or disabling symptoms, but rather a conflict with the outside world. The person attempts to change his environment or a relationship, or discharge internal tension through behavior, often delinquent or criminal in nature. His term "acting out" refers to a similar process in treatment whereby the patient, instead of experiencing a neurotic conflict with the psychoanalyst, talking about it in the context of the treatment, and remembering its roots and origins in the patient's childhood experiences and conflicts, behaves outside the analytic treatment situation in such a way as to prevent himself from remembering the original trauma and experiencing the concomitant pain. Today, many people use the term "acting out" indiscriminantly and not with this precise definition of "behaving instead of remembering." However, their use of the term does suggest that certain people seek to eliminate internal psychological conflict by externalizing it onto the outside world.

August Aichhorn (1925, 1964) was greatly impressed with Freud's teachings and applied them to his work with Viennese delinquents. He viewed deviant behavior as expressions of wishes for gratification and trained his staff to gratify these wishes. Such gratification would result in a neurotic conflict between a wish and a prohibition against the wish. The therapist would then be used by the adolescent for the gratification of other infantile wishes, and a classical clinical transference would be established. The delinquent would reenact with the therapist the wishes, conflicts, fears, and prohibitions from early childhood. These would be analyzed and understood, and the symptomatic delinquent behavior would disappear. Aichhorn noted, however, that with a certain kind of delinquent, no therapeutic relationship could be easily established. If by chance a relationship was established, it seemed that the delinquent did not experience the therapist as a separate person, but rather as part of himself. A narcissistic transference had been established. Many times the patient viewed the therapist as an idealized part of himself, ascribing to the therapist certain ideal qualities that he fantasied he had or would achieve one day. Aichhorn realized that it was necessary to try to work with this kind of delinquent by quickly establishing a narcissistic transference bond. His work with the "juvenile imposter" foreshadows some of Kohut's later contributions and some of our own work in dealing with disturbed delinquents and their narcissistic transferences (Marohn, 1977).

Franz Alexander (1931), like Freud, observed that certain criminals acted out of a sense of guilt. Often they experienced neurotic guilt because of internal wishes, desires, or fantasies which they felt were wrong and prohibited. Their criminal behavior was an attempt to behave in such a way that the external world would punish them and set their conscience at ease. An example well known to the police is of the person who confesses to crimes he has not committed. In therapy it is necessary to uncover the psychological crime for which the person feels guilty and attempt to resolve the neurotic conflict. One of our male patients, from an inner city gang, had been impotent even though he bragged about his sexual exploits. Stealing cars was a way of reassuring himself of his masculinity, but he would invariably be caught in the "act" by driving at night without headlights, driving the wrong way down a one-way street, or parking the car in front of the owner's house and repeatedly returning to use it. Therapy was directed at helping this boy come to grips with his own sexual prohibitions.

Building on Freud's formulation about character disorders, Kate Friedlander (1960) postulated that delinquent character disorders needed to be converted into neurotics by blocking the avenues for "acting out" discharge. This creates an internalized psychological conflict which can then be worked with therapeutically. While Aichhorn emphasized creating conflict by gratifying the infantile wish, Friedlander attempted to reverse the process by reinternalizing an externalized internal conflict, or in other words, by converting motor behavior to internal affect, thought, or fantasy.

Similarly, Anna Freud (1956) viewed delinquency as a failure of the socialization process, that is, a failure of the child to internalize controls initially placed on him by parents and other authority figures. She also noted, however, that some delinquency develops because of the chance availability of delinquent peer groups onto whom adolescents may displace their investments as they are in the process of separating from childhood and parents. Our experience causes us to doubt whether delinquency ever develops by chance. The choice of peer groups is related to the adolescent's psychological stage, level of development, or need for certain kinds of relationships. Youths may belong to a gang not only because the gang exists in their neighborhood and no other groups are available to them, but also because gang membership and what the gang stands for resonate with their own values, psychological defenses, ways of coping, wishes, and fantasies. The intense loyalties of some gang members to their cohorts is an example of how membership in such a peer group can become paramount in the member's life. The very same youth who flaunts society's laws and mores with impunity will adhere scrupulously to rules and norms of the gang. Such intense fervor suggests more than simply chance membership. Beneath it may live a desperate need to belong or be completed by another.

Johnson and Szurek (1952) also focused on delinquent value systems and problems in superego development. They described delinquent children who were responding to and gratifying the unconsciously transmitted deviant urges and wishes of their seemingly upright parents. Brian Bird (1957) added to this paradigm the observation that the delinquent child, although responsive to the parental unconscious, had developed no psychological skills for coping with his own internal wishes. Such formulations for delinquent behavior are often uncovered in family therapy. For example, the father of one of our boys expounded at length on how he had always taught his son to be polite and compliant with the police because if he were a gentleman, some night when he was caught by the police after curfew, he might be excused. Furthermore, he boasted, he taught his son never to steal anything of consequence, that is, taking a car battery was all right, but stealing a car was absolutely forbidden. He noted that his son reminded him very much of his own father, perhaps pointing to a generational transmission of delinquent patterns. Another father once explained that his 14-year-old son stole a car. The father grinned proudly and said, "I didn't even know he could drive."

Glover (1950, 1960) distinguished two kinds of delinquents: the structural and the functional. The structural delinquent shows significant psychopathology, not necessarily of a delinquent nature, both before and after adolescence. As a child or adult, the patient may have psychiatric problems other than delinquent behavior, such as neurotic or somatic symptoms. In contrast, the functional delinquent experiences a temporary imbalance during the adolescent maturation process which results in delinquent behavior. Baittle and Kobrin (1964) utilized this formulation in their study of a delinquent gang and noted that the leaders of the gang were structural delinquents and occupied a place in the community power structure just below the top. This suggests that family strivings to achieve in a delinquent sociocultural milieu are manifested in fairly stable character pathology in the offspring, whereas children from other families may have been part of the gang's activity simply because of the need to work through and discharge maturational tension. The Baittle and Kobrin work is a compelling example of the integration of psychoanalytic and sociological data.

As already mentioned, Peter Blos (1966, 1967) has offered a variety of psychodynamic explanations for delinquency: the difficulties encountered in separation/individuation; the child with precocious ego development who develops exquisite sensitivity to the cues and needs of adults and learns how to maneuver and manipulate quite successfully in the interpersonal world; the delinquent's decreased use of verbal modes of communication in favor of action; and the symbolic communication through the delinquent act of an underlying wish or conflict.

This underlying symbolism may be highly personal. For example,

Bloch (1952) describes the "delinquent integration," as an exaggeration of the normal tendency to integrate an interpersonal relationship. Thus, delinquency "always involves a relationship between people, real or imaginary, and the delinquent act functions to integrate this relationship in such a way as to avoid or minimize anxiety." One of our patients snatched purses, and it was not until he raped a woman that his underlying dynamics became evident. It was not simply that his violent activity escalated without treatment; his urges to do violence to women were integrated in the less violent delinquent act of purse-snatching, a temporarily satisfactory compromise solution. In other words, snatching purses symbolized this boy's urges to do violence to women. Had he been treated earlier and this dynamic understood, the escalation to rape might have been prevented.

Fritz Redl's (1957, 1966) monumental contributions to this field have revolved around the vicissitudes of ego development and ego functioning in relation to the everyday tasks of the child. He has underlined the importance of a psychodynamic understanding of the delinquency in an attempt to engage the child therapeutically, and has constantly emphasized the importance of the school teacher and child care worker in assessing and modifying delinquent behavior. His psychological insights permeate residential treatment in this country through his writings, lectures, classes, and consultations.

Winnicott (1958, 1973) held that delinquency represents the early and primitive object hunger for the mother who was once possessed, but later lost, and whom the delinquent hopes to recapture through his behavior. Winnicott sees this solution as a sign of hope because we know that the delinquent is still searching and has not given up.

In our own work with hospitalized juvenile delinquents, we have developed a treatment program, and parallel to this, engaged in an investigative research project (Offer, Marohn, and Ostrov, 1979). From January 1969, through November 1973, 93 delinquent adolescents between the ages of 13 and 17 were screened for admission to the program. Sixty-six were accepted for admission, while 27 were rejected either because they gave evidence of organicity with conclusive evidence of brain damage, epilepsy, or gross mental retardation, or because they were overtly psychotic and, therefore, could not engage in either the research work or an intensive treatment program. Some were excluded because they were not sufficiently or significantly delinquent. Others were excluded because they did not require institutionalization, and outpatient treatment seemed to be indicated. At this time in our work, we did not set criteria for treatability; the questions we asked at screening had to do with whether or not the adolescent needed institutionalization in order to help him engage in treatment or to set limits on his disruptive behavior. Of the 66 delinquents to whom we offered hospitalization, 55 were admitted, and are the research subjects upon which a separate monograph has been based. Though our own treatment philosophy and practice are based on experience with many additional patients since 1973, we do have a considerable amount of data about these first 55, and describing them will give the reader a good picture of the kind of patient with whom we work.*

Although we try to maintain a balance of about half male and half female patients on the unit, the ratio turned out to be 55% male and 45% female. Thirty-one percent of our patients were black, 68% white, and 1% Latino. At admission, the mean and median ages were 15 years, six months and 15 years, five months, respectively. Fifty-three percent of our patients came from intact natural families, 18% from families consisting of one biological and one stepparent, 16% from one-parent families, and 13% from adoptive families. Eighty-four percent of the families were intact. Our patients came from the entire range of socioeconomic status groupings. Forty-nine percent of our subjects came from the suburbs, and 51% came from the city of Chicago. Of these latter, 54% came from community areas of the city whose delinquency rates were at least one and a half times the city norm. All of our subjects had siblings: Thirteen had one sibling, 15 had two sibs, 15 had three or four sibs, and 12 had five or more siblings. Eleven were firstborn, 22 were middleborn, four were the youngest in families, and 18 were stepchildren or foster children.

It was not necessary that an adolescent have contact with the juvenile court or with a law enforcement agency or be adjudicated as delinquent in order to fit our definition of delinquency. Our definition was

---

* For a complete description of the population sample and the research results and implications, see Offer, Marohn, and Ostrov (1979).

a more informal one, i.e., an adolescent who engaged in activities or behavior contrary to the mores and standards of society, whether these behaviors were known or unknown to authorities. Our teenagers were referred to us for evaluation and treatment because of runaway, truancy, theft, shoplifting, burglary, vandalism, arson, rape, assault, sexual promiscuity, and drug abuse. Forty-four percent of our subjects were referred by the juvenile court or by the Illinois Department of Corrections. Forty-three percent had been incarcerated or held in a detention center, the median time being three months. Twenty-five percent had been hospitalized in a psychiatric hospital, with an average length of stay of four months. Seventy-eight percent had been in treatment at one time or another and 29% were in treatment at the time of referral to our program. Fifty-seven percent were attending school and 43% were not at time of admission. Ninety-five percent of our teenagers had been arrested previously. Of those arrested, about half had been arrested five or more times and half had been arrested one to four times prior to admission to our program. According to their parents, the majority of our subjects (53%) first broke the law before they reached the age of 12, and half of those who were arrested were arrested before the age of 13.

Data collected over that five-year period can be organized around four factors or psychologically meaningful parameters of delinquent behavior. These motivations exist in some delinquents in relatively pure form, but in others appear to be part of a very complex relationship contributing to the final common pathway of delinquent behavior. For purposes of discussion and classification, we have described four formulations for adolescent delinquency: the impulsive, the narcissistic, the depressed borderline, and the empty borderline (Marohn, Offer, Ostrov, and Trujillo, 1979).

The *impulsive* delinquent shows more antisocial behavior than the others, both violent and nonviolent. He is considered quite disturbed by his therapist, socially insensitive by his teachers, and unlikeable and quick to act by most staff members. Yet, he seems to have some awareness of a need for help. His delinquency derives from a propensity for action and immediate discharge.

The *narcissistic* delinquent sees himself as well-adjusted and nondelinquent. However, parents and staff recognize his difficulties in adapting, and characterize him as resistant, cunning, manipulative, and superficial. He denies problems, only appears to engage in therapy, exaggerates his own self-worth, and in his delinquency tends to use others for his own needs, especially to help regulate self-esteem.

The *depressed borderline* delinquent shows school initiative, is liked by staff, and tries to engage with staff therapeutically. Relationships with parents lead to strongly internalized value systems, and these delinquents show a considerable amount of guilt and depression, from which delinquent behavior serves as a relief, but also an anaclitic need for objects to which they cling and for which they hunger.

The *empty borderline* delinquent is a passive, emotionally empty and depleted person who is not well-liked, is an outcast sometimes, needy and clinging at other times, and whose future seems pessimistic. These adolescents behave delinquently to prevent psychotic disintegration or fusion and to relieve themselves of internal desolation.

These factors are found in all socioeconomic groups, regardless of race, sex, or age, and add a psychodynamic perspective to understanding and working with the delinquent adolescent.

Whether or not our population is representative of American delinquents is impossible to answer. Surely, though, our teenagers are typical. When we say that the conflicts, challenges, and problems of the delinquent and his family can be understood psychodynamically regardless of race, neighborhood, or social class, we talk of our experiences with many delinquent adolescents.

Research findings help us understand the delinquent; so do the writings and work of others. But our most fruitful learning came from working together, day after day, thinking and arguing, rethinking and reformulating.

2

Framework

Our philosophy of treatment is based on many experiences with disturbed adolescents who stayed on our unit from a few days up to as long as two years. They were in constant contact with the staff and their behavior was observed, assessed, and engaged. Each adolescent's response to our interventions was, in turn, scrutinized and the knowledge gained furthered our ability to observe, assess, and plan treatment.

The first decision to be made is whether the delinquent needs to be hospitalized or can engage in some kind of outpatient individual or family treatment. William Easson (1969) presents a useful framework for making this kind of differentiation. If the adolescent has the capacity to use another relationship to sustain himself in psychotherapy, hospitalization will not be necessary. Most of the teenagers referred to us have made previous abortive attempts at therapy—family therapy, individual therapy, counseling, group experiences or whatever—and have not been able to sustain themselves in the treatment relationship. Many became so overwhelmed by therapy that they ran away or dropped out of school—they needed the support of an inpatient or residential setting to maintain themselves in psychotherapy. For many adults a psychotherapy experience alleviates anxiety; for many adolescents it may be quite disruptive. The adolescent is attemping to separate from childhood and no longer has the sustenance and the psychological support of his parents. In therapy, feelings from childhood and childhood relationships with parents are stimulated. This is frightening, and many

19

adolescents run from this. Beset by psychological and physiological changes and seemingly inexplicable mood swings, the adolescent may discover that to engage in the therapy experience, where more problems and feelings get stirred up, is more than he can handle. The hospital supports him in therapy by providing other adults and peers to talk to, to support him through tasks he needs to master, and to deal with therapy spillovers. A locked unit is a necessary intervention because it blocks the momentary impulse to run.

OBSERVATION AND ASSESSMENT

All behavior is important, all behavior has meaning, and all behavior is subject to analysis. This is not restricted to patient behavior. The staff must be willing to look at their own behavior and conceptualize its importance in the overall treatment experience.

Some disturbed adolescents have tremendous difficulty in verbalizing their feelings, and often consciously deny, suppress, or disguise them. The adolescent presents us with behavioral cues rather than verbal cues; these behavioral cues must be studied with great care. It is only through long and careful observation of the adolescent's behavior throughout the day that one can arrive at some understanding of the nature of his ego deficits, and can formulate a plan to help strengthen his coping abilities, repair the deficits, work for the mastery of new skills, and begin engagement in psychotherapy.

Observation starts from the moment of screening and continues during initial hospitalization with a comprehensive psychiatric evaluation consisting of diagnostic psychiatric interviews, psychological testing, physical and neurological examination, various biological laboratory tests, school testing, family interviews, and various research inventories.

As part of the research, we developed a staff structure for observation and data collection in which each adolescent's behavior is reviewed by the staff three or four times a day. We have seen consistently that various research maneuvers enhance rather than interfere with clinical work, precisely because they stimulate curiosity, ask new and, at times, embarrassing questions, and are provocatively challenging to the clinical staff.

Our patient's day is organized around what we call the *basic structure* of the program, that is, those regularly scheduled, virtually unchangeable activities which form the backbone of the unit and in which every patient participates. This includes waking up; meals; attending ward meetings and therapy sessions; going to school, O.T. shop, and gym; observing study hour and quiet hour; and going to bed. We observe the adolescent's behavior highlighted against this basic structure, the unchangeable program activities, as well as during the nonstructured parts of the patient's day.

Once observations have been collected and shared among the staff, a process of assessment takes place in which we begin to draw inferences regarding deficits, conflicts and patterns of behavior. The inferences and assessments which we make are drawn from our knowledge of dynamic psychiatry, relying on empathy and introspection. We move from manifest surface phenomena to latent content. On the one hand, we attempt to place ourselves in the adolescents' shoes and try to understand what it is like to be experiencing what they are experiencing. We try to do this objectively and with some distance lest we overidentify with the patients and become so fused with them and their experiences that we cannot assess their condition dispassionately. On the other hand, we attempt to monitor our fears of closeness so that we are not rendered incapable of empathizing with what is happening to the patient, maintaining instead a very distant stance, observing but not interacting.

Countertransference responses or reactions to patients are diagnostically useful, and staff members need to grow in self-understanding so that their feelings can be helpful rather than inhibiting. As staff members examine their own feelings, they convey to their patients that self-awareness is valuable and that monitoring one's own behavior, thoughts, and feelings is useful.

Our adolescent patients, both in treatment sessions and in the hospital milieu, will repeat patterns of feeling and behavior that arose earlier in life, and all staff members, especially the therapist and the chief of the unit, will become objects of transference. Peers, too, may be drawn into transference reactions, and the patient is likely to recreate on the unit pathological family interactions from his home life.

All these phenomena are grist for the therapeutic mill and are grappled with and assimilated into a therapeutic understanding of the adolescent.

It is important that we also recognize that a patient's associative responses to his transference to the therapist may extend beyond the limits of the therapy session and may show themselves in various kinds of behavior on the unit—true "acting out." Adolescent patients do not necessarily bring their concerns to the therapist in verbal associations, but instead often express their concerns behaviorally in school or on the unit. It is the therapist's responsibility, with the help of the staff, to try to understand the meaning of those behaviors in the light of the clinical transference.

A developmental assessment embraces several views of adolescence. We can assess how the delinquent has navigated the separation/individuation struggle facing every adolescent. For example, many teenagers engage in delinquent behavior because of their difficulty separating from mother and the psychological ties to childhood. Or, we can look at the adolescents from the point of view of object relations. In what way do the adolescents seek gratification? What use do they make of other people? For example, does the other person serve solely to fulfill certain narcissistic needs for the delinquents? Is their relationship with someone else serving primarily to elevate or regulate their self-esteem? Do the delinquents' use of others indicate that they have little capacity to soothe and calm themselves?

We have noticed in the family backgrounds of our delinquents a tremendous amount of inconsistency, variability, and fluidity in the parenting process. Frequently, adequate family histories are not available, and often our family assessments are retrospective extrapolates from the behaviors the delinquent shows us on the unit. After awhile, many of our patients are calmed by the recognition that the pattern of life on our unit is pretty much the same from day-to-day; from this, we have inferred that, for most of them, growing up was chaotic, inconsistent, and variable.

When assessing the individual, we must not be too eager to dismiss or minimize the existence of profound disturbances by pointing to apparently well-functioning areas or by accepting rationalizations. We must address the delinquent's actual functional level. For example, many borderline psychotic teenagers function well in certain kinds of verbal interactions; they participate actively in school, or in psychotherapy sessions, or in daily ward meetings, but when one gets to know them, one finds emptiness and lack of psychological structure. Some staff members cannot appreciate how very disturbed many of these teenagers are. The bright, cute girl with some artistic talent engages in drug dealing and prostitution seemingly because of disordered communication in the family. When we get beyond this interactional explanation, we understand the terrible depths of despair that she experiences and her constant craving for a sexual and/or drug experience to help herself feel alive and whole.

Our staff is not immune to, and must guard against, common prejudices that can interfere with good assessment. For example, the seriousness of a delinquent act cannot be determined on the basis of whether or not the offender is male or female, as is often the case when delinquent acts are handled informally at the police station. The police tend to excuse or minimize delinquency by girls while boys who may commit the same acts will be regarded as potential criminals. In many instances, it is only much later on, after the delinquency continues to escalate, as it often will, that the girl comes to the attention of the authorities. She then appears to be much more seriously delinquent than the boy who was attended to by the authorities much earlier in his career. To reiterate, we must be careful that our own prejudices don't cloud the picture.

We often hear: "You and your program are trying to impose on this black ghetto delinquent your white, middle-class values with this psychoanalytic theory, and, man, you're not talking his language." We are told that because people are of a different culture or social class, they cannot be assessed psychodynamically. This is simply not true. Not only can an upper middle-class youth from a white suburb be assessed in depth, but a black youth from the inner city can, also. If and when we infer accurately about either adolescent's behavior, we can help him gain insight. For instance, he can learn that when he gets nervous, he hits somebody, and that he gets nervous because he begins feeling warmth and affection for someone else. Such learning is not bound by race or class. This is insight—important insight—the kind of insight we try to develop in the staff and in our patients.

We must distinguish the seriousness of the delinquent's pathology from the frequency or social impact of his/her delinquent behavior. For example, a boy who witnesses and participates in a gang murder is not necessarily more disturbed than a boy who runs away. Similarly, a girl who runs away frequently is not necessarily more seriously disturbed than a girl who has run away only once or twice. We do not assess the seriousness of delinquency only from the external behavior, or only from the kind of reaction it stirs up in us because of its specific nature, or only from the social condemnation attached to the crime. We make a psychological assessment of the delinquent's character structure and personality development. The external behavior is important, but it is essential to decipher the psychological dynamics and structure that eventuate in individual or multiple acts of delinquency. This process of diagnosis and prescription of treatment is in itself dynamic and relies on constant observation and assessment of our patients' verbal and behavioral feedback.

Many psychoanalytically oriented psychotherapists deal only with what their patient brings to them verbally in sessions. This is a serious mistake in working with behaviorally disordered teenagers. If an adolescent behaves in a disruptive way on the unit, he may be attempting to communicate something to his psychotherapist; disturbed adolescents communicate largely through their behavior. Consequently, we expect the therapist to talk about certain behaviors in the session because the patient has already brought them into treatment by his activity on the unit. Also, the ward staff targets certain behavior and says to the patient, "Being 10 minutes late for school today is important. You need to sit down and figure out what's going on with you," and to the therapist, "Bill was 10 minutes late for school today; we want you to be aware of this. We expect that at some point or other, you'll try to deal with it in your therapy sessions." Ultimately, the delinquent can begin to perform some of these psychological functions for himself. The adolescent can eventually learn how to remain calm, how to delay gratification, and how to set his own limits, but, he can achieve these only in the context of an individual therapy relationship.

The hospital milieu is necessary to support that relationship, to precede it, and to teach the patient how to engage in it.

Our assessment of the adolescent includes observing his interactions with his family on the unit. In some treatment situations, families are viewed as foreigners or invaders; in others, as people who have to be watched and supervised. In many situations, the staff expects parents to exert their "noxious" influences on their "innocent" children once again. By participating in family visits on the unit, we try to become part of the family system and assess its interactions.

PLANNING

On the basis of sound observations of data, as well as subsequent assessment of and inferences about these data, treatment planning can begin.

Easson's (1969) philosophy of treatment is based on the idea that patients need to be met at their developmental levels and provided with psychological tasks to master which do not overwhelm them with anxiety, but which do present them with optimal anxiety and challenge. Our assessment of how the adolescent deals with basic structure gives us a baseline determination of his ability to cope with various kinds of psychological tasks. It gives us an initial reading on his developmental level, and provides us an immediate opportunity to determine whether or not we need to provide more staff support and external interventions, or less, and whether or not the delinquent is in a position to start taking on other kinds of psychological challenges.

We like to conceptualize the therapeutic milieu for the behaviorally disturbed adolescent as having three levels:

The *first level* consists of Easson's (1969) "Sameness, consistency, permanence—monotonously from one day to the next" (p. 77), or Redl's (1966) ". . . repetitive maneuvers in their life space" (p. 87). Here we mean a dependable environment with a basic structure for the entire program. This includes an "unbreakable" (i.e., physically safe) environment with nonbreakable furniture; a secured space with no potentially available drugs or weapons; a schedule of *when* things get done—meals, wakeup, bedtime, classes, ward meetings; an understanding of *why* things get done—a basic philosophy and value system held by the entire staff and demonstrated through consistent messages to patients despite diversity of staff personality and opinion; and an understanding of *how* things get done—fulfilling the needs for safety and consistency for all the patients with affective involvement at a level the adolescent can handle.

The *second level* of the therapeutic milieu embraces the development of the essential tasks of all adolescents in our culture—school, activities, peer group relations, increasing capacity for verbal expression of needs and feelings—and makes participation in these activities both a goal and an expectation for all in the program.

The *third level* of the therapeutic milieu involves developing individual treatment approaches to help each adolescent experience some level of success. This is Aichhorn's (1925, 1964) idea of tailoring the environment to individual needs as understood through psychoanalytic insights into each child. This interest in and response to each adolescent's individual needs, defenses, and deficits can only occur within a safe and consistent structure (level I), with the tasks of everyday living for the adolescent (level II) clearly spelled out so that recurrent problems in behaviors are clearly apparent.

The purpose of all of this is, as Easson (1969) states, to bring the adolescent to the point where "His inner struggle is then more focused on his personal emotional conflicts rather than on an instability in his environment" (p. 78). As the dynamics of each individual are clarified through an understanding of behaviors in different areas of unit life and through an understanding of how space, time, objects, and persons are used by each patient within these settings, an individual, consistent treatment approach can be agreed on by the entire staff. It is based on what the patient lacks internally and what he needs to develop.

Once a patient can follow the basic structure, a great deal of psychological energy is freed to enable him to cope with other challenging and clearly growth producing tasks. When the adolescent no longer struggles with decisions about getting up in the morning or going to bed at night, about whether or not he will do his homework, about whether or not he should let his personal problems spill over into all contacts with other people, then a tremendous amount of energy is freed to focus on academic achievement, learning how to introspect, discussing transference reactions, and working out peer related problems in group meetings. The basic structure provides staff not only with a therapeutic tool, but also with a gauge for determining when the patient may be ready for more challenging and demanding tasks. For example, one boy was having great difficulty talking about his problems in his therapy sessions. Although he continued to function quite well in the classroom, it became clear as we assessed the situation that the very act of going off the unit was more than he could handle, as every bit of energy was channeled into struggling with very strong urges to run away. We decided that he would no longer leave the unit to go to school, even though he was functioning well there. Once removed from the frightening experience of leaving the unit, he felt supported and safe enough to begin discussing with his therapist those very problems and urges which beset him. He had been able to keep these problems from interfering with his performance in the classroom at the expense, however, of his investment in therapy.

After pooling our assessments, we begin to plan treatment at daily team meetings. We review the activities of the previous week, including behavior that occurred in the gymnasium, school, unit, or individual or family psychotherapy sessions. We formulate and reformulate our understandings of the delinquent, his family, and problems, and from this process prescribe or modify treatment interventions.

As we collected data and listened to what the patient just described had to say in his therapy sessions, it became clear that leaving the unit for school was extremely overwhelming to this young man. If he were to deal meaningfully in therapy sessions with a number of his problems, he might very well lose control of himself when he got off the unit. This is similar to what happens when a suicidal adult patient is hospitalized, and his suicidal urges disappear; the patient goes home every weekend on a pass, and the therapist wonders what happened to the suicidal urges. Many patients cannot bring to psychotherapy the depths of their despair and the seriousness of their problems when every day they have to pull themselves together to go to school or when every weekend they have to leave the hospital to function at home. We know from work with some adult patients that in order to get to the depths of their depression and deal with very intense suicidal urges, we can't send them home every weekend. This knowledge helped us reformulate the treatment program for this delinquent boy whom we removed from school. Subsequently, he was able to invest more in individual psychotherapy.

On the surface, our program might resemble a behaviorist or learning theory model because we do use restrictions, we do take away privileges, and we do grant privileges and responsibilities when appropriate. However, there is one crucial difference—the patient does not "earn" increased responsibility. He is provided with either lessened or increased responsibility based on staff assessment of his growth and need for the kind of atmosphere which will promote psychological growth. Sometimes it is necessary, therefore, for a patient to have virtually no privileges or responsibilities so that he might deal with only the most basic internal stimuli, like the feelings that are stirred up in his interactions with the staff on the unit. Other patients, after a period of time, may fail to grow in a structured environment and need to be given privileges and responsibilities, sometimes despite their protests that they are not ready or despite their "messing up." Such new responsibilities create enough anxiety in the adolescents so that they are prompted to grow and master a new situation, rather than simply avoid it. No two patients are the same; one patient may need to stay longer at a given "privilege" level before he moves onto the next. Our goal is not simply to teach adaptation to an environment, as is sometimes the goal in a behaviorist approach, but to produce internal psychological changes in the adolescent. In fact, many delinquents can adapt readily to most any controlled environment, thus, the old prison adage "good inmate, lousy citizen."

At one time we were particularly concerned with how to deal with violent behavior. Initially it appeared that violent, destructive aggression by a patient against the staff was a result of rage and anger, possibly because he felt the staff had promised some kind of gratification that he had not subsequently received. For example, the first Christmas holiday on the unit was a warm family-like experience with the staff providing food and presents for the patients. Soon after, however, there was a near riot on the unit, and we realized we had misassessed and planned improperly. Proper planning for holidays on the unit and proper planning for the possibility of violent behavior on the unit must take into account the impact of gratification on the delinquent. Giving gifts and spreading warmth at holiday time seems the human thing to do. Making up for previous deprivations should avert violence, common sense tells us, and wars on poverty are based on this idea. However, simply gratifying deprived children is not the answer. It does not prevent anger; in fact, it may only suppress it, or even stimulate it. The delinquent is at times over-gratified and over-stimulated. He can no longer tolerate the internal feelings that might arise in a mother-child transference relationship with a staff member and needs to discharge such internal tension in violent and destructive behavior (Marohn, 1974).

In essence, a psychodynamic approach is really a research approach because it asks questions, observes interactions, establishes hypotheses to be tested, makes interventions designed to test out those hypotheses, and then observes new data as the patient responds and the process continues.

PROCESS

Any routine in the day can be analyzed in terms of observation, assessment, and planning. Examples are the wakeup routine and the bedtime routine.

Wakeup Routine

Staff observations of patient behavior begin with wakeup time. Everyone approaches the start of a new day differently—some people awaken slowly and need time to lie quietly in bed for awhile before arising. Others can awaken and immediately jump out of bed to start the day. Some people are cheerful in the morning; others are grouchy and noncommunicative. Some people are "morning people," most productive in the morning, others are "afternoon people," and still others are "evening people" or "night people." The existence of a circadian rhythm, an internal "clock," has been documented and is well known. It is this internal clock that in part governs hunger, sleepiness, and energy level. Superimposed on the internal clock is our psychological development, the value systems and sense of responsibility that may temporarily, at least, override the biological processes. That is why. even if sleepy, most of us force ourselves out of bed in order to start the day and accomplish the tasks and demands of that day. Often our meals are determined not so much by actual hunger but because the clock on the wall tells us that it's time to eat. When circumstances force us to go for long periods without food or rest, this rhythm is interrupted, and it may take several days before our internal clock adjusts itself again. Jet lag is an example of an interruption in that rhythm. And so, morning wakeup time is influenced by a number of factors—the residues of the night; our dreams, worries, and hopes; our own biological clocks; the outlook for the next day; and the sense of value and responsibility which have become part of our psychological makeup.

The disturbed adolescent brings to wakeup time all the elements mentioned above, plus the pathology that necessitated hospitalization in the first place. Many of our patients enter the hospital with day/night reversal patterns and disturbed sleep patterns. The regressive letting go at night that permits restful and soothing sleep is something deficient adolescents find difficult. Bedtime, therefore, becomes a frightening experience that frequently results in arguments and power struggles. Awakening in the morning, the disturbed adolescent is depleted of energy because of lack of sleep or fitful sleep, and is fearful that the coming day will only bring additional problems beyond his ability to cope. Here at bedtime and wakeup time, the staff becomes acutely aware of the very basic, primitive urges and longings of the patient.

We start the day with three separate wake-up calls 15 minutes apart. Each patient is called individually and has immediate contact with a staff person. They need this time and contact to "reenter." We try also to help them prepare the night before by organizing all the items they may need for the next day such as toilet articles, clothes, and school materials. Early in the program all the patients kept all their toilet articles in the respective male and female bathrooms. People used each other's things indiscriminately and the facilities were cramped, but the cogent issue is that on awakening, ego boundaries are more tenuous. The staff arranged opportunities for each patient to keep toilet articles in his or her own room. The morning traffic to the bathroom is planned in advance because we permit only one patient at a time in the bathroom, and now the facilities no longer seem cramped because the experience of getting ready for the new day is organized by the staff.

Beyond these basic treatment interventions, each patient may require individual assistance. For example, an adolescent, who upon wakeup, calls the staff and anxiously relates that he thinks he may have forgotten to do some homework exhibits a specific need for help. He may need a staff member to define verbally for him what he needs to do here and now—get up, wash, and dress.

Breakfast is a relatively quiet time. The staff reminds patients of their tasks that day, and helps them sort out the events and the anxieties of the previous evening and night from the upcoming events of the day. Many teenagers are unable to make such distinctions, and frequently, personal concerns, preoccupation with family problems, terrifying dreams, or an anticipated therapy session might interfere with the school work of that day. We help them to separate, distinguish, and learn to focus psychological energy and intention on the task at hand.

So, beginning with wakeup, through breakfast, and while waiting for the "school bus"—the staff member who accompanies the patients to school—we try to help the patient shape the attitudes necessary to carry him successfully through the day. A disturbing family session the night before should not interfere with the math class that day. The morning routine is devoted to gentle reminders of the time when the class starts, the book that is needed, and the homework that must be ready. The patient is reassured, though, that there will be a staff member available later to discuss the disturbing family session, that some of these problems can be discussed at the next family session or in the individual therapy session, but for now, the really important thing is the upcoming math class.

Bedtime Routine

For many disturbed adolescents, going to sleep at night is like a mini-death from which they may never awaken. All day long, energies have been channeled into trying to focus and stay in control. The process of breaking off contact with external reality is uncertain. For many, sleep means recurrent nightmares, and with the lessening of vigilance and the failure of the dream mechanism, anxiety and terror may plague them at night. The tendency of many delinquents to stay up late, sometimes until they are exhausted, may not be because they are rebellious, asserting their individuality, or being "tough," but rather because they are frightened of sleep and fearful of giving up contact with reality.

Shortly after the program began, the staff became aware of the great difficulty these patients have with times of transitions. We provide the proper psychological supports to help patients with these two most basic parts of the program by looking at staffing patterns, the number of staff members needed at bedtime and at wakeup time, and the balance of male and female staff to provide the proper kind of psychological support when it was most needed. This was not simply dictated by the idea that when patients are having difficulty more staff members are needed; rather, these decisions arose from a meticulous process of observation, intervention, and assessment of behavior that evolved into a staff workshop to discuss these experiences. Eventually, a new increment was added to our philosophy of treatment which focused on an understanding of our patients' needs in these areas, how we can assess breakdowns in these basic structures, and how we can prescribe help for the troubled patient.

The staff's attitude about the preparation for sleep has now become part of the unit care. Winding down from daytime tasks and the eventual preparation for bedtime is begun when the evening shift arrives at work around 3 p.m. Passes end early enough so that the patient can spend the next few hours on the unit in a quiet atmosphere before retiring for the night. Stimulating evening activities originally designed to exhaust patients did not do that; they only taxed psychological defenses and made sleep more terrifying and proved to be hyper-stimulating, making it difficult for the adolescents to quiet down. Therefore, a transition is made from the stimulation and pressure of attending classes, going to ward meetings, and having therapy sessions, to the slower paced leisure time activities of the evening. Evening transition activities might include table games, informal conversations with staff, puzzles, card games, and television viewing, always with the participation of staff members who serve as psychological support. Active games are stopped around 8:30 or 9:00 in the evening and emotionally charged conversations about intrapsychic and intrafamilial conflicts are discouraged. The entire patient/staff group is involved in the preparation and serving of hot chocolate. A hot beverage has a soothing and calming effect, psychologically as well as physiologically. Here it serves as a signpost that the evening is ending and bedtime preparations have begun. Like so many other aspects of the basic structure, it is predictable and a consistent signal, and to many of our patients whose lives have been extremely chaotic, whose environment has never been predictable or consistent, such a signal of the basic structure is soon noticed and gradually offers a new security.

The entire process of preparing and drinking hot chocolate becomes imbued with soothing and nurturing. Infantile longings find their expression in this socially accepted way, and there occurs a period of closeness between the patient group and the adult caretaking staff. During this time, the teenagers also begin to give cues that bedtime tonight may be more difficult than usual. For example, we have noted that a patient who stares out of the window a lot is probably responding to some form of internal distress, such as a wish to run away, the longing for an absent parent, or other infantile strivings that going to bed may have evoked. Bedtime is often the time that fears of abandonment emerge, and staff must be extremely sensitive to such fears so that sleep will come. Stimulating conversation and sexual references may also be cues that the patient is having difficulty going to sleep, is beset by troubling thoughts and feelings, and may need additional staff help. A fearful teenager may ask who will be working the night shift, and who will come to his room for bed check. This may be a clue that the patient would like several reassuring staff contacts during the night.

The actual hour of bedtime is defined by whether or not it is a school night or a weekend or holiday night because the demands of the next day will vary. As in the morning routine, with those patients who show difficulty handling the anxieties of the day, staff assists with bed preparation. The staff says good night to each patient and psychologically "tucks" him in bed, like the parent of childhood. Sometimes bedtime stories are read; some are childhood tales, others are interesting short stories. When we first initiated this practice early in the development of the program, it was enlightening to see street-wise, tough, incorrigible kids fascinated and comforted by bedtime reading.

Usually our adolescents are able to sleep throughout the night when adequate treatment interventions begin on the evening shift. We can assess whether or not there is going to be difficulty during the night, and whether it would be necessary for an additional staff member or two to stay on the night shift to help out. The work of the night staff member is a continuation of the work of the evening shift, checking on patients, reassuring them when necessary, but rarely needing to deal with some unanticipated crisis.

The main organizing principle around the bedtime is that the staff attempts to provide externally, by interacting with the patients, the kind of soothnig and calming function the patient cannot provide for himself. A predictable routine facilitates this, and various kinds of acceptable, yet not infantilizing, nurturing experiences enable the disturbed teenager to sleep.

It is this approach that needs to be taught to staff rather than any set of policies or rules or procedures. This is the treatment philosophy: One must examine behavior and attempt to understand it and base one's interventions on this assessment. In the very beginning, we were plagued with such questions as: What is our program? What is our approach? Don't we have a policy about this? As a result of watching our patients very carefully, responding to their behavior, using our own empathic and introspective abilities, sometimes intuitively, and talking with each other in an attempt to check out various perceptions with each other, we were able to develop a cohesive way of working together that eventually became conceptualized as a basic treatment philosophy.

Such a treatment philosophy may vary from unit to unit, from program to program, and in its intricacies and niceties, specific rules and policies will reflect the personalities of the staff. Our program is presented here in that light, namely, that specific measures and interventions should not be copied or followed, but rather the thinking and the process behind such interventions should be understood and then applied in the consensually validated manner of one's own program. We insist that staff think about what they are doing and attempt to conceptualize what they are doing.

Such an attitude can be taught, and can develop, but requires administrative and institutional support in order to flourish.

STRUCTURE

The processes described above are only one part of the development of psychic structure. Another necessary factor is the affective quality and the content of the attitude with which these processes are carried out. The affective quality must be one of warmth and empathy; the content of the attitude must be one of interest in the growth and development of the child. When these factors—that is, dynamic understanding, warmth, and interest in the growth of the adolescent—come together, and the adolescent has the capacity to comprehend them as such, the development of new psychological structure occurs. What we typically see in the initial phase of hospitalization, once the adolescent perceives that the staff means business, is compliance with the basic structures. The adolescent will carry it out because the staff is present and he doesn't want a confrontation. Gradually, an adolescent moves toward identification, carrying out the basic structure to please the staff with whom he has developed a positive, affective attachment. He may even, at this level of identification, fulfill the basic structure even when the staff is not around, but still because of attachments to them. Following the basic program structure based only on identification does not lead to structural personality changes. Identification must give way to internalization. This movement takes place when there is an adequate balance of warmth, non-narcissistic involvement of the staff, and knowledge of what needs should be fostered for growth and what needs should be frustrated for growth. This approach must be carried out in an integrated way.

We believe that true behavioral change and character organization take place only in the context of a clinical transference situation. Though one may gain conformity by external behavioral pressure, this is not real change. When a patient shows behavioral changes on the unit, we question whether it is because he has been influenced by external forces, or whether it is a manifestation of internal changes which have taken place. In some areas we would like to think it is both. For example, we clearly put pressure on our patients to begin thinking about their behavior, and try to teach them to introspect. We try to show them that behavior has meaning, and we target, or "flag," certain behaviors to say, "this has meaning, you'd better take a look at it with your therapist." This process of beginning to think about oneself requires external pressure and the facility, as Meeks has described (1971), for such work. Eventually, however, eliminating deviant behavioral patterns depends upon the patient using his newly developed method of introspection to work with his therapist in unraveling the complex of defenses, transferences, wishes, and conflicts that have developed over the years.

Another way of looking at how the process of change occurs is the classical psychoanalytic model in which identification is viewed as a psychological process developed from dosed frustrations and resulting in the formation of psychological structure. When the mother is unable or unwilling to perform certain functions for the developing child, he experiences frustration but may begin performing these functions for himself. For example, a child may ask mother to make a sandwich for him, but the mother may be busy or may refuse to do so because of her sense of the child's increasing abilities. The child may experience some mild disappointment, but may learn, by having watched mother previously, to do it alone. In this process, the child has internalized not only the mother's caring, but also the ability to perform the task alone, resulting, therefore, in self-gratification. Similarly, the mother admires the child's drawing of stick men, and in her praise provides what Kohut (1971) describes as the mirroring response wherein the child experiences himself as the "gleam in mother's eye."

At some point, the mother, either because she is busy, or preoccupied, or decides not to do so, does not provide such mirroring and frustrates the child. If such frustration is tolerable, the child will experience mild disappointment, but will begin performing such self-assessment and self-praise for himself, thus, again, internalizing certain maternal functions, which lead eventually to self-esteem formation. As these experiences repeat themselves time and time again, the growing child develops identification and internal representations not only of the self, but of others. When such frustrations are massive, or unpredictable, when there is inconsistency in the mother/child relationship, or a consistent lack of warmth, the child cannot develop internalized representations of himself and others, and psychological functions, psychological structure, and the whole process of identification is seriously disrupted.

We encourage growth in both the staff and the patients. We try to grow in our ability to introspect, empathize, use intuition, and know theory in an attempt to understand the experiences of a delinquent. Essential to any attempt to conceptualize is the appreciation of time spent together thinking and talking, challenging each other, brainstorming, and trying to understand the work. Our staff met regularly in daily, formal, and informal conferences on the unit, in daily team and staff meetings, in regular ward meetings with our patients, in weekly case conferences with outside consultants, working together for several years attempting to conceptualize our program. We pushed our patients, our staff, and ourselves to look at and understand everything, and we relied heavily on introspection, attempting to understand our reactions to the behavior of our patients and our staff, and on empathy, attempting to understand and appreciate vicariously what our patients and our staff were experiencing.

There must be scheduled times for the staff to get together to share their observations and engage in the assessment process. There is a basic structure, too, that occurs within the staff—time spent at the end and beginning of each nursing shift and between the two shifts to discuss the patients' activities; daily report sessions before the ward meetings to familiarize the entire treatment staff with patient difficulties; reports from the "school bus" to the school staff about patients' behavior; daily team meetings at which patient treatment plans are formulated and implemented; weekly supervision of ongoing psychotherapy as well as regular supervision of the work of staff of all disciplines; weekly staff meetings where general staff issues are discussed; regular case conferences with outside consultants to focus on treatment issues; frequent meetings of the administrative staff to monitor the working of the rest of the staff and of the administrative staff itself; and a weekly Adolescent Program Review (APR) meeting when the administrative staff and the therapist provide each patient with feedback about his performance in the past week and give him an opportunity to discuss his own concerns and questions about treatment. These are organizing principles of the therapeutic program. Not only do they serve as scheduled activities around which staff and patients can organize their day, but they constantly reinforce and convey the importance of psychological self-awareness and self-observation.

From time to time, it became clear that certain problems and difficulties had arisen which could not be addressed within the context of the basic work structure, and specialized workshops needed to be held to confront these issues. Conceptualizing a camping program and transplanting the therapeutic milieu of the hospital to a campsite; realizing that violence escalates from verbal abuse to property abuse to physical violence to person and eventually riot; understanding the role of table games and other leisure time activities in the context of the overall treatment program—these resulted from time spent together as a staff attempting to understand and develop the program further. Regularly scheduled inservice training courses on adolescent development and pathology, milieu therapy, family therapy, and individual psychotherapy of the adolescent, as well as intensive supervision of other staff members and trainees, are essential supports. Writing papers or books, preparing presentations for professional audiences at all staff levels, and regular feedback from research investigations are yet other parts of the framework within which staff can grow and treatment can occur.

A clear-cut authority structure on the unit gives the staff in the program the freedom and capacity to work. When the authority structure becomes fuzzy, the chief is indecisive, or the staff is not sure about policies or the rules, the unit is ripe for some kind of disturbance

(Marohn, Dalle-Molle, Offer and Ostrov, 1973). If the policies of the unit or the authority structure become vague and deficient, the patients, themselves, will many times provoke some kind of authoritarian response in order to reestablish a hierarchical structure (Marcuse, 1967). Our staff makes the decisions. An egalitarian treatment approach is not suitable for delinquent adolescents. All still need parenting, and parenting includes taking responsibility. One aspect of the ever present authority structure of the unit is the APR where the chief of the unit, the activities supervisor, the social work supervisor, the ward staff supervisor, the school principal, and the therapist meet to discuss the adolescent's progress or lack of progress for the past week. They then meet with the teenager, discuss with him his own impressions of the previous week, give feedback about activities and provide him an opportunity to raise any questions he might have about his treatment. This and other events demonstrate that our unit operates under a shared authority, but final authority is not vested in the therapist. We give the adolescents an opportunity to participate in that structure, encouraging their comments and questions and asking them to provide us with feedback. However, we do not disguise the fact that we run the program. The staff's requests or orders may be questioned by the patient later, but at the time they are made, they are not open to negotiation.

3

The Experience of Psychotherapy

Previous attempts to postulate a treatment philosophy for adolescent inpatients have arisen from either empirically derived pragmatic approaches (Beckett, 1965; Holmes, 1964) or extrapolations of Freudian structural theory (Easson, 1969; Redl, 1966; Redl and Wineman, 1957). A pragmatic approach does not usually rest on a theoretical base which places it on a continuum with other forms of psychotherapy, and extrapolations of Freudian theory frequently falter when metapsychology is extended to interpersonal and group interactions on a psychiatric unit. General systems theory provides opportunities to conceptualize the interaction of a therapeutic milieu, to measure the dynamics of that organism, and to test out certain hypotheses about milieu therapy (Marohn, 1970).

An open system consists of component parts which relate to each other according to some sort of schema. This open system is in dynamic interaction with its environment, maintains a homeostasis internally which involves a steady movement of component materials, attains an independent state of its own, and develops increasingly complex states of organization (von Bertalanffy, 1962). In Allport's (1960) terms, in an open system ". . . there is intake and output of both matter and energy; there is the achievement and maintenance of steady (homeostatic) states, so that the intrusion of outer energy will not seriously disrupt internal form and order; there is generally an increase of order over time owing to an increase in complexity and differentiation of parts; finally, at least at the human level, there is more than mere

40

intake and output of matter and energy; there is extensive transactional commerce with the environment."

One can view a therapeutic milieu from any of these vantage points. The maintenance of homeostasis, however, is particularly crucial in the treatment of the acting out adolescent, who is hospitalized because of his inability to maintain internal homeostasis and whose internal disruptions manifest themselves in delinquent behavior. The hospital milieu consists of both patients and staff, and the component parts of interaction are the intrapsychic and group process dynamics of patients and of staff. We view the therapeutic milieu as an open system and will describe the interactions of the component parts of that system, emphasizing what factors tend to disrupt the homeostasis of the organism and what remedial measures are used to maintain or regain internal harmony. This will be a cursory survey, and we will return to many of these issues later.

Patient's Intrapsychic Dynamics. Various "parts" of the intrapsychic system may be deficient and result in a disruption of the adolescent's functioning. Such psychological deficits result in an inability to modulate, channel, and control impulses. A structured program partially compensates for such deficits. For example, the patient who has struck another is helped to think about his behavior, just as the patient who misses class is encouraged to contemplate his difficulty getting to school; these interventions foster an internal capacity to monitor one's own behavior. Superego deficits or lacunae are often responsible for the delinquent behavior of many adolescents; therefore, a theft on the unit is taken seriously and dealt with immediately in the community meeting. Some adolescents struggle with urges of greater intensity than others; specific intense transference responses unique to a particular adolescent's psychic development may result in a traumatic state (Marohn, 1974), whereas another patient may not respond with such intensity to a similar situation. The milieu attempts to preserve homeostasis by anticipating the specific and peculiar transference issues for each patient and by attempting to respond appropriately. For example, if a patient is excessively sensitive to criticism in school, such responses can be anticipated by the therapist, teacher, and ward staff, and the patient can be helped to view criticism issues in a more benign way.

Patient Group Dynamics. Several issues in patient-patient group interactions may disrupt the milieu homeostasis: competition, antistaff group formation, scapegoating, contagion, and acting out through other patients. Patients may compete with each other to be the favorite, the sickest, or the most obnoxious patient on the unit, but this is countered by a staff attitude that no patient is "better" or "worse" than another, but all patients are struggling with an illness and attempting to grow and mature psychologically. Antistaff attitudes and behavior are frequently a part of group formation on an adolescent unit, and it is necessary for the staff to intervene quickly and support strong therapeutic alliances and positive ego ideals. Thus, the staff demonstrates that "we talk about problems here instead of acting them out." Frequently, adolescents may project their own internal difficulties onto new patients or the more psychotic patients, or may act out through other patients. For example, a newly admitted patient who is frightened is labelled by the other patients as being "too sick to be here" because they resist recognizing their own problems and need for help. The staff must respond behaviorally to these challenges to community harmony lest contagion and riot result (Marohn, Dalle-Molle, Offer, and Ostrov, 1973).

Staff Intrapsychic Dynamics. Just as patients bring to the treatment situation intrapsychic deficits, so may the staff. The defenses one uses to deal with one's own internal conflicts may reduce the capacity for self-observation and cause blind spots. Staff members may have serious difficulties in structuring an adolescent's life on the unit because of their own structural deficiencies, such as difficulty in controlling their own need for gratification. A staff member may struggle with his own delinquent urges or a severely punitive superego. At times, a staff member's needs for narcissistic gratification may interfere with his capacity to be objectively therapeutic with patients whom he may view as peers, friends, or his own children. Personal therapy or analysis may be necessary, but certainly all staff members should be involved in a continuous supervisory process and taught to engage in self-reflection. The staff needs to rely on mutual feedback with other staff members and trust each other enough to be able to seek and accept help.

Staff Group Dynamics. At times staff may not be able to communicate openly with each other or may compete with each other because patients have succeeded in splitting staff into good and bad objects. Such splitting attempts resonate with staff members' wishes to be the favorite parent, or the favorite child of the administrative staff. These problems demonstrate a breakdown in staff equilibrium and are remedied by open communication, mutual feedback, mutual help, and constant self-analysis. Staff must be interested in working with adolescents, must receive adequate pay and adequate learning rewards, and must be constantly open to fresh ideas so that the system is capable of growing. All staff members need to be included in the decision-making process and share in the development of a philosophy of treatment.

Patient-Staff Group Dynamics. Certain kinds of treatment situations, such as a camping trip, open the therapeutic community to the danger of role diffusion. Patients may view staff members as fellow campers rather than treatment agents, and under additional demands and stress, staff may readily slip into more adolescent peer-type behavior. The whole community must be particularly sensitive to such issues and recognize that such diffusion can lead only to frustrating experiences for patients and staff. Confusion over leadership roles may cause the patients and staff to act out in order to provoke a leadership response and the reemergence of a more structured hierarchy.

Patient-Family Dynamics. Each adolescent patient is part of a family system, nuclear and extended, real and fantasied. Although we recognize that family dynamics and communication are important, uncovering dynamic meanings is only part of the treatment process. Structure building in both the adolescent and the parents is crucial, and so we intervene primarily through modalities we feel are best suited to achieve structuralization—separate work with the parents in parents' group, marital therapy, and parent casework and work with the delinquent adolescent in milieu and individual therapy, attempting to help him modify the parental imagos, or lack thereof, he holds internally. Formal family therapy provides opportunities to build on the gains achieved elsewhere, especially by providing channels of communication and opportunities to correct transference distortions, but often the uncovering of dynamic meanings and communications cannot be attempted until they can be attended to by stronger and better structuralized psyches. Tom cannot recognize how he feels worried about his mother's mental health and how he feels guilty about his wishes to mature until he can differentiate his needs from his mother's.

Dynamic Interaction with the Environment. The life of the therapeutic milieu is also influenced by the outside world. A very obvious example, of course, is the admission of a new patient who brings to the unit many aspects of "the street culture"—his slang, his costume, his music, or his drug preferences. These impinge on the milieu, confront staff with new challenges, and encourage preexisting liaisons among patients on the unit. Moreover, in a general sense, the life of patients and staff is markedly influenced by activities in the outer world. Budget cuts may decimate staff; threatened budget cuts may increase the anxiety level of patients about the future of their treatment. The intrusion of the television camera crew to get a "story" on threatened budget cuts or other publicity that a particular research project or treatment program may warrant affects the activities of the milieu. Court decisions granting "rights" to adolescent patients influence the kind of behavior teenagers show on the unit. Increasingly, adolescents express certain issues in treatment by signing out of the hospital rather than by more violent behavior. At the same time, staff and therapists may feel bewildered by new laws and policies, by court decisions and bills of rights. Their sense of confidence to help and to treat may be undermined. Such a situation complicates treatment because of the adolescent patient's need to idealize the treatment team, particularly the therapist and the chief of the unit, and to rely on staff to provide a consistent and stable structure.

The hospital milieu is a community and a social system consisting of patients and staff who live and work together for varying periods of each 24-hour day, the former having demonstrated considerable difficulty in living in the outside world, and the latter being relatively healthy and able to function, though bringing their own unique personalities and neurotic configurations to the treatment situation. One danger in any treatment milieu is that treatment is viewed as the responsibility of only the staff. At the other end of the spectrum, there is also the danger of staff members not having respect for themselves as agents of treatment, a particularly crucial problem in dealing with adolescents with impulse disorders. There needs to be a clear-cut differentiation between staff and patients, because the "generation gap" serves a necessary psychological function.

There is a living and vibrant interaction between staff and patients and among the various components of the treatment milieu (Marohn, 1969, 1970). It is not so much that patient conflicts are expressed in staff conflicts, or vice versa, but rather that, in any well functioning treatment milieu, most components of the system are struggling with analogous issues simultaneously. Each component of the system in its own unique way reflects the sophistication or primitiveness of its psychological functioning. Patients' struggling in a ward meeting with the issues of intimacy and closeness may parallel the staff's struggling with issues of getting closer and more meaningfully involved both with each other and with patients. As such, then, the milieu is an open dynamic system which, though it responds to outside influences, has a life of its own, establishes its own culture, expectations, philosophy, policies, and rules reflecting the personalities of that particular group of people. As such, one unit will appear different from the another, but there are some basic principles which apply to all psychiatric milieus. Leadership is always a crucial issue. The knowledge of that leadership, whether it is vested in a single authority or shared, how it functions, and who is responsible for what—all are pivotal issues that need to be understood. Without such knowledge, the patient-staff group will need to test out the reality and presence of that leadership (Marohn, Dalle-Molle, Offer, and Ostrov, 1973). When leadership organization is certain, staff and patients challenge each other, question each other, struggle to work out conflicts and problems, and constantly question the culture and philosophy of the unit. Without a known and felt authority structure, no one, neither staff nor patients, feels comfortable or safe enough to work and grow.

Nonetheless, there is always the danger of rigidity or bitterness in a treatment program where staff and patients rely on previous experience to resolve new problems and new challenges. New patients and new staff members inject welcome new life and blood into the treatment situation. Yet, at times, they can overwhelm and seriously disrupt the system. Adjusting to changes and continuing the therapeutic work can be accomplished only through frequent team, staff, and community meetings where communication is open, direct, and task oriented. Staff meetings can become obsessional experiences, but if they are used effectively to communicate, they form the foundation for an effective treatment milieu.

Hospital treatment of adolescents creates a milieu with a unique flavor. If we recognize that the primary psychological tasks of adolescence are to effect a psychological separation from the infantile parental imagos, to integrate into the personality structure not simply the physical changes of adolescence, but more importantly, the increase in sexual and aggressive drives and activity, to master and capitalize on the newly found cognitive skills and curiosities of adolescence, and to transform significantly primitive narcissistic structures and firm up a sense of self-cohesion and identity, then certain treatment principles naturally emerge. To devise a suitable treatment program, one must understand what normal adolescence is all about, diagnose accurately in what way a particular adolescent has failed in the maturational process, and facilitate the staff member's interventions as a more or less healthy parent surrogate whose job it is to foster the maturational process.

Adolescence is a developmental phase in which there is mourning as one separates from the infantile ties to the parents, ego depletion as one struggles to integrate increased drive, and periods of threatened fragmentation as one's tenuously established character defenses and resolutions to earlier conflicts are challenged, causing significant transformations in one's self-concept. Since the adolescent is involved in a separation-individuation struggle, he does not usually request help for internal pain as an adult neurotic might. The adolescent who is brought to treatment is usually one who has showed significant disruptions and has little ego capacity to engage in a meaningful therapeutic alliance on an outpatient basis. He will have enough psychological energy to engage in a meaningful therapeutic alliance only when other kinds of ego tasks are not demanded; consequently, adolescents are hospitalized when there is a need to provide externally those kinds of ego functions which the adolescent lacks internally or when there is a need for some kind of ego support which is lacking in the family or the external environment (Easson, 1969).

As noted earlier, the role distinction between staff and patients is critical on an adolescent unit; the staff cannot become friends or peers of the adolescent. They must be fully capable of saying no or setting limits and confronting the adolescent with his behavior. If a staff member is unable to do so, the adolescent then is unable to effect a psychological separation from childhood, in much the same way that the wishy-washy or ineffective parent complicates the adolescent's separation task. Adolescents need a generation gap, someone to butt up against, as they work out their own individuation problems (Marcuse, 1967). Since the adolescent is in the hospital because of significant ego deficits, the entire milieu is organized around providing external ego support and ego functions.

Since a considerable amount of psychological energy is required to work in therapy or deal with the problems that occur in interpersonal relationships, a structure is provided which is not questioned, but frequently tested. The adolescent does not have to struggle with issues of when to get up in the morning or when to go to bed at night, or whether or not to attend school, for these decisions are taken for granted, and his efforts are directed toward other more difficult tasks. As such, the milieu is also organized around helping the adolescent introspect and focus on the meaning of his behavior. The adolescent is frequently advised to discuss a particular issue with the therapist, and therapists are expected to be aware of the behavior of the patient on the unit because adolescents bring their problems to their therapist not only in verbal material in the session but also in behavioral communications in the treatment milieu.

Whenever a significant breakdown of the adolescent's functioning occurs, whether it be coming late for school or demonstrating seriously threatening or violent behavior, all else stops for a moment, and the staff members attempt to help the adolescent view what has just happened and to learn from the ego disruption that just occurred. Though on the surface many staff interventions might appear to be directed toward modifying behavior through a reward and punishment approach, it is in reality quite different, and decisions about tasks and privileges, restricting a patient to his room, or the use of restraints are all designed to provide an external ego for a disrupted and deficient patient ego, with the hope that eventually such controls will be internalized. We prefer to use external psychological controls—people—to help a patient settle down, or we may isolate the patient in his own room among familiar surroundings, rather than a seclusion room, to decrease the amount of external stimulation or to impress upon him the need to introspect. We will also use physical restraints and staff contact to help an adolescent reintegrate after a violent outburst or to help him forestall a significant disruption; and we will use medication to help the adolescent deal with overwhelming anxiety.

School and activities form the core of the hospital treatment program. The adolescent is action-oriented and activities help him not only to discharge internal tension, but also to master and integrate various conflicts and skills. School is the "work" of the adolescent. Here he can learn and master new intellectual skills and cognitive abilities, as well as develop important peer and socialization skills. Group meetings and group interactions also foster these phase appropriate developments and provide the adolescent patient with considerable opportunity for feedback from the all-important peer group which he utilizes in his separation-individuation struggles.

THE TEAM MEETING

The focus of the psychiatric team is the individual patient. The work of the team is to develop a treatment plan and to execute that plan, based on the understanding of the patient, his needs and problems, and the available therapeutic modalities. The patient can be understood as comprising a number of systems himself as well as being a member of other, larger systems. For example, the patient can be viewed as a somatopsychic system or as an intrapsychic system. The patient is also a member and subsystem of larger systems such as an interpersonal system, participating in two-party relationships. He is also a member of his own family system, nuclear and extended. He participates in a vocational and/or educational system and a cultural system with racial, ethnic, and social class variables.

Each member of the psychiatric team focuses on the patient from the viewpoint of a particular system. Expertise with given systems distinguishes the different mental health professionals. In our program, the *psychiatrist* is the team leader and chief of the unit, and has some familiarity with all these systems. The *psychotherapist* focuses on the systems within the individual, the intrapsychic and the psychosomatic, and attempts to modify the patient's behavior through psychotherapy and/or somatotherapy. His interpersonal relationship with the patient is referred to as the clinical transference, an expression of the patient's intrapsychic system. He may also work with patients in group or family therapy, but in our program the primary locale of his work is the dyadic relationship. The *ward staff* and *activity staff* relate to the adolescent primarily in the interpersonal system, but also recognize the kinds of family transference which the patient may establish in the hospital milieu. The *social worker* relates primarily in the family system, but in an interpersonal, vocational, cultural, and political way as well. The *psychologist* is the expert in diagnostic testing and research design, but adds his perspective on individual and group dynamics. The *educator's* focus is the intellectual and academic functioning of the child, quite distinct from a psychotherapeutic focus.

The treatment team, like any open system, is a complex of elements in mutual interaction (Marohn, 1970). The psychiatric team encompasses mental health professionals, their experiences, their training, and their ideas, and develops an understanding of a patient, a treatment plan for that patient, and its implementation. The energy for the team comes from the professionals' own identity and investment in their work and the mutual learning and professional growth which occur. The success or failure of the adolescent's hospital stay frequently depends on the ability of the staff to support and nourish each other, and on their not relying on patient success to enhance their professional status. A well-functioning team is characterized by harmonious working relationships, the resolution of work-impeding competition, the establishment of, and support for, team leadership, and open communication within the team, including the resolution of disagreements by open verbal confrontation, and not by displacement or other "acting out."

Examining two team meetings might clarify these concepts, that each profession focuses on a particular system in which the patient is involved and that the team, itself, is an open system. The following are descriptions of two team meetings to discuss Rachel's treatment, taken from notes compiled by the school staff and ward staff.

In the first team, the therapist reported that the psychotherapy sessions centered around Rachel's increased activity and her feelings and understanding of that. She expects that things will go wrong, and she believes that asserting herself causes problems which is why she feels responsible for any kind of acting up on the unit. Rachel feels that the more active she is, the more engaged she is in treatment, but she is also more responsible. She relates her sense of responsibility to the time when her father had a heart attack, and her mother blamed it on the children.

She feels that no one now can stop her from speaking up or from expressing her feelings, and she begins to be so carried away with her omnipotence that she sees everything around her as being affected by her. Talking about another patient being in restraints causes her to reminisce about her own experiences when she found restraints to be soothing and enabled her to fall asleep. She remembers that when she was at home, she liked to put her bed up against the wall so she wouldn't fall out. Restraints make her feel contained and give her a sense of security.

At the same time as she expresses a sense of omnipotent responsibility for others, there is also a sense of being more individuated and differentiated from others on the unit, as well as members of her family. She begins talking about her future, in that it might be a good idea to live independently and what that might mean to her. She recognizes that though her family might not change, she, herself, wants to change. The ward staff reported that she is talking more to other people rather than simply talking about doing so. She is using staff to help her interact more socially. She continues, however, to set herself up as a victim. She is making plans to get a haircut, and has called a local shop for prices and possible appointment times, and has made arrangements to go on a particular day with one of the staff members. She also needs to get glasses, and the chief intervened by emphasizing that glasses should be a top priority for her, even more important than a haircut. The social worker will need to explore whether or not the parents can afford this. The parents are quite in debt, and are not receiving Medicaid.

In the occupational therapy shop, she is someone who is easily over-looked because of her lack of assertiveness. She has been working on a stuffed animal project and not only enjoying it, but completing the project quite adequately. In school, she has been making some pro-gress, is more active in discussions, and at times shows some sense of humor about making mistakes. She expresses concern about environ-mental pollution in social studies discussions, and is having some diffi-culty in math with addition. Her vocational outlook seems to take a religious bent, and even though her preoccupation with religion has decreased, she indicates a desire to work with church groups in the future. Her probation officer plans to discontinue his involvement with her because most of her needs are being serviced in the program.

At a team meeting two weeks later, the therapist reported that the sessions focused on her feeling guilty that she is withholding dreams, and not talking about certain things. Rachel feels responsible for the mess that one of the patients made in the girls' bathroom, and thinks that possibly she did it. Yet she is able to recognize this has to do with the guilt she feels over her anger at her parents' failure to provide her money for her glasses and her haircut. For the first time she jokes with her therapist. The ward staff reported that she became quite angry, and threw a chair, and afterwards asked to be placed in restraints; this was not done because she was able to ventilate her feelings as well as maintain control. This seemed to be related to her increasing anxiety about going out for the haircut, and as she talked with the staff mem-ber who was to accompany her, her picture of the trip was "garbled and confused." When she was told that they would not be going out for the haircut, she was relieved, calmed down, and did better.

The chief commented that Rachel is quite ambivalent about moving ahead, and she needs a good deal of support in order to help her re-cognize that to move ahead does not mean losing our support. Despite this, she continues to work well on her projects in the occupational therapy shop. While this is going on and the patient is struggling with issues of separation, her parents express their concern about losing one of the family session co-therapists who would be on vacation. The father himself frequently feels cut off from the mother when she pays attention to the children. The father feels that Rachel is the only child who really engages with him, and went so far as to talk a bit about the incest of several years ago. The father increasingly appears to be a forlorn character who has no way to get his needs met. The finances are almost nil. Despite these difficulties, Rachel continues to function adequately and do competent work in school.

These vignettes illustrate how different professionals have a different focus in describing the patient's behavior as the team works together as an organic entity to understand and conceptualize what is happening in the patient's treatment. In these examples, data from a variety of sources indicated that the patient was struggling with issues of separation. She showed a capacity to master these conflicts—to step back, take a look at them, and even joke about them, and to continue to function in important areas of her life—even though experiencing considerable turmoil over her sense of omnipotent merger with others, the concomitant sense of responsibility for everyone, and her anxiety over beginning to individuate and move towards a more separate existence.

INDIVIDUAL PSYCHOTHERAPY

Change, internal change, can occur only in a transference relationship. By this we mean that previous experiences, traumata, deficiencies, defenses, characterological patterns, and the like can only be changed when situations psychologically similar to their origins are reexperienced and hopefully understood, and new patterns experimented with and developed. Only in a transference relationship can there be a shift of internal forces, changes in internal imagos, and modifications of internal structure. Our purpose here is not to review the techniques of insight psychotherapy or psychoanalytically oriented psychotherapy, but to show how this approach can be integrated with a milieu approach.

The delinquent patient is admitted to the hospital because he is handicapped and cannot mature as an adolescent, cannot attend to the developmental tasks of adolescence, and cannot master the internal psychological and biological changes as well as the newly developed peer experiences and relationships. Outpatient psychotherapy can work if the adolescent has sufficient external ego derived from a parent or a friend to engage in such psychotherapy. Psychotherapy and the relationship with the psychotherapist are, of course, ego supportive, but also ego challenging and ego depleting, as transference phenomena are stimulated and the ego and the defenses are attacked.

As we have emphasized, everything in the hospital milieu precedes and facilitates the self-observing ego hoped for in the individual psychotherapy. Stimulating experiences are made more manageable for the deficient ego, unnecessary or less important ego tasks are temporarily set aside, and overwhelming ego tasks are minimized. The ward staff and the therapist alike must keep in mind that though treatment is ego supportive, it is also ego stressing because of the difficult task of self-observation and the transference issues that are stimulated. Of course, not everything in treatment is related to the central issue of self-observation, because in the treatment process some ego skills develop automatically as conflicts are resolved and the natural push to maturation and health expresses itself. The healthier teenagers involve themselves with a peer group without necessarily thinking about why they had earlier isolated themselves. There does seem to be a natural tendency in the adolescent to mature, develop, and move toward a healthier adulthood. The self-observation of psychotherapy is only a way station or a means to the end—that of growth. Other means are experimentation with peer experiences, the mastery of other kinds of ego tasks in school and in recreation, and the untangling of a pathological family web. The use of drugs, engaging in sexual activity, violence, theft, and running away from the hospital are indications of interferences in that movement toward growth and obstructions in the self-observation process of psychotherapy; in such instances, the adolescent acts out instead of verbalizing. Missing a class in school, for example, indicates a problem in the path to maturation. In and of itself, missing class may not be destructive to treatment, but it is taken seriously as an indication of a serious breakdown of the adolescent's movement toward maturation. Such a breakdown is expected to be dealt with not just by the ward staff or the school staff, but is also to be taken up by the therapist in the treatment session.

Many beginning psychotherapists rely on a model of psychotherapy which directs the therapist to deal solely with whatever material the patient brings to him. This, perhaps, may be useful when dealing with adult neurotics in psychoanalysis, but whether or not it is useful in the psychotherapy of adolescents, particularly in the hospital treatment of delinquents, must be evaluated.

Any behavior that occurs in that treatment setting, whether the patient directly verbalizes it with the psychotherapist or not, is in our opinion being "brought" to the therapist. Any bit of acting out which occurs in the hospital is the adolescent's way of bringing to the therapist's attention deficiencies, problems, conflicts, or specific transference issues, which are displaced from the individual psychotherapy situation yet must be focused on and hopefully understood and verbalized. The psychotherapist must take all behavior seriously, especially that which does not occur in his office, and work hand-in-hand with the rest of the treatment staff in communicating to the delinquent that all behavior has meaning and all behavior must be understood, an idea which delinquents cannot readily accept.

Adolescents cannot attach themselves to the psychotherapist who carries the burden of a parental transference. The therapist who expects his delinquent patient to come to him seeking help or eager to discuss an argument with a teacher is being unduly optimistic. Many delinquents, however, want to "save face" and, despite protest, will engage in a treatent relationship because of pressure from parents or court.

A treatment alliance need not involve the patient's liking the therapist; many beginning therapists expect gratitude and positive affection from their patients, something that is contrary to the very nature of the adolescent process. The problem, of course, in working with many adolescents, and especially delinquents, is that specific transference issues such as the over-idealization of the parental figure, the hungry longing for maternal gratification, the wish to defeat the parent, or the mistrust of the parents' consistency and dependability, may many times interfere with the therapeutic alliance. Consequently, there must be considerable external support for the psychotherapy alliance; ward staff members frequently and consistently encourage the hospitalized delinquent to bring issues to the therapist and take note of the patient's missing or keeping a therapy session.

Certain kinds of behavior are considered so indicative of internal conflict that the return of certain kinds of privileges and responsibilities on the unit occur only when these behaviors have been "worked on" in the psychotherapy session. Such "work" in the beginning may be only taking note of a fleeting affect that the delinquent discharged through some kind of antisocial act, but as his ability to engage in psychotherapy grows, it may later take the form of understanding specific transference issues which cause the aberrant behavior. These concepts are further demonstrated by considering the therapist a part of the management team that makes decisions about the adolescent's treatment plan and privileges. The therapist does not make these decisions by himself; nor does a separate administrator. Thus, the patient learns that the therapist, though important, does not carry the burden of treatment alone, and the daily living activities of the milieu are extremely important in facilitating, supporting, preceding, and enhancing the ultimate benefits of individual psychotherapy.

Although individual psychotherapy is characterized by therapeutic alliance, self-observation, and empathy, these processes occur in the milieu as well, but less distinctly. Reality-testing, interpersonal feedback, and confrontation characterize the milieu, but may occur in individual therapy as well.

Many beginning psychotherapists are deceived by the power of their verbal interpretations and by the illusory establishment of a relationship. Often the only hope of the inhospital phase of treatment is that we try to provide a situation in which a therapeutic alliance can be developed and begin to be utilized by both patient and therapist. Many neophyte therapists are caught up by their own importance and approach the patient as someone to be understood solely by them, and consequently do not look for, or demand, an alliance of the patient. They may confuse the concept of a treatment alliance with positive feelings for the therapist and become dismayed when their patients do not like them.

On the other hand, the psychotherapy novice expresses and experiences many tensions with the rest of the treatment staff and, on many occasions, overidentifies with his patient, whom he defends against the confrontation of the staff. He is frequently pleased with the antisocial behavior of the patient because of his own angry competition with the rest of the staff, or believes that there is something cathartic about patients acting out antisocially, as if delinquency were something that needs to be discharged, never to recur. We have also noted that a therapist sometimes utilizes cultural differences between himself and his patient to excuse or rationalize certain kinds of behavior. It has been our experience that race or socioeconomic status does not significantly influence the meaning of disruptive behavior. Many therapists attempt to demonstrate their social consciousness by pointing out that certain kinds of impulsive and disruptive behavior are commonplace or normal in lower socioeconomic subcultures, such as in the black ghetto; our experience has been that this reflects a subtle depreciation of the patient. Therefore, we uniformly apply the same kinds of expectations and diagnostic attitudes toward disruptive and impulsive behavior, regardless of the patient's socioeconomic background. Certain factors may, of course, influence our mode of intervention, as well as our understanding of specific transference issues, but no one is excused from owning his behavior, accepting the responsibility for it, for understanding it, and for attempting to modify it. Culture does not change basic psychopathology, although it may influence its expression.

Delinquents are hospitalized because they are psychologically deficient and they are not able to grow or master the developmental tasks of adolescence. A therapeutic environment is one in which the deficient ego is supported and presented only with tasks that it can master, rather than tasks which overwhelm it. For internal change to take place, some capacity for self-observation must be developed; this is precisely what individual psychotherapy is all about—it is the self-observing function of the therapist and staff that is internalized among others. This work really begins in the milieu when the ward staff member notes a bit of behavior, calls it to the delinquent's attention, and then helps him to look at it, or many times helps him to stop it and then look at it. The responses of the staff are not just verbal, but convey strong affect. It is this kind of communication to which the deficient ego can respond. Forcing the patient's attention inward precedes, supports, and eventuates in the insights gained in individual psychotherapy. Insight may not always be recovering a primal scene memory. It may be helping a tough, violent delinquent realize that when he gets scared he wants to hit someone, and that sometimes he gets scared when he likes someone or longs for affection. The "oriented" of "psychoanalytically oriented psychotherapy" does not refer to free association and the couch, but indicates that when we work with delinquents we keep our wits about us and rely on our theoretical formulations.

It is quite clear that the hyperstimulation of the transference situation can frequently lead to a traumatized, overstimulated, and disrupted ego, with the patient behaving violently in an almost random discharge manner (Marohn, 1974). Violence is an ever-present problem in attempting to do meaningful psychotherapy with delinquents. Violence must be prevented before it occurs in order for the unit to be safe for growth and for therapy to occur. Violence to property precedes violence to person. Threats of violence must be dealt with, and violence by verbal abuse cannot be tolerated. An adequate and consistent staff must again provide external functions for the already disrupted egos of the delinquents. Medication, physical restraints, and isolation in the patient's own room, not a bare and unfamiliar seclusion room, are tools we have used as external ego supports and to decrease internal stimulation, in the presence of contact and work with milieu staff. The psychotherapist must be keenly aware of the damage that he can do by prematurely forcing a delinquent to deal with certain issues, by ignoring signs of disruptive behavior, and by subtly or overtly promising the patient the longed-for parental gratification that many delinquents defend against. We know that many delinquents feel more comfortable when they can idealize their therapist or mirror in their therapist their own powerful and omnipotent fantasies. The therapist must be sensitive to the delinquent's need for such a narcissistic relationship and must be comfortable enough with his own self-esteem to permit such transference to unfold. He must be keenly aware of the delinquent's sensitivity and that a most minimal slight may precipitate a period of psychotic disorganization and fragmentation, an outbreak of rage as the delinquent attempts to gain control over his world, or a period of severe disillusionment and depressive withdrawal.

To see all antisocial behavior on the unit as the acting out of specific intrapsychic issues is a mistake in many instances. It may not be that specific neurotic-like conflicts are being externalized, but it may very well be that the patient has regressed to a period of fragmentation and ego disorganization, in which thought and action are no longer differentiated, and in which the boundaries between the internal and external worlds have become blurred. Exploring with the patient the reasons for such disintegration is important, but frequently emergency measures must first be provided by the therapist and the staff to shore up and reestablish tenuous ego functions.

The individual treatment situation is central, or better said, focal. It is the primary transference relationship in the hospital; it is the therapist's responsibility to direct and organize the team's understanding of the patient, and it is through this primary treatment alliance that self-observation, self-understanding, and conflict resolution, as well as ego growth, are channeled.

Since the individual psychotherapy is so pivotal and so imbricated with transferences, it is also the treatment situation that is the least consciously appreciated by the patient, usually repressed, and quickly terminated as the adolescent grows and matures toward adulthood. It is, of course, not in the nature of adolescence to cling to the parental figures of childhood, and our experience has been that as our delinquent patients grow, they terminate. Some terminate abruptly, while some terminate by forcing us to do the termination ourselves, but they do terminate, and seem to have internalized something from the therapeutic experience.

The psychological development of the adolescent forces us to view this time of life as a unique maturational phase. The uniqueness of this period has implications for treatment. The teenager must experiment with, master, and integrate his genital sexual urges. He must establish some kind of psychological separation from the parents of infancy. He or she experiences significant transformations in his own narcissism, or self-love, with vacillations in self-esteem, swings between grandiosity and feelings of worthlessness, depreciation and de-idealization of parents and authority, and idealization and worship of his own heroes. This means, of course, that adolescence, particularly middle adolescence, may involve a considerable amount of internal turmoil with no apparent disturbed behavior, or it may result in tumultuous behavior, including a fair amount of expectable delinquency, until the adolescent finally achieves a stable personality or character structure as seen in late adolescence. At this point, he has developed a capacity for longer-lasting relationships and a certain amount of intimacy, with quiescence and calm following the storm (Offer and Offer, 1975).

In the process of separating himself from his parents, the adolescent deprives himself of their psychological support; no matter how helpful parents want to be, the adolescent cannot accept their support because it is too much like being a "baby." Furthermore, giving up the parents of childhood involves some mourning and grief; consequently, adolescents are frequently depressed.

As we described in Chapter 1, Anna Freud (1958) has described various ways in which teenagers break the ties to their parents; in most instances, the average healthy adolescent will use many of these methods. The hallmark of health in adolescence is probably the gradual, rather than precipitous, manner in which the separation is achieved. The healthy adolescent will utilize a variety of psychological maneuvers rather than relying simply on a single way of separating from the parents. If the teenager is attempting to separate from his parents by displacement and has already achieved a new infatuation, it may be very difficult for anyone, including the therapist, to try to establish a meaningful alliance with this teenager. On the other hand, if a love affair has just broken up, or if the teenager has not yet established an important new relationship, the teenager may readily displace his intense feelings onto the therapist; this may enable him to establish an alliance readily, but it may also, of course, create problems if the alliance blossoms into an infatuation. With only displacement in his repertoire, he may then, fickle person that he is, readily break off the relationship with the therapist and attach himself to someone else.

The teenager who deals with intense affectionate feelings by reversing them into opposite feelings feels guilty about hating and being angry with the very people he cares about, and so frequently this teenager is depressed and guilty. This teenager is in pain and may readily share his depression with a therapist and may eagerly seek some kind of help.

Other adolescents may deal with their wishes to cling to their parents by trying to separate in a paranoid manner, that is, by accusing parents and other authority figures of attempting to dominate and control their lives. With these adolescents it is difficult to establish a relationship. Other adolescents may deal with their attempts to separate from the parents by regressing to a more infantile level of development and here, of course, the therapist may readily establish a relationship with the dependent, clinging adolescent. A relationship may be readily established, but the adolescent may resist growing up.

It is clear, then, that the manner in which the adolescent separates psychologically may facilitate or hinder his ability to relate to another adult. The relationship with an adult is always a fragile and delicate matter, and the adolescent's degree of attachment and ability to work therapeutically may fluctuate greatly within a single hour. Adolescent attachments are unpredictable and fickle, and one must never feel secure about the working relationship with a teenager.

Meeks (1971) makes a number of practical suggestions that one can use to determine whether or not an adolescent is capable of establishing a treatment alliance. Certainly we must determine that the patient is motivated, that he is capable of some kind of basic trust in another human being, that he is experiencing some pain which prompts him to seek help, that he hopes that there is a possibility of receiving help, and that he wishes to change some things about himself or at least change his present circumstances. It is helpful if an adolescent can talk about his feelings, giving them names, and expressing some of his own ideas and plans. It is also useful if the adolescent has developed some capacity to abstract, to think in something other than concrete terms, and to be able to try to talk about problems and feelings rather than discharge them simply in activity.

However, most adolescents do not come to us this way; they are action-oriented, they speak in concrete terms, they see nothing wrong with themselves—it is their parents they wish to change, they do not trust adults, and in no way do they want to be treated like a "baby" and ask for help. Most adolescents find it difficult to seek help or to admit they have problems because such attitudes are experienced by them as signs of weakness and as signs of "badness." However, very concrete, mentally dulled, violence-prone teenagers can be helped to introspect. For example, one very tough boy, a violent teenager from a disrupted family and a ghetto background, frequently threatened staff and attempted to engage in fist fights on our unit. With the help of a very direct and confronting therapist, he was able to learn that, when he got angry, he was really frightened of something, and that usually what frightened him was that he was beginning to experience some kind of affectionate feelings for another human being. Such insight was a milestone in this youth's development.

We look for some capacity on the part of teenagers to look inside themselves, to introspect. Do they get up in the morning and, recognizing that they are in a bad mood, attribute this to "getting out on the wrong side of the bed," or do they say that it might have something to do with some problems or worries about their family, friends, or school? Do they minimize difficulties or do they express some curiosity about why they do certain things and why certain things happen? Even such minimal curiosity is substantial evidence of a psychological mindedness which many teenagers may not demonstrate spontaneously, but which can be demonstrated when someone spends time talking with them.

Frequently, the interviewer must be sure that the difficulties the teenager is experiencing are indicative of problems, and he must unambivalently and decisively confront the teenager with that definite possibility. Only then, when the teenager is confronted with a somewhat firm and confident adult position, can he relax comfortably and share his own doubts and concern about his personal life.

It is, of course, important to recognize what phase the teenager is in as far as the separation process is concerned. If the teenager is in early adolescence and is, for the most part, still attached to his parents, he may find it difficult to begin relating to another adult. If, on the other hand, he is in middle adolescence and is attempting to separate from his parents, he may readily engage with a family physician, a school counselor, or a therapist. If he begins feeling towards that other adult as he had felt towards his parents, that is, wanting to be taken care of, but also wanting to flee such a dependent relationship, at some point or other the treatment alliance may falter. At that point it is important that the helping adult skillfully minimize the amount of anxiety that the teenager is experiencing. It is often useful to find out, in assessing whether or not a teenager is capable of establishing a treatment alliance, the nature of his previous experiences with other adults; has he been able to accept help, has he been able to call on people in time of need, etc.?

Some common problems arise in working with teenagers. Since teenagers are attempting to separate from the parents, privacy becomes terribly important. Teenagers frequently have secrets with each other or whisper things in confidence that in themselves have no particular value, but parents frequently believe that some secret plot of dire consequence is being hatched. The only dire consequences are those which ensue when the parents attempt to find out what the secrets are. Diaries, written but unsent letters and notes, and other secret treasures all represent an adolescent's attempt to exclude others and heighten the importance of oneself. Parental prying into adolescent secrets represents serious interference with such attempts at individuation. Although the individuality of the teenager must be respected, privacy can never be absolute and must always be subject to the recognition that the teenager is not yet completely emancipated or responsible for himself and, indeed, expects and requires a certain amount of parental care and guidance.

The developmental tasks of the teenager and adult problems with them become considerably more complicated in the hospital treatment situation. For example, when two teenagers pass love letters back and forth, is this the expression of adolescent maturation? Is it play-acting and experimentation in an attempt to integrate sexual feelings? Could it reflect the adolescent's separation need to keep things from adults and to have something special with a peer? Does it represent the displacement from an intense transference situation in therapy in which feelings are being experienced in another relationship instead of being brought into the treatment situation—in other words, a true acting out? Or is it an unconscious attempt on the part of one or both parties to resist the treatment orientation of the unit? All situations must be assessed on an individual basis.

It is useful to begin with some understanding of normal adolescence and normal parenting and then begin deducing appropriate therapeutic principles therefrom. The fact that certain behaviors occur developmentally in normal teenagers does not mean that adult responses appropriate to that situation are always appropriate to the treatment situation. For example, in the hospital we do respect the privacy of each teenager's room much as parents should; yet, we recognize that there may be times when it is necessary to intrude in the teenager's privacy even though he may object. Sometimes it is necessary to search rooms for drugs or weapons, but this is never done without the teenager's knowledge and is always done in his presence. We do become quite suspicious of pairing off, surreptitious conversations, and the exchanging of written notes. Our experience has generally been that these are attempts to withhold or withdraw from treatment, to defend against or resist the treatment process, or, in the extreme, to plot sexual escapades or run away. In many ways, after all, the hospital is not a "normal" environment for the adolescent. We put patients under a good deal of stress and create a highly observant atmosphere, in which they are confronted with stimulating experiences, with close physical and emotional contact with others, and with the burdens of intense transference situations. In such a "hothouse," staff vigilance is essential to curtail patients' acting out their difficulties in ways which are either destructive to their own growth and development or destructive to their own or someone else's therapy.

The outpatient therapist guarantees confidentiality and shares with the teenager whatever his discussions or conversations have been with his parents or other authorities, but not vice versa, although there are occasions when some things need to be discussed with parents, but then only in the presence of the teenager. On the other hand, in the hospital situation, it is clearly understood that the therapist meets with the team and has informal discussions with other staff members about the nature of the psychotherapy sessions. In this kind of situation, in order to foster and facilitate a multidisciplinary team approach, it is not possible to guarantee the teenager strict confidentiality of the treatment room, and the therapist can only indicate and promise that he will use his discretion in what is shared with other staff members. He cannot be bound by a promise of confidentiality because it must be assumed that the responsibility of confidentiality becomes the responsibility of all the staff and no delinquent adolescent will profit from a situation in which he is able to split one staff member from another. The obverse may also occur when a patient selects out his favorite staff member and begins sharing "secrets" and embarrassing problems with that staff member with the promise that it will not be discussed with the therapist. In some instances this may be useful practice and an attempt by the patient to deal with the anxieties of the transference situation, but again there can be no such confidential or special relationship and the information needs to be shared with the psychotherapist, as the patient expects that it will be. Most adolescents understand that it is this kind of confidentiality that exists in the hospital treatment situation, and fully expect that their conversations will be shared throughout the staff. The therapist is, of course, under no obligation to share anything verbatim, and whether he shares the intimate details of many of the patient's associations, fantasies, and experiences is his own judgment because it is, after all, a therapeutic responsibility to integrate and organize the meaning of the psychotherapy material in an understandable and workable manner for other members of the treatment team.

Because many teenagers need to separate from their parents by disagreeing or rebelling, the teenager who says "no" may frequently mean "yes." Many teenagers cannot agree to seek help or admit to having certain problems that require help; consequently, they rely on parental authority to get them help. Many teenagers are vociferous in their unwillingness to engage in treatment, but do so reluctantly because of parental or other pressure. They need to save face because they could not openly admit their need for a dependent relationship on an adult or that they have problems—statements which they frequently experience as signs of weakness. As a result, those legal authorities who seek explicit agreement by teenagers to various treatment maneuvers are overlooking and underestimating an important aspect of adolescence, that reluctance must not be interpreted as refusal. A teenager's unwillingness to pursue a particular therapeutic course may simply be that he is hoping that parental authority will step into the breach and provide the reassuring controls. It is important, therefore, that the therapist not be unwilling to use his own authority in insisting on a particular plan of action with the teenager. This does run the risk of forcing the teenager into a dependent position which might precipitate flight, but frequently the teenager will respond with comfort to firmness and a sense of authoritative direction.

The therapist who presents himself as a peer confuses the teenager. He may be like an older friend, but it is important to recognize that every therapist will be viewed to some extent by the teenager as a parental figure, and the teenager's need to protect himself from too much closeness with the parent will unquestionably arise in the treatment relationship as well.

Many therapists, and other staff as well, have their own unresolved difficulties stemming from a failure to have worked through certain developmental tasks of adolescence. Staff members may have their own problems in accepting authority and rebel at the slightest possibility of anyone attempting to be firm with them. This will make it difficult to help the teenager who is rebelling against legitimate authority. Similarly, staff members may themselves have sexual difficulties, and this may make it difficult for them even to listen to a teenager's recounting of his own sexual problems; a moralistic, impatient or dogmatic attitude about masturbatory guilt or sexual experimentation may interfere with being an empathic listener. Many staff members find it difficult to accept the idea that a teenager idolizes them or thinks that their ideas are valuable. On the other hand, it may be difficult to recognize that a teenager who is negativistic may still, however, be listening carefully to the therapist. The therapist who demands absolute compliance from patients, and who may be used to getting such compliance from adult patients, may find it difficult to deal with an undependable and frequently uncooperative teenager.

Because adolescent patients are rarely compliant or cooperative, the therapist must distinguish a working or therapeutic alliance from a positive transference; adolescent patients, particularly delinquents, rarely evidence positive feelings towards their therapist. Conversely, a negative transference is not to be equated with resistance or an untreatable patient. An inexperienced therapist may eagerly terminate with a treatment case because he is confronted with a negativistic, depreciating, critical, disparaging patient, whose negative transference be cannot understand. The adolescent's negativism arises from his disillusionment that an idealized parent has failed to materialize, and the therapist confuses this negative transference with the absence of a therapeutic alliance.

At the other extreme, we have often seen compliant adolescent patients who conform to the requirements of the psychotherapy and milieu situation and who, after discharge, are unable or unwilling to continue in psychotherapy principally because no therapeutic alliance had ever been established. It is true that some adolescents leave therapy because the therapist served certain developmental functions for the patient—just as it is part of the adolescent process to separate from the relationships of childhood, so, too, maturing adolescents detach themselves from therapeutic alliances characterized by infantile ties. Yet, considerable ego support and external control are required before the delinquent adolescent can engage in a therapeutic alliance; many missing or deficient functions must be provided by the staff or the patient must be relieved of a number of psychological tasks in order to invest in the psychotherapy relationship. Staff support is required in order to assist the adolescent to begin to identify symptomatic behavior and initiate the process of introspection.

A similar problem is the confusion between a narcissistic transference and resistance. First of all, it is important to distinguish the patient's idealization of a therapist from the reaction formation or denial of aggression or hostility. As Kohut (1971) has described, therapists are not comfortable being idealized and frequently attempt to search for the hostility lying beneath the positive valence. Secondly, merger transference may also frequently be experienced as "resistance" in which the therapist is being utilized as a self-object and not experienced as a separate person. Consequently, interpretations about missing the therapist after an interruption are usually reacted to violently by the patient, but not because the patient is "resisting" the meaning of the interpretation, but because the interpretation is incorrect. The patient did not miss the therapist in the sense that he experienced the loss of another person, but rather the patient fragmented, and attempted to restitute or reconstitute himself through various forms of behavior or symptomatology because an important function not at all related to the person of the analyst or therapist had been taken from him.

Traditional models of psychic functioning, such as the repression barrier model of the unconscious, preconscious, and conscious systems or the structural or tripartite model of ego, id, and superego, are not very useful in understanding the difficulties of many of these patients. A self-object model, which postulates that certain psychic functions, particularly those of self-soothing, are missing and self-objects are utilized to complete deficiencies of the self-system, is more useful. Thus, the absence of the therapist poses a threat to the integrity of the self-system. The patient who continually expects the therapist to like the same kind of music as he does and read the same kinds of books and attend the same kinds of movies, and then is continually frustrated and disillusioned when he learns otherwise, is not attempting to identify with the therapist, but rather requires similarities in the therapist because certain activities of the therapist are required to mirror the patient's grandiosity and bolster his faltering self-esteem. To misinterpret this as a patient's attempting to identify with the therapist, whom he may have perceived as an aggressor in an attempt to resolve oedipal conflict, clearly misses the point. Such conceptualizations may not only create difficulty in the therapeutic relationship, but also may be experienced by the patient as an empathic rupture and a painful narcissistic injury. A third way in which narcissistic transference and resistance may be confused is that some resistance is not an inertia that needs to be overcome by interpretation, but rather an important and necessary defense against fragmentation which might be brought on by the kind of overstimulation that some patients experience when the therapist accurately empathizes with their needs.

"Countertransference" problems also interfere with the establishment of a therapeutic alliance. Here it is important to distinguish true countertransference, that is to say, reactions of the therapist to the patient which are derived from unresolved transferences from the therapist's own early life, from more neutralized affective reactions to the transference of the patient. An example of countertransference would be a therapist's own unresolved conflicts over individuation; these create a blind spot, making it difficult for him to recognize that a patient's flaunting of authority in an attempt to be independent has its roots in psychological conflict. On the other hand, irritation and anger at a patient's persistent attempts to challenge and ridicule the authority of the therapist are expectable and useful reactions, which can give the therapist some clue as to the meaning of the patient's behavior. Such a reaction need not be evidence of countertransference, though the manner in which the therapist behaves in response to such feelings and such a challenge may have countertransference aspects.

Countertransference problems frequently arise from the therapist's own narcissistic fixations, which may cause him to reject the patient's idealizations or to distance himself from mirroring or merger, but which could also cause him to encourage idealization, mirroring or conformity in order to avoid a patient's anger or attempts at differentiation and autonomy. Frequently, a patient's "resistance" and the therapist's belief that the patient is "fighting" him are a misinterpretation of the experience that the adolescent is utilizing the therapist as a self-object, when the therapist is incapable of empathizing with this intense deficit and need of the patient's. It is difficult to empathize with this situation because one is not treated as an independent and autonomous being, but rather as an object to be possessed, manipulated, dominated, and used. Often, such merger may go on silently, and the therapist may not notice the use to which he is being put by the patient. As a result, much of the patient's psychopathology may seem to disappear.

Frequently, when the delinquent adolescent has been hospitalized and many of his deficient psychological functions are being compensated for by the hospital milieu, or when a merger transference has begun to be established and the mere presence or existence of the therapist begins to make up for certain psychological deficits of the patient, acting out behavior and obvious delinquent pathology subside. It is difficult, then, for many staff therapists, particularly beginning therapists, to recognize the patient as having problems. Such a "flight into health" by the patient begins precipitating wishes by therapists to discharge the patient, and they have great difficulty saying no to relentless testing and demands for passes and an early discharge date. The delinquent is fearful and uncertain of entering into a treatment relationship and exploring the nature of the merger transference if the therapist and the staff are not empathically in tune with the extent and seriousness of his own psychopathology. Programs which foster the perpetuation of community and family ties and expect patients to go home every weekend, for example, may place such challenges and demands on adolescents that they cannot enter into the kind of treatment relationship necessary for the exploration of their pathology.

Often the therapist believes that a patient is resisting his interpretations when, indeed, the interpretation is not being resisted in the sense that an id impulse is being defended against, but rather the interpretation is "incorrect." The interpretation may not be imprecise, inaccurate, or wrong in content, but rather it may not be directed at the level at which the patient is functioning. Interpretations need to be made on the basis of current experiences in the treatment situation.

Therapists frequently understand, correctly so, that whatever the patient talks about in a session has some relevance to the transference; however, this is not to say that whenever a patient talks about an external event, the feelings about that event or the experience of that event have necessarily been stimulated by transference strivings. On the contrary, bringing the event into the session has some transference implications and, more often than not, a therapist is more successful when he talks about the event having its parallel in the analytic or therapeutic relationship. However, the therapist often fails when he attempts to convey the idea to the patient that the real meaning of the event lies in the transference experience. The patient is unable to accept these interpretations, not because he is resisting the emergence of an instinctual impulse or the transference phenomenon, but rather because he has enough reality-testing to know that there is a real life outside the analytic or treatment relationship, and that the therapist's focus is simply wrong and diminishes the import of that eternal reality. An adolescent needs to cling to his reality-testing fervently.

Another difficulty that therapists experience, particularly in the beginning phases of their training, is the need to avoid the implications of transference entirely. Many therapists prefer to view the therapeutic experience as one that can be understood only in terms of cognitive theory, while others state explicitly that certain kinds of patients are to be viewed primarily and solely as suffering from biological or biochemical disorders and that their communications have no real meaning and need not be attended to. Yet, these therapists must still learn how to talk with patients and will undoubtedly be involved with communications that need to be understood and responded to.

Novice therapists may exhibit their particular difficulty in accepting the transference experience by such responses as "I am not that important," "There is nothing wrong with her," or "I don't like him." The first position is often the result of the fact that the therapist's own narcissism has not been attenuated sufficiently and the transference idealization is experienced by the therapist as a reality experience rather than a phenomenon emanating from the patient's past and not really based on the worth of the therapist. On the other hand, therapists who require narcissistic feeding may not reject the transference idealization of the patient, but may accept such a transference as a reality, enjoy it, seduce the patient into subtle reinforcement of the therapist's needs, and never come to grips with the transference distortions. Finally, the therapist who rejects the patient may be doing so either because the transference is anxiety-ridden for him or because the transference is of such a nature that it does not reinforce certain of his needs. The patient is then experienced as an impossible or difficult human being.

As stated in Chapter 1, our work (Marohn, Offer, Ostrov, and Trujillo, 1979; Offer, Marohn, and Ostrov, 1979) suggests the existence of four major dimensions of nonpsychotic delinquent behavior: the impulsive, the narcissistic, the depressed borderline, and the empty borderline. Each subgroup may represent different problems in the establishment of a therapeutic alliance. The impulsive adolescent will find it difficult to tolerate a transference of any nature and will need to discharge through action rather than engage in verbal interactions. The narcissistic personality disorder may defend against engagement with a therapist in order to avoid self-esteem fluctuations or personal injury. While ordinarily a depressed patient has a low energy level, yet desires treatment to relieve himself from suffering, an adolescent who is acting out delinquently in order to relieve himself of depression may find it difficult to engage in therapy because painful affect precipitates the need for action and distancing. The empty borderline, because of the need for merger and self-object relating to prevent fragmentation, may readily engage in a therapeutic alliance which will be fraught with many delicate problems as one attempts to forestall psychotic regression or as the patient attempts to flee from merger and fusion anxiety.

The adolescent who seeks out or initiates treatment with a clearly demonstrable potential for a therapeutic alliance is rare. Most adolescents will require an external ego and external self-objects, often in a hospital setting, in order to engage in a therapeutic alliance. Quite obviously, at the outpatient level, such external functions are provided by parents or family in either collateral or family therapy work.

OUTCOME OF THERAPY

Questions about dropouts from therapy continue to plague us. At follow-up, most of our patients are doing well. Although many continue to check in with the staff at intervals in the first few years after discharge, most discontinued outpatient therapy within three to six months.

One year following discharge, we began contacting the 55 delinquent subjects reported in the research work (Offer, Marohn, and Ostrov, 1979), who form the core of the population we treated. We were able to obtain data on 89% of our subjects who were eventually interviewed about 21 months after discharge. Our average subject had been arrested 1.7 times, spent 1.5 months in a correctional facility, and 21 days in a mental hospital. Thirty-nine percent had used no drugs in contrast to 18% on admission. And 28% had used only marijuana. Twenty-six percent had used heavy drugs such as psychedelics, speed, uppers or downers, in contrast to 63% at admission. Seven percent used heroin, in contrast to 19% at admission. At follow-up, 85% used no alcohol or used alcohol moderately, while 15% used alcohol to the point of drunkenness, in contrast to 15% and 41% respectively at admission. At follow-up, half of our subjects had been rearrested, in contrast to the 91% who had been arrested prior to referral. Of those rearrested, half were status or minor offenses, while half were major.

Seventy-nine percent of our subjects felt positive or very positive about themselves, 9% were ambivalent, and 11% were negative or very negative about themselves.

In addition to these research interviews, we have had numerous further contacts with our core population, as well as with all other delinquents we have treated. Most of our patients have been provided some form of therapy after discharge. For many of them, the termination from the hospital is a stormy disruptive time; for others, it initially appears to go smoothly, but the delinquent adolescent usually drops out of outpatient therapy quickly, often within three months, even though a therapeutic alliance seems to have been established. Our first response to these data was that this indicated a failure to have established a therapeutic alliance, or that the adolescent had, indeed, not yet been ready for discharge. However, on further contact, we find that these patients are doing quite well and have quite obviously internalized something of the treatment program. What becomes clear is that part of the adolescent maturation process, which had been derailed and which was again reestablished through our therapeutic efforts, leads to separation from the hospital and from the therapist, who now becomes part of the adolescent's earlier life and must be left behind.

CASE HISTORY

Theresa, 15, was admitted because "everybody says I am crazy." Since early in grade school, she had viciously assaulted other people either on her own or in gang activity. Just prior to admission she had been caught carrying a gun on a school playground. She boasted that she frequently carried a gun, had shot one person, and had fired at many others. She described herself as being the "chief" of a gang of 75 girls, some as old as 21 years of age. She maintained her leadership position through aggressive, hostile attitudes and behavior. The gang fought with other black girls' gangs while at the same time abusing, humiliating, and assaulting white teenagers. Her parentage troubled her; her mother was white, her father was black, and she was raised by a black woman to whom she had been given. She saw herself as black, but the daughter of a "white bitch."

On the unit she showed a marked intolerance of anxiety, which she usually mastered by a defensive toughness and bravado. For example, during a teaching conference when a staff member left the room while Theresa was being interviewed and was visibly anxious, she shouted, "She can't do that, walk out of my meeting. I am the one to walk out." Initially, the staff and her therapist tried not only to calm her, but also to help her begin to recognize that she was frightened.

She was described by one consultant as "really falling apart with nobody to fight against." Sometimes she would hold her head and at others her entire body while rolling around on her bed as if she were "going to explode." She was exquisitely sensitive to the problems of other patients and frequently found herself getting mixed up in their difficulties and conflicts. Her inability to differentiate herself showed in needing to fight in order to feel different. Therapy was directed at helping her accept contact without feeling absorbed.

Her self-revulsion and frequent attempts at self-mutilation alternated with grandiose attempts to control the unit, openly defy the staff, and intimidate other patients. She would talk in therapy about her father's wish she had never been born and her mother's promise to return some day to claim her; both these attitudes were repeated in a narcissistic transference when she alternately felt attacked by her therapist or glorified in her omnipotence in her therapist's eyes.

Because she manipulated the staff into giving her direction, structure, and identity, she was provided with an atmosphere during her

two-year hospitalization that helped her move from panic and fragmentation, through omnipotent struggles, to a capacity for self-
observation.

The patient expressed concern about whether or not she would serve
certain needs of the therapist, like being a therapeutic success or failure, as indeed she had so often fulfilled the ambitions and needs of her
foster mother. Making this issue explicit helped to resolve it. She
recognized that she had changed and was unable to return to her life
of violence even though her current adjustment was in some ways
more painful. Follow-up psychological testing demonstrated that the
patient could now experience and tolerate affect, knew that she was a
troubled person, and had conscious ideas and fantasies, however poorly
integrated. A self-cohesion had evolved which enabled her to engage
in relationships with people rather than break away to prevent fusion
or merger. Yet, she could separate from her "white bitch" therapist in
only an abrupt manner, running away from the hospital and returning
twice. The third time she stayed away. Later, she returned, on drugs,
pleading to be readmitted. She was refused, and began outpatient
therapy.

The stormy separation demonstrated that Theresa still utilized her
therapist for essential psychological functions and that to leave the
hospital could be accomplished only under her control, as she struggled
to regain omnipotent control of her world. Drugs were an attempt to
replace the soothing functions of the therapist, and the demand for
rehospitalization represented the hoped for reunion in a maternal symbiosis. Refusing such a request and deciding not to rescue Theresa was
based on the recognition that she had developed the internal resources
to individuate and grow, even though her behavior seemed to suggest
that she was not ready for discharge.

Of course, such seemingly premature termination of therapy may
also reflect incomplete work which can be finished only in adulthood
and which is now temporarily suspended because of the unavailability
of external support outside of the hospital setting and the shift of
energies outward to family, peers, school, and job.

TRAINING ISSUES

Parallel problems occur in training psychotherapists where considerable support by the staff and the therapy supervisors is required to sustain the therapist in the challenges and demands of his work with our delinquent adolescent patients. The emergence of a transference may cause such fear in the therapist that the patient, sensing such insecurity, may choose to leave treatment rather than persist. The therapist may also be buffeted by depreciation and challenges in the experiencing of a negative transference; he may choose to see this as resistance and prefer to terminate with the patient. Such responses indicate an overwhelmed and frightened therapist who requires a considerable amount of empathy and support from the permanent staff. Because of the transferences that the staff experience towards therapists and because of the beginning therapist's difficulty in accepting help, this supportive alliance is not easily accomplished. The relationship with the supervisor cannot be limited to the psychotherapeutic material, but needs also to embrace the entire process of being a member of a staff. Eventually, the therapist, too, develops an internal structure, a way of approaching data, of inferring, and of intervening, which sustains him even in the throes of such a stormy period as Theresa's discharge.

The experience of psychotherapy is both the patient's and the therapist's. It occurs in the context of a living hospital milieu which engenders and sustains the working alliance and highlights the multifaceted transferences. It culminates in a termination, sometimes stormy, and often imbricated with maturational thrusts.

4

Person

Hungry infants cry out in distress. They are responding to internal tension that they cannot identify or define. The distress is real and they express themselves in the only way they know. They are letting the "outer" world know of their "inner" turmoil, unaware even that there is an "outer" world. They are picked up, gently held, and fed a bottle, after which they are put back to bed and blissfully fall asleep. What has happened? The unnamed inner tension has been eased: The belly is full, the infant is dry; he is neither too hot nor too cold. "All is right with the world," and so sleep is quiet and serene.

Infants, of course, do not "know" that mother has heard their cries, determined that they are hungry, warmed a bottle, and then fed them. But they "know" the experience of being lifted carefully, of being held against a soft body, the warmth of the milk—these things they feel, smell, hear. They incorporate the pleasure of the situation, the gratifications, the sense of well-being. Infants are completely oblivious to the "other" in this transaction. The mother who responded to them, held them, fed them, talked gently to them is experienced not as a person, separate and distinct, but rather as an extension of the totally self-centered universe. The total experience, many times repeated, is absorbed rather than known. This symbiosis, begun in the womb, continues in the infant/mother relationship.

In the healthy development, this symbiosis is gradually replaced by internalization of the "other." Somewhat older infants also cry in distress when hungry, but now are aware of stirring in the kitchen, footsteps, and perhaps even a reassuring voice. They have learned by this

76

time that this combination of events in the past resulted in feeding and the relief of tension. If the experience of the mothering has been satisfying and regular and predictable, the relief of tension occurs even before being fed. A psychobiological pattern emerges. They can now tolerate an interval between their first cries and the moment when the bottle arrives. Infants still do not "know" there is a person, a mother, out there who hears their cries and anticipates their needs; they are simply "aware" in a visceral sense that the stirring of footsteps eventuates in satiation. Healthy development must encompass this symbiotic beginning. Eventually, the child must move away from this symbiotic state. The formation of psychological structure depends on the gradual loss of that symbiosis, the later even more gradual internalization of the mother, eventual individuation and awareness of the mother as a separate person with her own boundaries and affective responses, and the replacement of the internalized mother by functions the child then performs smoothly and automatically for himself.

This gradual shift from relying on the mother to relying on oneself to perform certain psychological functions occurs when the child begins to identify with the mother's caring functions. Identification results from dosed frustrations; when the mother is unable or unwilling to perform certain functions for the developing child, he experiences frustration but may begin performing these functions for himself. For example, a child may ask his mother to attend to a minor bruise. The mother may choose not to take care of it, but tell the child to wash and bandage the injury. The child may experience mild frustration, but learns to do it for himself. Similarly, the mother admires the child's drawing of stick men and in her praise provides what Kohut (1971) describes as the mirroring response, wherein the child experiences himself as the "gleam in mother's eye"; at some point, the mother, because she is busy, preoccupied, or decides not to do so, does not provide such mirroring and frustrates the child. If such frustration is tolerable, the child will experience mild disappointment, but begin performing such self-assessment and self-praise, thus, again, internalizing certain maternal functions, which lead eventually to self-esteem formation. As these experiences are repeated time and time again, the growing child develops his own psychological structure and is capable of such psychological functions as soothing and calming himself, monitoring his own behavior, modulating urges, and delaying the need for gratification. Furthermore, he develops identifications and internal representations not only of the self, but of others.

Psychological structure develops as the child integrates dosed frustrations. However, when such frustrations are massive or unpredictable, where there is a lack of consistency in the mother/child relationship, the child is unable to develop internalized representations of himself and others, and psychological functions, psychological structure building, and the whole process of identification are seriously disrupted. We see this in many of our delinquents who have no sense of themselves or of others, who have no experience of the outside world as predictable, who have no capacity to represent or describe themselves or others, and whose experience of the world is of responding to stimuli, waiting for something to happen, and of never being under their own control. They have no capacity to initiate games or projects; they have no capacity to plan or anticipate the future.

The existence of deep disturbances in the individuation process of infancy becomes increasingly apparent during adolescence, which, as Peter Blos (1967) has demonstrated, can be viewed as a second period of separation and individuation. Since one of the major tasks of adolescence is the separation from the internal representations of the infantile parents, and given the fact that the original experience of their parents did not lead to clear-cut differentiation, with their parents not experienced as well-structuralized internalized objects, our delinquents find it difficult to achieve such individuation. For many of them, the experience of their parent needs constantly to be reinforced by concrete interaction with the parent rather than with an internalized image of a parent. Consequently, much of their delinquency is an attempt to provoke limits and to induce a parental response.

Harry, for example, invariably provoked fights on the unit with another patient, a repetition of events previously occurring in his family or in his peer relationships. His behavior assured staff involvement and the very predictability of his provocations provided for him some sense of psychological organization. Other adolescents compensate differently. They experience the lack of structure as a feeling of internal emptiness and void which they attempt to fill by promiscuous sexual activity, exciting behavior, or drug experience. As well, they frequently rely on responses of the external world to give them some sense of internal cohesion and internal life.

Disturbed parent/child boundaries are manifested from the very beginning of the adolescent's hospitalization, as he begins to adapt to a new environment. Separation from home and family is often painful and disorganizing. The home situation may be extremely pathological, chaotic, or unsafe, yet it is familiar and known, and the youngster has found ways of coping, maladaptive though they may be. The hospital, on the other hand, is completely unknown, unfamiliar, and frightening. The staff, no matter how benign or skilled at their jobs, still represent something strange and foreign to the newly admitted patient. At first, the staff is seen as one conglomerate, a mass of authority. Although there might be 25 staff members around, many delinquents cannot separate out individuals; they experience them all in the same way, the "other"—an indistinct, unclear blur. For example, when Barry, a 15-year-old, wanted anything, he would plaintively call out "staff," exactly as the two-year-old cries "Mommy." He would also hang around the nursing station window, even when no staff members were present, in what appeared to be an attempt to be near the source of nurturing, glass enclosed and sterile as it might seem to others.

In time, familiarity with surroundings and other individuals adds definition and aids the process of differentiation. But familiarity alone does not suffice. Patients, even when they recognize individual staff members, tend to misuse names, sometimes appearing unable to distinguish one staff member from another. For example, in the O.T. shop, two staff members are Elaine and Marlene; frequently patients will call for Eileen, Marlain, or Arlain. Because the names sound similar, one might be tempted to explain away these "unintentional slurs" as resulting from cognitive deficits or inattention. But differentiation is more than a cognitive problem. Attention to linguistic nuances, particularly in regard to a person's name, must be preceded by an ability to differentiate psychologically between individuals. What is important in this case is that the two workers are experienced as one function, rather than two individuals. The similarity in sound does not cause the confusion, but rather makes the adolescent's inability to differentiate all the more obvious.

As some initial adaptation to the unit takes place, the adolescent begins to make global differentiations. Usually he begins first to identify the chief of the unit as a separate entity. This takes place because the chief is highly visible and leads daily ward meetings. Often this identification takes place even before the therapist is seen as separate from other staff. Kurt had seen his therapist several times a week for a period of four weeks before his therapist went on vacation. While on vacation, his therapist sent him a postcard; Kurt not only did not have the slightest idea who the card was from, but also had to be reminded that he had actually seen someone on a regular basis during the last few weeks.

The adolescent's difficulty differentiating others is evident with other patients as well as with staff. For example, normal youngsters can engage in horseplay, roughhouse with each other, and have a great deal of physical "play" contact which can be broken off at any time because a healthy ego can distinguish "play" from aggressive activity and because there is respect for the other person's boundaries and limits. The disturbed adolescent with serious ego deficits cannot do this. Especially when control of aggressive impulses is required, physical contact, even of the most benign sort, can create a situation where the boundaries of the disturbed adolescent begin to dissolve and he merges with the "other" until there is no separateness or awareness of the "personhood" of the other. Soon the "playful" action gains momentum and takes on a life of its own, generally now beyond the control of the one who initiated it. Often, one or both parties get hurt, and the adolescent who started it winds up bruised, confused, and bewildered because he was "only playing."

The ability to differentiate others is inextricably tied to the ability to view oneself as a separate individual. Delinquents show poor self-cohesion—their experience of themselves is vague, diffuse, and fragmented. They find it very difficult to distinguish between inside and outside, although superficially their reality testing appears intact. Their relationships are symbiotic in nature and characterized by wishes to merge and to fuse with other patients as well as staff. Unlike normal teenagers who build on, yet move away from, parental support and find greater and greater support in the world of other adults and peer relationships, disturbed adolescents seem to have little capacity to turn to other adults or peers for their own psychological sustenance. Instead, these adolescents hunger desperately for the staff and the therapist to make themselves complete and whole, yet fear such an experience either because it leads to fragmentation or because it stimulates needs that can be neither gratified nor denied. Though these adolescents seek merger with a nurturing and parenting person—a self-object relationship—such self-object relating also stimulates a good deal of anxiety, particularly about the loss of one's identity.

Some delinquents provoke the staff to become more and more involved by exhibiting more and more regressive behavior on the unit to the extent that the patient is almost encapsulated in a womb. Margaret provoked the staff to notice her and set limits on her; providing her with contact calmed her, until she demanded almost constant attention, having regressed to the level of a psychotic merger transference where, whenever staff left her, she became disruptive and omnipotently regained staff involvement.

Regression is an important part of adolescent development; the adolescent returns to unresolved childhood problems dealing with separation/individuation and attempts to resolve more satisfactorily these difficulties. He also dips back into his childhood experiences to gain some support from earlier solutions to similar conflicts; with the additional psychological skills of the adolescent and the availability of newer identifications, more mature solutions will result. Our patients, fearing infantile dissolution, are not able to regress and resolve childhood difficulties. They can only repeat the very pathological solutions from childhood against which massive defensive walls, usually of denial, have been established.

Winnicott (1958, 1973) described the "antisocial tendency" by which he refers to his belief that the delinquent symptom is an attempt to find the originally lost, but still longed for object, the mother. Because delinquents are still seeking gratification, Winnicott is optimistic about delinquents and their opportunities for cure. It is certainly true, as we have stated, that many of our delinquents demonstrate this object-seeking tendency. Their delinquency is repetitive, forcing authority figures, parents, our staff, and the therapist to deal with them and their behavior. They act as though they are attempting to master some painful experience from the past. This makes work with delinquents relatively encouraging because one can be certain that eventually the delinquent's pathology will become obvious if only the environment, and particularly the therapist, are attuned to meet it and seize the opportunity to turn it to therapeutic gain.

It is interesting to note that once a patient has identified his therapist as a separate entity, a plateau occurs, and no one else becomes individuated for awhile. At this point, the delinquent can experience only a dyadic relationship, suggestive of an exclusive mother/ child relationship. This two-party relating, anaclitic in nature, is a progression from experiencing the therapist as an extension of himself. The patient/therapist tie recreates the early situation of mother-and small child. But it is still too early to permit a third party to disrupt this attachment.

Not until some sort of resolution takes place can separate and distinct triadic object relating begin. It is a long time before our adolescents can see and accept that therapist and staff have a relationship with each other. For example, Laura became angry when seeing her therapist talking to other staff members in the nursing station and proclaimed, "You have no other reason to come to the unit except to see me." Very gradually, the conglomerate mass of staff begins to separate out to be unique people, who look, dress, and behave differently, who work different shifts, and who are known by different names. As this differentiation begins to occur, psychological structures begin to develop, and with effective psychological structures comes the possibility of better mental health.

The ability to differentiate others is inextricably tied to the ability to view oneself as a separate individual. Delinquents not only show difficulty differentiating others, but also show poor self-cohesion—their experience of themselves is vague, diffuse, and fragmented. They find it very difficult to distinguish between inside and outside, although superficially their reality testing appears intact. As we have described, their relationships are symbiotic in nature and characterized by wishes to merge with the other person as well as tremendous anxieties about such fusion for fear of losing identity and autonomy. In many instances their parents have not demonstrated clear-cut boundaries, and the delinquents have experienced nothing "to push up against." For many of them, the experience of their parents needs constantly to be reinforced by concrete interaction with the parent rather than with an internalized image of a parent. Consequently, much of their delinquency is an attempt to provoke limits and to induce a parental response. It is not surprising, then, that the patient spends much of the early hospitalization "pushing up against" the strong boundaries of a healthy staff group. What staff members attempt to convey through attitude and behavior is: "I'm me . . . an individual, a person. I respect myself enough not to let you walk over me, and I respect you." Confronting staff boundaries is a frustrating experience, but if experienced in increments he can handle, pushes the adolescent to learn self-other differentiation.

Delinquents externalize internal conflicts and deficiencies. Friedlander (1960) wrote about changing the delinquent into the neurotic, much as Freud (1905) had seen perversions as the antitheses of neuroses. Friedlander's proposal is that, by blocking the avenues for discharge, the externalized neurotic conflict can be reexperienced by the acting out delinquent as an internal, painful, and therefore more motivating experience. As was mentioned previously, many of our delinquents do not show such internalized structuralized conflict, but some do. For example, Carl stole cars repeatedly, but assured his arrest by driving the wrong way down a one-way street, driving at night without lights on, or repeatedly parking the car in front of the owner's home and returning again and again to drive it off. Carl was in considerable conflict over his own sexual urges and had repeatedly proved to be impotent, though he projected the image of a tough, gang-oriented delinquent. Treatment was oriented to helping him resolve some of his internal prohibitions against phallic aggressiveness; this conflict had been expressed in auto theft. Yet in the very delinquent act itself, the prohibition again reemerged in his repeatedly precipitated capture.

There are other motivations for the delinquent symptom. Many delinquents are functioning at a very primitive psychological level, and they are unable to distinguish inside from outside. As Kohut (1971) has described, much acting out behavior is really not the externalization of an internal conflict as we might view it, and not even a discharge of tensions, but rather the demonstration that the person has regressed to such a primitive level that distinctions are no longer being made between thought and deed, between feeling and behavior, between the inside world and the outside world. The delinquent acts because to him such activity is analogous to the internal experience. In many of our delinquents, thought does not intervene between impulse and urge and motor behavior, and the delinquent's experiences of these phenomena are one and the same. Others behave violently simply because they are experiencing a traumatic state. That is to say, they are experiencing overwhelming internal stimulation, often having to do with affectionate longings and longings for nurturing. These transference experiences become so intense that the adolescent is psychologically ill equipped to understand, limit, modulate, and tolerate them; what we see in a good deal of violent behavior is a massive motor discharge phenomenon, comparable to an overwrought infant screaming because of internal stimulation or similar to an overwrought, tired, and highly stimulated child having a temper tantrum (Marohn, 1974).

Other delinquents act violently simply because they are enraged at some narcissistic injury or narcissistic slight. They expect themselves to be able to control the world, and they expect certain important people in the world whom they have idealized to respond appropriately and instantly to their needs; any delay, any modification, any hesitancy, any mistake is experienced by such narcissistically vulnerable delinquents as a terrible rupture in empathy, a painful experience involving loss of self-esteem or the threat of psychotic fragmentation, and the result is rage. Such rage expresses not only the delinquents' unhappiness with themselves and with the outside world but is also an attempt to control and dominate the outside world and restore some kind of grandiose equilibrium.

Another area of difficulty for adolescents with behavior disorders is experiencing and identifying affect. Many of them cannot and do not experience emotions because feelings have been denied; instead, they express themselves in behavior. Their tolerance for painful affect is minimal, and as soon as they begin to experience some sadness or depression or anger, they must deal with it immediately by behaving in some way that eliminates the internal pain and creates some kind of pain or distress in the outside world. This kind of alloplastic solution is exemplified in the behavior of George. This tough delinquent boy frequently, in an almost paranoid manner, challenged someone else to a fight. As he explored this further in his therapy, it became clear that as soon as he began experiencing some kind of affectionate feelings for someone else, or longing for some kind of transference nurturing, he became anxious, and such anxiety was as intolerable as the nurturing wishes. Consequently, he would feel like hitting someone and would frequently provoke a fight or challenge someone to a fight. Delinquents then convert one kind of feeling into another kind of feeling. They convert feeling into external motor discharge and have little capacity to think or conceptualize what the feeling is that they are experiencing and to delay action.

Many delinquents do not experience an internal world; they are empty, they are void, they experience only the affect of internal psychological hunger, an affect which disappears when they engage in some kind of activity or with some person that fills them. Few have the capacity to introspect about their internal psychological world, whether it be to identify ideas or to identify feelings. These delinquents must begin to recognize that there is such a void, that there is such a hunger. They must be taught to distinguish one kind of feeling from another and helped to see that their external behavior indicates the existence of some kind of feeling. As a result we live by the rule "all behavior has meaning," and attempt, by targeting behavior and teaching the adolescent to introspect, to help him understand the relationship between external behavior and internal feelings.

Many of our hospitalized delinquents are like the traditionally described "character disorder," a fairly stable personality structure in which internal conflict is constantly externalized, and internal pain and conflict are experienced only when the person meets some obstacle in the outside world. Yet, the adolescent personality structure is not quite stable even though many do show repetitive patterns. But unlike character disorders who may function more or less successfully and avoid obstacles in the outside world, most delinquents are not "smart" —they repeatedly get into trouble. They are not successes, but "failures." They behave as though they were attempting to resolve some kind of internal trauma, and repeatedly engage in object-seeking behavior as if to resolve some kind of internal deficit. Their lack of psychological sophistication and the presence of psychological deficits makes it unlikely that they could become successful character disorders and function comfortably in society, simply avoiding those pitfalls which would lead to difficulty. In the hospital environment even the more or less stable character disorder, including the traditional "psychopath," will run into obstacles and will be forced to deal with the internal consequences of such confrontations. In the character disorder, the character armor and the behavioral symptoms are a compromise between the impulse-urge and the conscience-prohibition; in many delinquents, the impulse and the guilt are experienced separately. The conscience does not operate in a mature manner, as an integral part of the overall psychological makeup, modifying behavior automatically and silently without one being aware of its operation; the delinquent's conscience and its guilt show after the fact, in a painful, devastating way which must either be denied, appeased, or mollified by provoking punishment from authority figures.

In classical psychoanalytic theory, the superego is that aspect of the personality which performs certain kinds of specialized ego functions—the prohibitions, the goals and values (ego ideal), and the self-judgmental and self-critical functions. Much, of course, has been written about delinquency as a result of superego problems. For example, Johnson and Szurek (1952) have described superego lacunae existing in the families of delinquent children; as a result, the children were behaving in ways that gratified the delinquent urges and wishes of their seemingly upright parents. Of course, all children meet certain narcissistic needs for their parents, but many of the delinquents we have seen are exquisitely sensitive to the demands, needs, and claims of their parents, and, as a result, much of their behavior is an attempt to thwart their being used for parental narcissistic gain. This is recapitulated many times in the hospital and in the therapy situation—as soon as the delinquent becomes aware of the fact that the therapist is achieving some kind of gratification from the delinquent's progress or behavior, the patient feels used, mistrusts and is disillusioned with the therapist, and often regresses. Of course, we do see the opposite constellation as well; namely, that the delinquent behaves in a way which is designed to gratify and give pleasure to certain staff and therapists. Most of the delinquents we see are not motivated by the unconsciously transmitted delinquent urges of their parents, but are responding to the more universal narcissistic needs of parents.

The delinquent's superego tends to be primitive. Most delinquents are not immoral or amoral, but have well-established systems of morality. They have their own rules, and they know the rules and mores of society. The mechanisms by which they judge themselves and monitor and modify their own behavior are seriously deficient. Their superegos are harsh and punitive judges after a crime has been committed, not managers that modify, control, channel, and direct behavior. Time and time again, delinquent activity on the unit is met by much harsher responses by the patients themselves than by the staff. Furthermore, our delinquents are unable to comprehend complex problems of morality. They see solutions as either black or white. They give evidence of an omnipotent, cruel, harsh, and powerful superego which permits no compromises and which gives no respite from its punitive activity. As a result, they become enraged with parental mistakes or failings and reenact this by responding to staff errors or deficiencies with harshness and rage. Changes in superego functioning are not ends in themselves in therapy; rather, developing a more flexible and nurturing superego evidences other kinds of psychological changes that are occurring in the teenager as therapy progresses.

A milieu is as therapeutic as the ward staff who people it. Ideally, the milieu provides the benign background in which disturbed adolescents are given an opportunity to grow. A staff member must be relatively healthy and well-differentiated and possess a secure sense of himself. He must be reinforced by other staff members who derive gratification from the work goals they share. Ideally, in interactions with patients, behavioral responses from each staff member should be similar so that consistency is gained; however, the affective responsivity and personality of each staff member are different. A competent staff member represents a healthy auxiliary ego, helping the disturbed adolescent hold back impulses which are constantly striving for immediate gratification, and a more flexible superego, modifying a severely punitive conscience. The staff member helps the patient test the reality in various situations and uses himself in such a way that the patient can temporarily borrow his support to nurture and sustain his own faltering and weak ego structure.

Much of what we have described about the delinquents' pathology, however, does have its counterpart in the staff. Quite obviously, any staff members who have difficulties of such severity as these delinquents cannot function adequately. However, there are lesser forms of such pathology; some staff may be attracted to this kind of work in order to utilize the experience for their own psychological healing. Such is not necessarily a bad motivation, but needs to be assessed. Staff members often project their own needs and fantasies onto adolescents. Frequently, because a teenager is attractive, verbal, bright, or reminds the staff member of someone from his or her own past, the staff member attributes to the delinquent certain abilities, wishes, and aspirations which bias the diagnostic assessment. Consequently, his deficiencies and limitations are not appreciated and he is viewed as functioning at a higher psychological level. Also, some staff members are so frightened of merger and fusion with their clients that they maintain great emotional distance and are unable to achieve the optimum amount of psychological objectivity and distance. They gratify the delinquent's every wish, miss his pathological functioning, are not perceptive to his clues and subtle threats of delinquency, and consequently fail the delinquent in crucial ways by not providing the kind of differentiation and limit-setting that are so necessary to his therapy. Furthermore, a staff member can slip out of the therapeutic relationship with a patient and begin viewing himself more as a buddy or an older sibling. In this instance, the staff member does not recognize that the teenager not only experiences him as an older sibling or peer, but also idealizes him. If the staff fails to use such leverage to help the teenager develop controls, for example, an important therapeutic opportunity is missed. Staff members must be "above reproach" and aware of and in control of their own delinquent tendencies or competitive feelings, because the teenager may readily model himself after a personal idiosyncracy, a depreciation of treatment or a delinquent suggestion.

Staff members who seek narcissistic gain from relationships may encourage the delinquent to try to fulfill the staff member's needs and will not permit the delinquent to realize his own growth potential, separateness, and individuality. Such staff members are also a considerable drain upon other staff, because they utilize staff relationships not just to support, but actually for the maintenance of their own self-esteem economy and their own psychological well-being. A most extreme example is using staff meetings for self-therapy, and frequently a fine line must be drawn between group process to work out staff difficulties and group therapy to resolve personal problems.

What we look for, then, are well-differentiated, fairly autonomous human beings, who have rather healthy personal lives, and who may be in therapy themselves in an honest attempt to better understand themselves. The fact that they are somewhat adolescent in their own behavior, the fact that they may be attempting to better understand themselves through the job, the fact that they may have had stormy periods of adolescence, do not deter us. For a long time many in the field said that the ideal staff member for working with adolescents was a middle-aged woman who had already raised her own children; certainly such a person is an asset to any treatment staff, but our experience has been very positive with a young adult, himself just beyond late adolescence, who is capable of getting in touch with his own adolescent experiences, and who may also serve somewhat like an older sibling or peer and be idealized by our teenage patients.

Staff members must be comfortable enough to turn to other staff for support and help with introspection despite fears of closeness, rejection, or embarrassment. Some do fuse with other staff, have no ideas of their own, and imitate rather than learn staff roles; such people prove to be a drain rather than an asset. The defensive staff member who needs to do everything himself, who believes himself infallible, who cannot support someone else's ideas, or rely on another person to help him in a decision-making experience, will also not work out well. Staff disagreement, discussion and resolution are crucial to the therapeutic process because they lead to and support healthy differentiation. If staff members are not able to disagree openly and disagreements are submerged, inappropriate, critical, and rigid responses to patients result.

Staff gratification cannot come from the patients' getting better or from the patients' expressing pleasure or gratitude. Staff satisfaction must come from the quality of one's own work, from the nature of the relationship with other staff members, and from one's own growth and learning. Gratification derives from inservice training, research, and seeing one's work as part of a larger exploration into the nature of disturbed adolescent behavior—attempting to understand its causes and ramifications, while learning something about modifying it. A program thrives on a research orientation, a commitment to staff training, and the development of assigned trainees. New staff members are welcomed as people who challenge us, present their own creative ideas, and help us not to become encrusted with old policies or calcified rules.

We emphasize staff training. We teach the staff that they, themselves, are both agents of assessment and agents of treatment. Most delinquents not only try to split staff by attempting to set up one staff member against the other, or one staff member against the therapist, or the therapist against the administrative structure of the unit, but also try to establish very special relationships with some staff members. We try to provide an atmosphere and culture in which our staff constantly attend to and confront each other, asking each other about the work, trying to help the other understand his or her own work. The ability of staff to talk openly and frankly with each other is essential, particularly when serious problems do arise.

For example, very early in our program, Sam had returned to the unit from a camping trip and had brought with him a large rock, unknown to the rest of the campers. During the camp-out, this near-psychotic boy had been out of control, mutilating small animals, and there had been quite a debate about how to intervene. Some of the staff on the unit, particularly the male staff, tended to see this as normal "boy" behavior. One day on the unit, Sam showed his large rock to one of the male staff members, and even playfully threw it at him. The staff member felt uneasy about this kind of activity, but dismissed it as the kind of horseplay that adolescent boys engage in with each other. This staff member's first mistake was to view himself as an adolescent boy, rather than as a milieu worker. During the following days, when Sam started body punching with him, the staff member was still oblivious to the fact that this boy was losing control of himself. Only a few days later, when Sam participated in a riot on our unit, did it become clear that he had evidenced an escalation of violent behavior which eventuated in a serious outbreak.

An outbreak of violence need not be a tragedy, and the same process and principles of monitoring, confrontation, and feedback can result in a valuable post-mortem assessment. The riot helped us learn something about violent behavior and the importance of staff members as treatment agents (Marohn, Dalle-Molle, Offer, and Ostrov, 1973). We now know that after there has been an outbreak of violence or some form of assault on the unit, we can usually look back and find an undetected escalation of violence from verbal violence, such as name-calling, obscene words, or threats, to violence to or misuse of property, such as writing on the walls, scratching up the tables, or cutting up the seats of the chairs, and then to violence to persons. It took us a long time to recognize this, but as a result, we now intervene very early, as soon as we recognize that someone is being verbally abusive or as soon as we hear a verbal threat of violence. We convey our concern about how serious the behavior is and how serious it could become if unchecked.

This is not at all unlike other interventions on our unit. If, for example, food is taken from someone's meal tray, it becomes a serious issue on the unit. Many delinquents will not accept the fact that an apple taken from somebody's lunch tray is serious; they contend, "We are all thieves anyway, what the hell difference does it make what we do to each other?" Besides, they insist, an apple is of little value. Actually, the theft is of great importance because it indicates that a patient is behaving delinquently instead of dealing with a feeling or talking about a problem. We immediately make that kind of delinquent activity on the unit the focus of our ward meetings. We do not always discover the culprit, but we are usually able to help the group progress from refusing to talk about problems and minimizing the seriousness of their behaviors to accepting the fact that there are important things that need to be discussed. In these meetings we try to develop a unit culture that stresses thinking before acting, respecting oneself and others, and learning how to solve problems.

Through such ongoing training, we repeatedly demonstrate to our staff that all behavior has meaning and can be understood. If we successfully demonstrate this to our staff, then we can eventually demonstrate it to our patients.

We want staff members to have psychological structure—to be capable of performing crucial psychological functions for themselves. But this is not synonymous with rigidity wherein one imposes his own internal psychological solutions on others. Rigidity may frequently mesh with the delinquent's need for structure in the beginning of treatment and cause a nice therapeutic match. Eventually, however, as the delinquent needs to grow and develop certain functions for himself, the rigid staff member cannot permit such to occur. When we talk about the ideally structuralized staff member, we refer to the staff member's ability to grow and learn to identify affect, to use it both in understanding himself and in understanding others, to be able to communicate values, beliefs, and feelings effectively. We want a staff member to be decisive and to be able to recognize that decisions, though firm, are not necessarily perfect, and that in many instances there may not be a "right way" to do something. However, the staff member to be decisive and to be able to recognize that decisions, understanding that firmness is not arbitrariness, but a reassuring experience to an unstructuralized delinquent. In other words, the staff member's self-esteem system must be in a fairly decent homeostasis. It derives support from his outside personal relationships and from valuing himself as a professional. To be a milieu therapist is to be a professional. The milieu therapist does not serve at the prescription of the psychiatrist; he possesses a modality of intervention and a set to principles to guide him which, though comparable to and able to be integrated with individual psychotherapy, are not defined by the psychotherapist's viewpoint.

We look for staff members who can tolerate being utilized by our clients as narcissistic objects because delinquents will turn to them for the completion of their own personality and for performing certain functions that they lack. Staff members must not become disturbed when such demands are made, when they are used as pieces of furniture and dictated to, when their very humanity may enrage a patient, when requests for attention are incessant. For example, on one camp-out, staff acted silly and joked around with each other in response to how intensely they were being used by the patient-campers to help them function. The staff can achieve some distance from the situation only by being able to recognize the desperate deficiencies of our patients.

A hierarchical organization of staff is crucial to the work with delinquents. Not only must the delinquent be able to push upward, but staff must in turn be able to identify clear-cut lines of authority, clear-cut differentiation between certain functions and roles on the unit, and the different levels of problem-solving and responsibility for decisions. The affective presence of the chief is crucial to the maintenance of a well-functioning unit, as our study of a hospital riot demonstrated. Just as the staff must be constantly vigilant in working with delinquents because of the possibility of the breakthrough of delinquent urges and delinquent behavior, so too, must the staff be constantly monitoring how each of them is fulfilling certain responsibilities and meeting certain functions. The chief is frequently called on not only to fill the cracks and function for other staff members, but must himself "push back" and demand that staff members perform certain tasks and functions when his assessment so indicates.

Staff members who are punitive about the emergence of any kind of wish for gratification or who, themselves, overidentify with such wishes for gratification, have considerable difficulty in working with delinquents. Their work becomes either a moral crusade to stamp out sin and evil or a vicarious exploration of the shady side of life.

The interface between staff and patients is a continuously dynamic series of interactions, a process with shifting boundaries, spontaneity, and variations on themes. The delinquents' themes are their pathology, their motivations, and their attempts to heal themselves; although each delinquent is an individual, there are similar patterns, presenting themselves with a myriad of expressions. The staff's themes are an internalized treatment philosophy, awareness of oneself relying on the support and feedback of other staff members, and recognizing oneself as an important force and means of intervention and change. How any staff member performs his job rests on his ingenuity and individuality, for to attempt to mimic another person is fraudulent and doomed to failure.

At this interface, the delinquent's need for self-object relating and merger with another begins to show itself; some are able to utilize such self-object relating and grow in the relationship. The staff member then is able to share this sometimes burdensome experience with other members of the team and the therapist, and such data are useful in developing the treatment plan. Other patients, though seeking self-object merger, are frightened and anxious and defend themselves against it; the staff must provide some "distance" and not move in too quickly, but in a proper dosage so as not to overwhelm a hungry and devastated primitive psychological organization. Other adolescents hunger for self-object merger, engage with the staff member readily, but quickly begin to fragment, seeking more and more involvement with the staff in a regressive pull to a primitive level of infantile functioning. It is important that the staff try to thwart such overwhelming regression before it leads to serious disruption and violent assault and before treatment is abruptly terminated by one of the two parties.

At the same time as our patients give us clear clues to their wish to engage with us, we will unquestionably miss some of their messages. This is inevitable, though staff needs to sharpen its awareness of these issues. Such "mistakes" may frequently lead to an outburst of rage, expressed verbally, but usually in some kind of major acting out. It may, for example, take the form of a request to be discharged, or a demand for a privilege or a verbal or even physical assault. This may mean not that the staff has made a serious error, but that the patient is experiencing a break in empathy. This experience can be used diagnostically to understand the patient further and to help him understand himself.

Though the kinds of transferences the patient establishes may become most focused in the individual psychotherapy sessions, some emerge on the unit, and patients may demand a merger or mirroring experience with staff members, may idealize or depreciate staff members, and may precipitate in staff members various kinds of counter-responses based on these projections. Some readily assume, for example, that the patient who constantly depreciates the staff is really not engaged in treatment; he may, indeed, be engaged, but in the only way he can engage, depreciating and condemning the utterly imperfect staff.

At the interface, the staff prepares the patient for psychotherapy, by targeting certain behaviors, helping to introspect, fostering and facilitating self-awareness, and eventually supporting a process which becomes the bedrock of individual uncovering psychotherapy.

Similarly, as the staff member has served as an external ego, or external self-object for the patient, the emphasis shifts to the other side of the equation, with the patient assuming progressively more psychological and self-functions for himself. Here, the staff member may feel less important, may begin wondering whether or not, indeed, he is worthwhile at all, and may question whether or not the patient needs the hospital. The patient may fear growth and maturation, recognizing that he needs the staff members less, fearing rejection and abandonment by a wounded staff member, or expecting abandonment as a recapitulation of the family pathology wherein his previous futile attempts to separate and individuate eventuated in rejection. The termination process, usually viewed superficially, is a painstaking period in treatment. Only too often, a patient's readiness for discharge is assessed on the basis of how well or how poorly he handles passes or family sessions; but more important than that is whether or not various kinds of psychotherapeutic activities and psychological functions have been internalized by the patient and can stand the test of separation from the supportive hospital milieu and the daily contact with the therapist's world.

As the patient separates and individuates, the nature of the interactions at the interface between staff and patients changes. Limits and affective staff responses have led to the establishment of self-boundaries and the patient's recognition of his/her own individuality. Earlier, limits and affective responses served to indicate that external psychological structure is available and to replace internally absent functions; they also established clear-cut differentiations between patient and staff, which are vital to patient growth.

As the patient's awareness of staff availability and staff psychological support begins to develop, the staff's physical presence is no longer needed and the interface becomes more ethereal, involving glances, looks, words, and the like. Many patients at this changing interface do not require physical proximity, and are supported and enriched by seeing staff at a distance. This reflects a growing sense of object constancy, a trust in staff availability. The adolescent experiences parental nurturing in through the benign monitoring of activities, such as when staff sits in the nursing station and watches the dayroom, or asks a patient to check in when he leaves the dayroom; when patients are accompanied on the "school bus" by a staff member; or when a patient's schedule is kept in the nursing station; and when his treatment is reviewed in the weekly team meeting and in the weekly Adolescent Progress Review.

The activities of the superego begin to be modified, and as staff demonstrates a certain tolerance for psychological problems, yet an abhorrence for certain kinds of delinquent discharge, the delinquent, too, begins wondering about his motivations, begins to be able to soothe himself, becomes more tolerant of his deficiencies and mistakes, and begins to replace a primitive morality with a morality that may occasionally enrich or gratify him and which is capable of reaching out to others and recognizing their needs. This morality embraces the legitimacy of one's own needs, feelings, and wishes.

5

Time

The development of a sense of time is a cornerstone in the construction of reality in the infant. As Piaget has described, this sense of time is put together one step at a time (Flavell, 1963). The child begins with "local time," relating it to the terminal points of his own movement. The child gradually develops a conceptual grasp of "lived time," that is, internal subjective time, as intervals between events and the succession of events is learned.

Because the child perceives that the ordering of external events is related to the predictable gratification of needs, time thus becomes an internal organizer or pacemaker of the child's inner drive state. Time is intimately connected with the development of a capacity to delay; this delay between impulse and action is essential for the development of the intervening states of affect, thought, and fantasy. To be able to delay is to shift from a passive experiencing of events to their active mastery. To tolerate delay, one needs to learn that anticipation leads to eventual gratification and that delay is not arbitrary and unpredictable. The capacity to delay is related to a developing sense of trust and confidence in the environment and significant people.

In summary, the perception of time and the internalization of a sense of time are basic ego skills, parts of the basic neutralizing and organizing fabric built up and elaborated during psychological development. Time has its internal and external anchorings, both as internalized structure and as a basic interaction with the impersonal and personal environment.

Among adolescents who require hospitalization, it is no surprise that basic ego skills are deficient, with concomitant breakdown and failure of impulse control and with little capacity for delay. Time is one of the delinquent's enemies. To the adolescent on a psychiatric unit, time is endless; he is bored and may feel adrift in a sea of time. Many joke that a jail sentence would be preferable, because of its fixed time demands, to the indeterminant sentence of a therapeutic plan in the hospital.

We have already described how we create in our hospital milieu a set of expectations and predictabilities called the *basic structure*. In addition to a series of activities themselves, basic structure is a marking of beginnings and endings of time intervals as the adolescents progress through the day from waking up until bedtime. Time is marked in the conventional sense of hours or minutes assigned to various activities. However, the marking of discrete time periods is done primarily by staff. Our delinquents use the staff to tell time, and we notice that many tend not to use their own watches and clocks. The wakeup routine is initiated by the staff member on duty, and not by an alarm clock. The announcement of "O.T.!" shouted by the occupational therapist is like having Big Ben strike. Study hour is designated by staff at the same time everyday to help the patient develop a time interval to focus on school work. For those patients who find being on the unit too diffuse and stimulating, limited periods of time with the television or the stereo set are geared to the patient's capacities. Our patients welcome such limits and assistance. In such ways, staff structuring of time serves as an external pacemaker.

Learning the basic structure and internalizing the meaning of time intervals associated with it occur initially in the context of a patient-staff relationship. As we mentioned above, staff members become the timepieces by which the patient organizes his day. This may be part of the overall use of staff as self-objects, but it may also represent some patients' inability to use a clock or wristwatch. The clock face has no meaning for them in organizing their day or lives. Many have not learned to use a wristwatch, but not because of intellectual limitations; telling time has never been learned, often because of affective limitation and psychological deficit. A person who cannot invest in himself enthusiastically, recollect his past or anticipate his future does not measure time in the present. Eventually, the patient may begin using a wristwatch, an alarm clock or the clock on the unit; ultimately, time associated with basic structure becomes an internalized operation, an internal pacemaker.

In order to support and implement interventions regarding time, mutually held staff attitudes and norms are essential. These attitudes develop in part from a sense of time that the unit chief and administrators share, the importance they attach to time spent in meetings, promptness, time set aside for supervision and teaching, time to get one's work done, and the like. Patients on the unit are keenly aware of how staff handle time; the adolescents learn about time not so much from clocks, but from staff cues. This is particularly obvious in the early days following admission as the new patient is learning the structure of his day from wakeup through bedtime.

The newly admitted patient frequently has problems getting to a place on time. This may represent the testing of limits and of the authority structure of the unit, or the fears and anxieties about entering into the unit culture. The adolescent may protest "no one told me," or "I had to use the washroom" in explaining his failure to be at a certain place at a certain time. These statements manifest his underlying concern, and in many instances, are temporary. Chronic and repeated problems with time commitments demonstrate that many of our adolescents have much more complex problems with time, and, at a deeper level, with time orientation. Ted, a newer patient on the unit, came late to his first day's activities. For the next week he continued to come late until finally he began openly refusing to come to meetings and activities altogether. On one occasion, he stayed in bed with his pajamas on, covered with blankets, and refused to come to the afternoon ward meeting. He kept repeating to the staff "I won't go." When staff stopped dealing with his total and global refusal, but began looking at "first things first" by breaking up his refusal into smaller components, things became much easier. Staff looked at sequences like "How about getting out of bed, then we can talk about the next step?" Ted got up, appearing vividly less anxious, and then moved through getting up, getting dressed, getting his bed made, and finally being ready to face the anxiety about going to the meeting. Ted was quite obviously able to deal with and master only small increments of time, and by breaking up his responsibility to attend the ward meeting into smaller components, the staff was able to help him begin to face his anxieties.

Time is the warp upon which the structure of the program is woven. Scheduling a complex set of activities reflects staff priorities, and adhering to schedules becomes, hopefully, a group norm. For example, school classes are held in the beginning of the day until shortly after lunch. Occupational therapy and recreational therapy are scheduled at set times, negotiated by the staff, and subsequently supported and respected as far as their time boundaries are concerned. For example, five minutes preparing for gym and five minutes ending the gym activity are set aside and are not to be used for other purposes such as a psychotherapy session. Ward meetings and psychotherapy sessions are expected to start and end on time. What emerges then is a staff attitude that conveys a regard for predictability and for responsibility toward another, and an awareness of the importance of these principles for the adolescents' learning.

Many of our patients appear to have difficulty gauging time for a variety of reasons. Some display day-night reversals in their habits and sleep patterns. Others have led chaotic lives at home or on the street; others have been involved in frequent running away or intermittent detentions. For some, an unwillingness to accept the reality of time and its inherent limitations is a reflection of their omnipotence. Ernie, for example, sat in the O.T. shop with his back to the clock and ignored the notices to clean up, just as he complained angrily to his therapist about the clock in his office and the time limit on sessions. His defiance of and denial of the reality of time reflected a grand desire to control the environment and in so doing construct a self-serving universe. That his efforts took the form of omnipotent gestures, however, reflected, as well, his very real sense of powerlessness to exert control over the environment, others, and himself.

Many have virtually no sense of predictability. They live from moment to moment, and nowhere is this more apparent than in their productions on projective psychological testing, which is administered to all patients. Here, in the kaleidoscope of their perceptual world, impulsive nonreflective stories on Rorschach percepts indicate their very strong predilection for "thinking on the run." There are few references to, or uses of, the past as it might guide them to a solution in the present. For many delinquents, it is as if the door to the past has been prematurely shut, and they see themselves as thrust headlong into the present for which they are poorly prepared. While this hypercathexis of the present and of activity is a central characteristic of adolescence, many teenagers lack many of the prerequisite ego skills to gain from the present in constructive ways. Many of our teenagers spend a lot of time talking about, and engaging in delinquent activity simply because it gives them a sense of being alive in the present, but they are not able to grow from the present. It is not surprising, then, to find them investing little hope in the future. For some, their lack of investment in the future reflects their dawning awareness that their own behavior is unpredictable (Marohn, Offer, and Ostrov, 1971). Projective outcomes show little acknowledgment of the future, which is usually relegated to terse magical story endings where the favorite resolution is "and they lived happily ever after."

And so the time structure of the milieu becomes a crucible in which the newly admitted teenager tests his omnipotence, tests the consistency and predictability of adults, and gradually develops his ability to organize time. What starts off as staff's time to which the delinquent conforms eventually becomes, through identification, the patient's own time expectancies. Initially, it may be a shock to confront the orderliness and predictability of the day's activities as well as encountering staff members who adhere to and carry out a schedule. However, after initial surprise and a period of testing, constancy is met with welcome relief. In fact, before too long, the tables are turned, and the delinquents "expect" the staff to be on time. For example, we see patients reminding parents on visiting days of the time for the visit and when it ends. It is not uncommon for a patient to be seen waiting for a therapist who may be a few minutes late, looking at the nursing station clock, ready to scold the therapist.

Adhering to time limits and delineations is not just a capricious whim of the staff or a compulsive need to "make things neat," but rather an attempt to establish guideposts against which adolescent behavior begins to develop some meaning. We must remind ourselves over and over again that for most delinquents, behaviors are communications; without this understanding, one is presented with a multitude of intentions, excuses, and rationalizations about all the "little forgettings of everyday life." For example, Danny was not present when the ward meeting began. When staff went to his room to remind him, he reported that he forgot and just fell asleep. He was reminded by the leader of the meeting that people are expected to be on time, an expectancy placed on the staff as well. Two days later, Danny was late again, this time claiming that he needed to use the bathroom just prior to the meeting. Eventually, we discovered that Danny was frightened of facing the group because he feared being accused of a theft that had recently occurred on the unit. It is important that we at least be aware of and inquire into the possible communication of his behavior regarding the ward meeting.

This example could be multiplied a hundredfold for different activities, all having to do with the use of and regard for time boundaries. We adopt the view that the patient's behavior has its own idiosyncratic meanings, which may include rebellion and testing, a possible wish to be noticed, a fear of the activity or the meeting, or a difficulty engaging time and planning. Whatever the meaning, it is incumbent on the staff to first help the patients take responsibility for their behavior, and secondly help them understand its meaning. This stance is extremely useful in helping patients learn to make connections between their thoughts and feelings and their behavior, a deficiency common to all delinquents regardless of the kind of behavioral problems with which they present.

In providing a total treatment milieu for disturbed adolescents, Redl and Wineman (1957) point out that it is not enough just to fill up time for the adolescent in the institution. Rather, events and activities that provide ego support must be developed. Initially, delinquents view time as something to fill up, and they seek to escape boredom or the discomfort of their own bad feelings and uneasy state of being. In one sense, then, how adolescents view and experience time is a metaphor for how they experience themselves. For many, the experiencing of time is an awareness of their own lack of continuity, or lack of stability or self-cohesiveness. This can be evidenced in how fragile a perception some of the patients have about the flow of events in the day, and how much staff contact is required to help keep them in order. For instance, Ernie became agitated one Wednesday morning and kept coming out of his room yelling for the staff. When the staff talked with him, it became apparent that he had mixed up his days and thought it was Thursday. At this particular time, had it been Thursday, Ernie would have had a scheduled activity. Such was not the case for Wednesday. However, his therapy session, which was usually scheduled on Wednesday, had been cancelled. He was amazed and relieved when the staff member told him what day it actually was. What then followed was a recognition on Ernie's part that he was feeling alone, and indeed his cancelled session was a disruptive experience. So it is not unusual to find some adolescents carrying with them, on paper or in their heads, a detailed account of their day's activities, for in so doing they begin to gain a sense of existing in time.

There are different times. There is a time for beginning the day, the wakeup time, which on our unit is carried out by staff members awakening each adolescent individually. It involves a preparation for school, an awareness that the daytime staff is coming to the unit, and it is a time to get oneself "together," to assemble books, homework, and be ready for class. It is a time to clean up and dress, and to have breakfast together.

Then there is a time for going to and from school with the other patients and accompanied by the staff in our "school bus." School is a time for concentrating and focusing one's attention on intellectual tasks. Here, as in other activities of the day, problems with time manifest themselves in restlessness, an inability to delay, low frustration tolerance, an inability to pace oneself, and the like. There is a time for the daily ward meeting which patients and many staff members attend on a predictable basis to discuss issues of group living and express the major concerns of the unit. It is a time to meet with the chief of the unit, and a place to get information about events that affect the everyday life of the unit: visitors to the unit, staff's absences, patient's plans for discharge, and all those other ways of structuring and ordering time so as to make a chaotic life predictable.

There is a time to make things and a time to play, and a time to exercise sports skills. In school, in shop, and in the gym we see the more concrete aspects of practicing with the use of time, learning to wait, sequencing thoughts and actions, planning, beginning and ending activities. There is a time for psychotherapy sessions during which the adolescent learns to engage regularly with another human being with whom he can gain some self-understanding. Session time comes to be a focal point in the patient's day. There is a time for studying and for preparing school work. There is quiet hour time freed of activities and stimulation. In a sense, it is a transition from the daytime hours of activity and engagement to the evening time of contemplation and assessment. There is the evening time with a different, but not totally new staff, a period of more free time, of sitting in the dayroom, of watching television, of playing records, or of engaging in other self-selected activities which may include visiting with family. A weekend is quite similar to the evenings, and our patients view it more as their own time, and are subsequently confronted more clearly with problems they have in using leisure time as well as the challenges it provides for new learning.

Free time on the unit is the counterpart to the teenager's leisure time at home. Some of it may simply be unoccupied time, short gaps or waiting periods between two events, or time "left out" at the end of an extended, active, highly structured day or week. For many teenagers, these unobligated hours may be experienced as gaps during which they feel no attachments or motivations. They cannot define how the time is to be used or discern what goes on when the pace changes. This can be a frightening experience when teenagers find themselves feeling let down and losing meaningful attachments, especially as they disconnect themselves from staff who helped regulate day-to-day functioning and from tasks that are routine and predictable. During this open and undefined time, choices are made about the activity to fill it. Does the teenager have a readiness to enjoy, rest, relax, and use skills and capacities arising from inner resources? How he uses his free time depends on the gratification he derives from the activity, active or passive, simple or complex, individual or group, spontaneous or planned. It is not simply a matter of the disturbed adolescent lacking information of activities or lists of things to do that is the source of his problem. If this were the case, information could be readily supplied. Disturbed adolescents, because of their poorly developed and disorganized psychological functioning, cannot use resources and lack inner capacities and inner controls to seek ways in which activities can be sources of gratification.

Unobligated hours on the unit are not always anticipated with much enthusiasm as many teenagers begin to experience the loss and withdrawal of the staff. This is particularly true as the week comes to a close and the significant figures leave for the weekend, precipitating feelings that supplies will be cut off. Many complaints of boredom arise. There is "nothing to do" with extended hours of unstructured time. This replicates the experiences of many delinquents who wait around on street corners for "something to happen," eagerly anticipating some kind of excitement that will be provided from the outside. This boredom is often not a lack of things to do, but a sign of internal deficiency, a lack of initiative, an inability to nurture and gratify oneself, investments in primitive fantasies unrelated to the real world, or serious and primitive guilt. Boredom may escalate to increasing panic about whether or not one can maintain a sense of continuity without externally structured events providing a framework for self-definition. The staff must ride through much of the free time with the disturbed adolescent, and as at other times, nurture his ability to function autonomously. This process can only begin in the context of real staff contact.

Providing teenagers with alternatives is one way to help them become successfully involved in nonroutine activities. Helping them gauge feelings, providing them with support, and anticipating their readiness for particular stimuli are all important facets of the staff follow-through. Staff become important during these times because their observing participation facilitates an understanding of what activities mean for the adolescent and how they can best be utilized as tools for growth promoting experiences. If activities are viewed as a variety of isolated ways to keep the teenager busy and to release tension, a great deal is sacrificed in the overall therapeutic approach. Activity programs should not exist simply to tire and wear out teenagers in order to cut down on the likelihood of serious acting up behavior on the unit. An integrated activity program requires more than this.

How adolescents enter into activities reflects their psychological deficits and strengths. The teenager who waits around for something to happen, to be filled up, or to be nurtured, is the teenager who is experiencing internal emptiness. The teenager may not be able to survey the environment and see things which can be manipulated and used for constructive activity. For example, in the unit dayroom there may be puzzles and games to play or rugs which the group has decided to make for the unit. These activities are left out in the open, but often ignored by the adolescents, in spite of the fact that they are "fun to do." Frequently, it is not until the staff actively express interest that patients begin to invest in the activity and the project becomes a source of gratification. Similarly, a teenager may eagerly jump into an activity, not out of enthusiasm for the activity, but to compensate for withdrawal of significant figures and external structures. Very often, however, the teenager is unable to sustain the activity, as he becomes bogged down with increasing fears of abandonment.

Many adolescents' resources are limited to a passive incorporation of the television set. These teenagers rely on the staff to help them develop an ability to interact with the environment; this may require the use of the staff for extended periods of time before they are able to develop interests with growing awareness and competence. In each case, it is the affective involvement of the staff which is the significant and defining agent for activity progression.

Some adolescents involve themselves in activities like "a driven flurry." The impulsive adolescent may enter into a benign card or ping-pong game, and once in the game escalate noticeably and feel that things are out of control. He may explain the resultant aggressive behavior as a way of getting out some pent-up energy, but it is apparent to staff that his involvement is driven, and he is unable to delay or think before acting. Such escalation and increased aggressiveness can be terribly frightening for the teenager, and for other teenagers around him, as he becomes less and less capable of predicting his own behavior and the outcome of his actions.

During activities some adolescents attempt to determine the source of limits and controls within the environment. A patient who is testing the staff may miss a class or get sent back from school and then try to divert himself from his problem in a TV program or Monopoly game. Giving the adolescent time to think about his behavior and confronting him with the fact that his behavior has meaning are the really important messages.

Other teenagers enter group games and develop destructive relationships with peers. Enmeshed complementary pathologies may cause this. A teenager who exhibits himself as a clown pairs with a teenager who maintains his self-esteem through sadistic relationships. This coupling perpetuates maladaptive behavior for both. The staff needs to recognize such subtle interplay and must help patients look at the destructive elements in their group relationships.

And then there is a time for bed and sleep. Preparing for going to bed begins early in the evening, often around an organized activity which, as one staff member described, "gathers in all the impulses, and then slows them down as the game comes to an end." Later, other cues signal the approach of bedtime, such as making hot chocolate, reading a bedtime story, and finally the time spent by staff visiting each patient, saying "good night," and symbolically tucking him in.

There are many other markings of time in the experience of our adolescents on the unit. It is useful to look at the time before and after given events, the time of transition. Perhaps the most carefully appreciated and completely developed transition is the preparation for bedtime already described. However, there are numerous other transitions during the day requiring shifts of focus. The ward staff often reports that it is during the transitions between activities that destructive behavior begins to develop and staff intervention is required. Many adolescents seem to have little sense of transition and may appear aimless as they sit in the dayroom. On one side of the dayroom is the television set, an area described by one staff as the "waiting room," where patients may temporarily plug themselves in to fill in time and "wait" for something to happen. Some patients who are required to spend more time in their rooms prefer, nevertheless, this time in the room to the in-between times of going to and from activities.

One needs to understand the "moment-to-moment" orientation of many of our teenagers to understand the real distress they experience with schedule changes. For example, Kent, a 16-year-old and one of the few patients to wear a wristwatch that he checked constantly, was told that his O.T. schedule was changing, giving him a half-hour of free time. He was asked if he would like to use it to go the music room, but he became very tense and needed considerable staff help to fill up the free time. His sense of time constancy had failed him when he had to make changes. Karen, 14, anticipated her half-hour out of her room by planning time with a staff member. She was practicing setting her own limits and developing a sense of pacing herself. When she found herself going over her time limit, she seemed in near panic. Here, impulse control and the use of time come together as the patient makes tentative steps to develop her own pacemaker. Transition times were difficult for 16-year-old Ursula. The time for the therapy session to begin and end, and the time spent walking with the therapist to and from the office, were difficult, and the patient frequently used those intervals to ask all sorts of questions about unit rules and policies, decisions made in teams about her privileges, and the like. Initially, we saw a good deal of this as testing behavior; it was only later that we recognized how tenuous was her sense of self and her continuity in time such that talking about rules and policies helped her master these transitions.

Staff's acute awareness of the importance of time becomes an integral part of the therapeutic milieu. The staff schedule is posted in such a way that patients can anticipate who will be working what shifts and on which days. Respecting staff's importance in the patients' day leads to a sense of continuity. The staff announce to each other and to the patients when they will be gone on vacation, when someone is ill, or when the work schedule changes. After awhile, patients begin announcing to their peers that a probation officer or caseworker will be visiting the unit a particular afternoon at such and such a time. There is a pace on our unit, a tempo perhaps unique and idiosyncratic to ourselves which may be somewhat different on another unit, but nonetheless this tempo becomes a pacemaker, organizing and structuring the chaos of intervals, delay, waiting, and "boredom" that so many of our delinquents experience.

Up to this point, we have focused on the function of time as it is related to disturbed adolescents' learning to delay their impulses, then recognizing that the hospital milieu and the adults in it can provide a sense of predictability and permanence, and later developing their own pacemaker. Impatience and impulsivity are expressions of an early omnipotence and of magical thinking in which wish is action. A major goal of hospital treatment, by adhering to the basic structure, is to encourage delay so that feelings, thoughts, and verbalizations might begin to emerge.

If we look at the phenomenological world of the teenager, we might think of his experiences and attempts to organize time as related to a developing sense of self and self-continuity. Goldberg (1971) conceptualizes one of the experiences of delay or of being delayed as a continuum of tolerance for waiting and relates it to the development of a self-system. "Psychologically, there is a development of this principle from an incapacity to wait to a fragile and vulnerable organization which controls drives and external stimuli to a firm self-system which has continuity and can experience pleasure in waiting."

In our population, we have teenagers with primitive needs and organization who climb the walls when they have to wait, when they feel at the mercy of their drives and of those who will provide the reduction in their need states. Waiting is often viewed by these youngsters as a betrayal by the mothering person. Their self-image is tenuous and they experience considerable discontinuity. For many, their impatience is not only related to the lack of an available object, but to the instability of the self, a state from which they would like to flee in one way or another.

A major problem in waiting is illustrated by the experiences of 16-year-old Paul. He could not wait to finish a lesson in school, and wanted, instead, to jump to the end of the assignment. He could not tolerate not being first in line for anything. He could barely wait for visits from his parents who would bring "goodies." In almost all these instances, waiting was synonymous with being betrayed, unloved, and out of control. He saw himself as a "trained dog on a leash," which conveys both his sense of helplessness and his need for external regulators. Certainly there were many primitive and oral qualities to his demands, but it was striking to notice the instability of his fragile self-system, which was readily disrupted by the experience of anticipation. At these times he wanted to withdraw and talked of his favorite pastime, fishing, paradoxically an activity which depends heavily upon the capacity to wait. In fishing, he was able to turn the tables from being the passive party at the mercy of others to the active master where his waiting put something under his control. It provided his unstable self with a temporary sense of mastery. Many adolescents have problems in waiting, and it is important to assess this unique difficulty within the patient's overall psychopathology.

On the other hand, there are those teenagers who, though requiring hospitalization, show a relatively stable sense of themselves and of self-continuity. These are often the more depressed, neurotic-like delinquents, or those who have achieved an increased stability of self as a result of treatment. They go about their business, have things to do, structure their own time in leisure activities or in planning towards discharge. Time and waiting do not seem to have a disruptive effect. In fact, impatience in these teenagers, as in healthy adolescents, is not always drive-related, but due to an overall change of the self-system as a precursor to a prearrangement or reordering of that system. The impatience to leave after the adolescent has made substantial progress in treatment and his eagerness to try his wings are qualitatively quite different from the preemptory pressured experience of the patient who can't wait until his "sentence" is up.

Generally, teenagers stay in our hospital program from one to two years, a long hospital stay. Paradoxically, while daily time is highly structured, the length of stay, itself, is indeterminant. In a sense, how long one stays in the hospital depends on an assessment of the patient's capacity for delay, internalization, and the development of a more stable self. It is necessary for both patients and staff to set aside the time of the "outside world." The adolescent suspends his "passage of time" and participates in a clearly defined psychological moratorium. At the outset of hospitalization, he talks of "being here a month or so." As one would expect, he maintains the external pre-hospital frame of time reference. Or he may say, "Maybe I'll stay here until September when school starts." The teenager is being asked to forego the usual time frames of his life, though these may be diffuse even for the normal adolescent, and to tolerate a sense of indefinite time and even timelessness. During this transition, what is being substituted is that the hospitalization will be a time, though indefinite, to work on oneself, one's behavior, attitudes, and problems. After he has tested staff reliability and become more aware of his own serious intent to get help, he is more able to cope with waiting. It is at this juncture that one begins to see ambivalence emerge over the underlying wish to stay a long time, even forever. The staff sees the teenager forming attachments and finding a place for himself and anxiety may even diminish.

However, the passage of time as part of reality is always in the wings. It shows itself during visiting hours, family events, birthdays, and holidays. Nowhere is it more obvious than during the holiday season beginning shortly before Thanksgiving and lasting until after the New Year. Adolescents become particularly aware of how long they have been in the hospital, and painful feelings of separation are experienced and reexperienced again. Waiting may again feel disruptive and anxiety is intensified. The staff experiences an increased pressure from teenagers and parents for reunion, and even the staff members suspend the normal and ordinary expectations and view the holiday times as "special."

The admission of new patients to the unit and the discharge of others also brings time sharply into focus. Patients tend to think of their progress in terms of time, and how long one is hospitalized or how long one is in treatment becomes a way of measuring success. People who have been around longer feel pushed out by newcomers (Marohn, 1970). The admission of new patients once again brings into the unit the time of the outside world and reminds the hospitalized adolescent of the time interval between childhood and adulthood. Discharge raises questions of how the time has been spent and confronts all very sharply with the realization that the moratorium does not last forever. Those who remain behind begin to develop a sense of seniority, a continuity with the past and with the culture of the program, and become regarded as "old timers."

The program is organized not only around long-term hospitalization, but also around relatively long-term intensive psychotherapy. All the teenagers are seen in individual sessions approximately three times a week. Psychotherapy, except for goal-specific short-term therapy, is by its very nature uncertain in its overall time dimension, and has a sense of timelessness. The orientation of intensive psychotherapy is toward developing and understanding the relationship as it emerges between patient and therapist. Though it is a timed experience, being limited to a certain number of minutes per session, it stimulates regressive pulls having to do with the wish for an "externally gratifying parent/child unity." In these words, Bergler and Roheim (1946) describe the role of a sense of time in therapy by referring to the timelessness of the fantasy of mother and child being united endlessly.

At certain points in the history of the program, therapists were assigned to the unit for six-month intervals; gradually this has been replaced by longer rotations for trainees, and more patients are being treated by permanent staff members whose availability is not limited to a training rotation. The disruptions of psychotherapy after a six-month rotation of the psychiatric resident, for example, though providing ample opportunity to deal with problems of separation, were simply too damaging and could not be rationalized by training needs when they ran counter to the very cogent need to organize and structure the time chaos. Previously, some patients could use the therapist's six-month rotation as a way of fixing time. Now, however, the teenager is faced with more of an ongoing relationship. He marks time in months or yearly anniversaries in the hospital, and in so doing reestablishes a sense that his hospitalization is time limited. For those patients who were hospitalized elsewhere previously, the one-year anniversary often includes comparisons of how this treatment is different from the previous one. But the one-year period can also be a time of crisis when waiting turns to impatience or when a redefinition of the self takes place in reference to parents, therapists, the hospital unit, and one's own goals. Clearly, it is a time of assessment, reassessment, and turning to the future.

Many authors have described the rather unique quality of the normal teenager's experience of himself and time. Redl and Wineman (1957) refer to an adult's view of a teenager as being like a "speeding train," a hypercathexis of the present and of action. Bonaparte (1940) points to the prominence of instinctual life and daydreams in the adolescent whom she regards as having an illusion of eternity. Anna Freud (1958) also describes their preoccupation with new objects and with the present. Erik Erikson (1959) first called our attention to those ego states related to time in the teenager; he noted a "time diffusion" where one loses one's function of perspective. These are the vicissitudes of normal adolescence, a time of far-reaching reorganization of the self and the working through of the psychological separation from previous relationships.

This second phase of separation-individuation brings to the fore earlier deficiencies, and particularly so in hospitalized teenagers, given the occurrence of significant disturbances in their very early development. It is not at all surprising to find difficulty in waiting and feeble attempts to gain perspective. Some of our patients have foreclosed prematurely the past of their childhood; in some the past floods them and cannot be separated by any time interval or psychological distance; in others the future is vague and magical. Many teenagers cannot project into a future state or develop a picture of themselves in the future. For some a realistic view of the future can precipitate despair. For example, Art, a 15-year-old, was participating in a group discussion of future and school. Suddenly, he was gripped with a terrible sense of failure when he realized that he might be 19 or older when he graduated from high school. His voice was filled with despair and he questioned whether, indeed, he had, or wanted, a future. Six months after discharge and during a brief hospitalization elsewhere, he killed himself after a series of delinquent acts. While this extreme outcome is relatively rare, it is not uncommon that with the cessation of acting out, a period of depression and dysphoria results, as one is confronted with the temporal discontinuities of oneself, and the inability to project oneself into the future.

A time perspective is not easy to define or to teach, but it would seem to depend on a sense of oneself as a starting point. Building on that is a sense of continuity and the idea of an enduring self. One can describe the process of therapy in the hospital as moving from a fragile self, dictated by drives and the needs of the moment, to a more stable self that actively directs the teenager's efforts and goals. Such movement is achieved by the buildup of many daily occurrences interspersed with periods of regression. It is indeed a process and cannot be isolated at any point in time or circumscribed in any one single event. A brief vignette which occurred during the 18-month hospital treatment of a 16-year-old girl might illustrate an aspect of the process. Ursula was headstrong and verbal, constantly involved in testing, and involved in minor mischief on the unit. Her behaviors were very often in conflict with the rules and with the staff. She was contentious and vitriolic in sessions. Eventually, after a long period of intervention and confrontation regarding her behaviors and various attempts to resist and avoid engaging in therapy, she became somewhat isolated and depressed. One day in the therapy session she commented in a genuinely reflective tone: "You know, there is more behavior than there is me!"

What we provide in the intensive treatment of the hospitalized adolescent is a time to stop the frequently headlong flight into destructive behavior and learn to shift attention to oneself. This time affords the teenager the possibility of centering on himself, which, given the plasticity and potential push for growth of the phase we call adolescence, facilitates the development of greater coherence and sense of mastery. Out of this growth and change emerges a perspective or a sense that there is more than just the immediate present, that there is a past which one cannot deny and a future which one can anticipate.

6

Space

The young infant feels safe and protected in his mother's arms. When he cries in hunger or distress, he is often comforted, before food is even offered, by being held close to his mother. The infant who falls asleep in his mother's arms may awaken immediately when put into bed, only to quiet again when he is picked up and reassured by physical closeness. Even an infant who is only weeks old may scoot his way during the night to some corner of the crib, away from the empty space in the center toward some physical contact and protection. Physical closeness, small warm spaces, clothes and blankets that enfold and hold the infant—all provide him with physical and emotional security as he begins to make his way in the external world.

The infant experiences a sense of oneness with his mother; he perceives her as an extension of himself. For healthy development, however, this early symbiotic relationship must give way to a gradual process of separation/individuation. The older infant, though not yet capable of holding the image of the mother in his mind, takes delight in such games as peek-a-boo. The disappearance and timely reappearance of the mother are tremendously reassuring. The anxiety aroused by the hint of separation is assuaged by the immediacy of recognition and reunion. The infant, not yet capable of soothing himself, must rely upon the physical presence of another to soothe, calm, and reassure him. He has learned, however, that his cries of protest and distress result in the emergence, out of nowhere, of the mother. He lights up when she enters the room, delighted in part with his own abilities to summon her. If her responsiveness has been consistent, he will gradually develop some tolerance for physical separation and delay of gratification, confident that she will return. This early trust in the mother invariably influences later perceptions of the external world.

The infant's separation from the mother begins in space and is propelled forward by the infant's increased mobility. When the infant learns to crawl and walk, he can, for the first time, move away from mother. In a safe environment, supported by the mother's encouragement, the infant can explore and begin to master new surroundings. His efforts, at first, are generally tenuous. The child steps out on his own, but frequently returns to his mother, to touch the safety of home base. This phenomenon is repeated by the toddler time and again, and even the older child, through symbolic play, reenacts this rapprochement phase in innumerable games where home base represents security and safety from external threats.

Now, the toddler, who not long ago as an infant felt powerful enough to summon his mother from out of nowhere, still views events that occur in the environment as very much a result of his own doing. Inanimate objects take on human characteristics, events are personalized, cause and effect are personalized, and the entire human and nonhuman environment is blurred. The toddler, for instance, may enter a room filled with other children and toys, yet cling frantically to his mother's leg because he fears abandonment more than some external threat imposed by the environment. He holds on to her in an effort to recreate the comfort of being held, of being one with her. If the environment is indeed benign and dangers minimal, if he is reassured that physical separation does not mean abandonment, he will eventually be able to separate more easily from his mother and invest himself confidently in his surroundings. But this it not always the case. If the child feels overwhelmed by fears of abandonment, if the mother-child relationship is fraught with conflict and characterized by inconsistency, the child may well learn to perceive even benign environments as similarly unpredictable. In turn, he may avoid or withdraw from what he fears to be a hostile environment and cling even more desperately to his mother. If the environment is indeed injurious, the child, who does not yet readily distinguish between the animate and inanimate world, may view the mother as somehow responsible in that she was unable or unwilling to protect him. In either case, he is left fearful of being abandoned to unfriendly spaces.

On the other hand, a toddler may become eagerly involved with toys and other children. This may be an act of genuine enthusiasm by a child well on his way toward separation/individuation. It may be, however, that the child immerses himself in activity in an effort to ward off the painful feelings associated with separation. If his mother is in fact unreliable, the child may focus on attempting to control and conquer the environment and in so doing maintain a kind of equilibrium. Manipulation of the environment then acts as a buffer against the unreliable mother.

A child's approach to and involvement with the nonhuman environment are inextricably tied to early object relations. During the process of separation/individuation, a child may approach a new situation or surrounding with timidity, fearfulness, interest, or enthusiasm. Each of these responses, and more, can be appropriate, or adaptive, and not necessarily indicative of any serious problem. Over time, however, as the child grows, he must find his place in the world which inevitably involves finding his place in relation to others. His fears, anxieties, uncertainties, and methods of coping and adapting find expression in attitudes developed toward the external world (Balint, 1955).

Most of the hospitalized adolescents we see do not seem to have found their "place" in the world; they seem confused and uncertain about their relations to others and tend to view even relatively benign environments as hostile and overwhelming. Their response to external and internal threat, real or imagined, is varied, but their attitude, reflected through behavior, is not without meaning, but full of implications and purpose.

In an extreme case, for instance, a poorly differentiated adolescent, like a young infant, may seek a symbiotic union, living from object to object, fearful of being left to his own devices in terrifying empty spaces. Only when in close physical proximity to another, in touch with a safe object, does he in turn feel safe. Since he cannot differentiate, he cannot feel regard or concern for the other, only need. Because the other's importance depends on the functions it performs for the self, it is experienced as a part of the self, a self-object (Kohut, 1971). For this reason, most any object will do if he can only merge with it and cling desperately, struggling all the while with the fear that the object may fail or abandon him. When the adolescent is consumed by a quest for a symbiotic union, it is of no surprise that healthy interest and involvement with the world cannot fully develop. Furthermore, there is little motivation to learn about a world which in his own experience has proven, more often than not, to be exploitative, frightening, and disappointing. A safe retreat, in touch with another, seems preferable. On the other hand, another adolescent may appear comfortable in an environment, move from place to place freely, involving himself in activities. On closer look, however, it is apparent that he involves himself with a fury, moves quickly from event to event, activity to activity, incapable of maintaining interest or prolonged concentration. He is watchful, and moves in space in order to keep a safe distance. In this instance, the adolescent must avoid, or control, others—the unreliable and potentially dangerous objects. He must protect his vulnerability and structure his world so that he does not have to depend upon untrustworthy individuals. He cannot, however, develop any real skill in manipulating the environment or derive any lasting pleasure from it because potential success is constantly interrupted by a need to be vigilant. He relies on a kind of important omnipotence, and efforts to ward off dangers inevitably thwart the development of positive interpersonal relationships.

Toddlers who cling to the mother or immerse themselves in play may indeed be responding appropriately to the difficult and painful process of separation/individuation. Adolescents, however, who repeatedly cling to a safe object or keep a safe distance reveal dramatic impairment in the growth process. Their approach to the external physical world, their lack of sustained interest in the environment, and their use or misuse of surroundings are all indicators of the source, nature, and extent of their turmoil.

OVERVIEW

It is in this light that observations of the teenager can be useful as diagnostic tools. Space in the treatment setting provides the "holding" place for individuals whose internal structures and external supports are failing to keep them at a level of integration they and/or others can tolerate. An early and basic writing on the use of space in treatment is *The Mental Hospital,* a study by Stanton and Schwartz (1954) of a treatment ward for schizophrenic patients. Their observations on milieu have been added to in recent years by workers with children and adolescents—Bettelheim (1974), Redl (1966), Easson (1969), Treischman, Whittaker and Brendtro (1969). Each has contributed to the concept of structuring the residential space in treating children and adolescents with psychoses and behavior disorders. Each understands the opportunities for new experiences of consistency, safety, and growth within a well-defined, consistent, and human environment which modulates the life experiences to that level which is tolerable to the capacity of the individual. The successes and failures within that structure provide the raw material for therapy.

Not every consistent, well-defined and warm environment is therapeutic. Redl cautions:

> May I be allowed to add at least the demand that we become more specific about this point and stop confusing our own recreational taste buds, philosophical convictions, and habits of social interaction with objective assessment of what is or is not useful in the treatment of the patient at a given time (Redl, 1966, p. 73).

We conceptualize a safe, growth-producing milieu for delinquent adolescents as having three levels. Briefly restated, the foundation stones are the basic safety aspects of the physical environment such as the patient rooms, lighting, and windows. Secondly, there are specific considerations for delinquent adolescents, including plans for the use of time, space, persons, and objects. Lastly, there is decision making by the staff based on each patient's dynamics and psychological structure. At this last level of milieu organization, the staff member assesses the individual's needs, moment to moment, and decides either to maintain or to change the first two levels for this particular adolescent.

One of the basic differences between Stanton and Schwartz's work and that of ourselves and other writers is in the development of a milieu specific for a relatively homogeneous group of patients. Behaviorally disordered adolescents need an environment which helps them maintain their anxieties and feelings within a range they can tolerate. They must be helped to examine their behavior, acknowledge it as their own, and understand its effects on themselves and others. They must also be helped to name and identify the feelings that they experience and also to claim them as their own. Unacceptable behavior within a therapeutic milieu for delinquent adolescents needs to be understood, but not accepted, encouraged, or overlooked.

Whereas Stanton and Schwartz speak of the milieu as a holding and containing place between therapy sessions, we view the milieu as the place which supports the adolescents to do what they could not do on the outside—engage in productive learning, enjoy constructive activities, and explore their problems in living. Therapy will, in turn, deal with successes and failures in these areas.

New experiences and expectations for behavior change gradually produce in the adolescent conflict and insight within the therapy relationship. For all patients, safety is basic. However, structuring space for the behaviorally disordered adolescent provides a background against which problems in internal structure and control will become manifest. It is against this background that the adolescent can, with help, begin to take responsibility for his behavior and accept it as his own.

When we began to work with behaviorally disordered adolescents, we gradually recognized their inability to differentiate themselves from others, not just cognitively but affectively. Most evident was the abuse of other persons through physical violence. Gradually, as we dealt with such incidents, we became increasingly aware that space was either misperceived or misused. There was an apparent lack of involvement in surroundings, except as they met the immediate needs of the individual to express their internal world. The following report of a weekend day by a milieu staff member illustrates a patient's disinterest in the environment until it was changed; this disrupted her internal equilibrium, evoking anger and a sense of impotence.

It was a kind of unusual day with a feeling of some tension among the patients. Everyone slept late. Tammy was visited by parents and really seemed to enjoy it. Norine, Frank, and George then began getting up for TV and cards. Everyone was out for lunch but quiet. After lunch, Theresa, George, and Norine went back to their rooms. Mike read. Tammy wrote letters. I got the kids busy cleaning up the dayroom and Frank, Norine and George, Elaine and Mona began doing a thorough job *with Lorraine walking in and out.* At this time the patients asked if they could rearrange the dayroom and have their chairs facing the windows. I said no, but they could rearrange it in a different manner. This took approximately a half-hour and they also swept and mopped the floors. It looked good. *Then Lorraine saw the new arrangements and was furious and sarcastic.* Theresa also became enraged. It appeared to be a question of where the power was on the unit and Lorraine bitterly complained that it was mostly the new patients who changed (it), and that she had been here a long time and wasn't asked for her opinion of the change. Theresa just began swearing and refused to try to work something out with the group. Lorraine spoke with me and then Norine and said she felt better because it was more a matter of telling people how she felt rather than disliking the dayroom arrangement. Lorraine and Norine wanted the whole group to talk about it and asked for a ward meeting after visiting hours. The shift in power base was quite apparent and is indicative of a rather big change on the unit. The tension seemed to dissipate some after Lorraine and Theresa expressed their anger.

The environment had meaning for Lorraine, which was noticeable only when changes in the environment caused her to feel disrupted internally. The environment and the arrangement of the chairs had become for her self-objects, serving certain kinds of psychological function in order to maintain her equilibrium. Changes, without her participation, caused her a great deal of discomfort, and she became enraged at her inability to control the world around her, a world which she needed to be constant and consistent in order to hold her together. Thus, her rage at the rearrangement of the dayroom expressed her internal disarray, but the disarray could be dealt with therapeutically by the work of an empathic staff member. It was not simply catharsis of angry feelings that helped Lorraine and Theresa integrate, but rather the time spent by the staff in helping them channel and express their anger appropriately, and the work done by the staff in helping them soothe themselves.

We gradually learned that through the use of space we could help the individual and the group make primitive but necessary distinctions. As we began to define space as having certain functions, we could then help the adolescents learn the proper use of space through structure, rules and regulations, clearly assigned responsibilities and consequences associated with the use of space—all things being carried out by direct, secure, warm, and knowledgeable staff members. As a result, some of the incomplete differentiation, markedly impaired impulse control, and lack of self-soothing ability became more evident and amenable to change.

In recognizing and understanding these deficits, we attempt to structure the environment in order to decrease external diffusion, confusion and stimulation and to block expression of some impulses. Along with and through the structure, we attempt soothing and caring by the staff. For those patients who cannot tolerate personal contact, the structure alone can often provide comfort. By these measures we work toward increased differentiation of boundaries, internalization of conflict, delay of impulse expression, production of thought and fantasy, and a gradual internalization of good object representations. Thus, the milieu prepares the patient for individual insight therapy.

Rearrangement of the environment helps to achieve personality change and not simply external compliance. For a well-defined and coherent milieu to affect personality development, the use of space must be transmitted by a knowledgeable and caring staff. The staff must learn to accept the rage of frustrated omnipotence, of conflictual or direct impulse expression, without changing their ideas or attacking the adolescent. This sense of caring and competence is translated in the personal presence of the staff, and, for some adolescents, through the concrete rules and regulations regarding the use of space.

THE ADOLESCENT COMES TO THE HOSPITAL

The adolescent who is referred to us is usually in need of hospitalization as the result of several interacting factors: 1) strong conflicts;

2) poorly developed capacity to control needs and tensions and to carry out the tasks of daily living; and 3) lack of relationship ability to compensate for other ego weaknesses. If the delinquent's defenses were more stable, or he could trust enough to seek support from others or make use of available support, he would most likely not be hospitalized (Easson, 1969). We want to provide 24-hour nonhuman environmental and human supports "until the ego arrives" (Redl, 1966) and to help build a capacity for using human relationships to grow.

When delinquent adolescents enter the hospital, they carry with them a long history of misuse of place—explosions of inner turmoil have terrorized others in the school, on family outings, in the homes of friends, and in their own homes. The child, and then the adolescent, has for years been incapable of controlling the storm once it starts to blow, and he cannot do what is expected at a particular place and time. He has become, as many of our adolescents have described themselves, a "time bomb" with unpredictable explosions in various places: school, movie theaters, shopping centers, or the home, often in open confrontation with the police. Although they may claim to be in control of themselves, they actually feel the relief of this external control. Tammy Z's history demonstrates such an example:

> After continued episodes of acting up in school and at home, Tammy went to a supermarket and stood, omnipotently, in the parking lot, refusing to let cars pass until she was taken away by the police. Although verbally she has refused the efforts of school counselors and her parents to get treatment for her, Tammy's attempts to control the space around her forced the issue out into the open. Her desperate need for omnipotent control brought her into the hospital.

These delinquents enter the hospital with a history of misusing physical space to show their tremendous discomfort despite their knowledge of socially acceptable rules, regulations, and attitudes which define certain places for specific functions; their cognitive understanding is usually adequate but their affective responses primitive.

THE SPACE ON THE TREATMENT UNIT

All the space on the unit is defined very clearly for the incoming adolescents. This provides them knowledge of what is allowed and where. The adolescents are assured of the enduring configuration of the physical space. The unit does not change day by day, hour to hour, or minute to minute as do their internal feelings and controls. The environment must be the "good enough" mother against which the adolescent differentiates himself while being protected from excessive stimulation. He will be expected to participate as fully as he can in the program so that gradually his conflicts, needs, and deficits can be understood. This does not imply that the adolescent is put into certain environments which we know he cannot handle, but his failures too are studied, so that both the staff and the patient can learn from them.

Each area of the unit—dayroom, individual rooms, bathrooms, music room, kitchen, corridor, nurses' station, staff offices, and extensions of the physical unit such as the route to school, the gym and the shop— is clearly defined in terms of both purpose and expected behaviors for all patients. Consequences of not using the various parts of the environment according to expectations are also known. When a patient is unable to meet these expectations, the staff is alerted that something has gone awry, and the consequences are applied. In this way, the staff can intervene constructively.

> On his way to school with two or three other teenagers and a staff member, Bill starts pressing several of the floor buttons once they have entered the elevator. He belligerently refuses to stop when told to do so by the staff member. The staff member senses that Bill is having some difficulty making the transition from one space to the other, maybe from the protection of the unit to the elevator, or maybe moving into the school space and the classroom is distressing him. The staff member assesses Bill as being unable to handle the situation currently and he is taken by the staff member to the unit and to his room where the two of them try to understand what just happened.

The staff member holds to the principle "a place for everything, and everything in its place" and assesses inappropriate behavior in a given place as an indication that something has gotten derailed. Although this is not to be a punishment, the teenager might readily perceive it that way and the staff member will have to clarify her intervention. In temporarily limiting Bill's inappropriate behavior, he and the staff came to understand that he felt like eloping, and needed a staff member to accompany him to and from school by himself. As he and the staff understand his behavior in space, Bill might be able to verbalize what bothers him rather than giving direct expression to his impulses. Unless this behavior had been noted and intervened with, and later explored by the staff member and Bill, it could easily have been misread as simply a game, typical teenage behavior, an attempt to manipulate, to get out of the class, or "horseplay."

On the treatment unit, each space becomes structured with an adult ego serving as a repression barrier to motor discharge. Once the adolescent stops, he can learn to delay, fantasize, and plan, thereby holding in check those impulses which had previously been discharged immediately. Through these experiences in the environment, the patient will interpose thinking between feeling and behavior. It is through this blocking of impulses and help with calming down, naming feelings, fantasizing, thinking, and planning future situations that the adolescent who is used to speaking primarily through disruptive behavior and "empty" words can be helped to develop skills for engaging in individual therapy.

The space of the hospital setting can be considered as territories— claimed spaces. Lyman and Scott (1967) describe four:

Public Territories are characterized by an ambiguous "freedom of access," but not necessarily of action, within a legal, moral, and social structure. The public territory of the ward is the day area with freedom of access for adolescents, staff, families, and other visitors. It is structured by the rules and demands of the treatment philosophy and the guidelines of community living.

Home Territories, or private spaces, are ones in which members exert some control over an area which they regularly use, and in which relative freedom of behavior and expression of intimacy are permitted. The private territories of the ward are the individual patient rooms, the patient bathrooms, corridors for adolescents and staff and the nurses' station for the staff.

Interactional Territories are interpersonal spaces, which are usually mobile and fragile and envelop social interactions. The interactional territories on the ward are places where patient-patient interactions occur, such as the day area; places on the unit where staff-patient interactions occur, including individual patient rooms, day area, game room, and music room; and places on the ward where staff-staff interactions occur such as the nurses' station and the conference room.

Body Territories are the spaces occupied by the human body and are the most private and inviolate territories. Every staff, patient, and visitor has his or her own unique body territory needs.

In examining and describing a few of the major ward spaces and how they are used, the basic principles which are the foundation for our practices become evident. These can be applied to other spaces, in and out of the hospital, which can then be employed for therapeutic activities.

The Day Area

The Day Area is a common, public space for both boys and girls— the only public interpersonal space for adolescents on the unit. It is used for eating, watching television, playing games, daily patient-staff ward meetings, and for informal chats. It is frequented by visitors and contains the only patient telephone and the unit ironing board. It is a multipurpose room; this can easily lead to confusion and clashing of interests, but can also promote growth in delay of gratification, planning, and sharing.

It is a supervised interpersonal space. A staff member is present here at all times to provide the necessary external ego and a sense of safety, and to help the patients redirect those impulses which interfere with successful completion of their goals. The immediate physical presence of a staff member becomes a partial barrier to misusing one another and the environment. Often one who is feeling empty, overwhelmed, or wants to stir others up, starts to brag of past delinquent escapades, drug usage, or sexual experiences, and as the talk gets louder and more spirited, each patient is confronted with tensions beyond his limits. Sometimes tensions build over the use of the television or the telephone or "heavy rap sessions" with peers about personal problems. Each one of these situations requires a different response, and each one calls for a different degree of staff involvement.

Distinctions must be made between what the staff will do and what the staff and adolescent will do together. For instance, stirring up others with talk of delinquent escapades is met by immediate staff intervention perhaps by redirecting conversation or sending the individual to his room.

On the other hand, for some time early in the life of the unit, the teenagers would fight over the use of the telephone. The problems were resolved by group work accomplished by staff support, guidance, and participation. After several weeks of work by the patients and the evening staff, the following communication emerged:

Rules for Use of the Phone

The following rules for use of the phone were thoughtfully worked out with the kids and announced. Periodic meetings should be held to go over these rules for the benefit of the new patients. Changes of the rules or exceptions are to be made when indicated as long as they are made in a very thoughtful manner and recorded, *but staff discretion should always take precedence over these rules.*

1) The phone is to be used from 8 a.m. until ½ hour before the first bedtime which means until 10 p.m. Sunday through Thursday; 12 midnight Friday and Saturday; and 11 p.m. when the bedtimes are extended one hour on the night before a holiday. Of course, on a holiday like New Years Eve, an exception might be made to let the kids call their families to say Happy New Year. This is the kind of exception that might be made after careful consideration of the staff.

2) Kids who receive emergency phone calls outside of the usual phone times may receive them if the staff knows the nature of the call and has decided that the kid *can* and *should* deal with the stress involved rather than waiting till later. Rarely should this be necessary.

3) As with everything else, we are not here to solve these kids' problems for them when they are able to solve them without us or with our help. Therefore, if there is an argument over use of telephone, we are available to assist in helping the kids work out a resolution as long as they maintain control over themselves. Of course, in the event of an impossible situation around the phone, the staff may find it necessary to restrict the parties from use of the phone until something can be worked out. The kids know that they can ask each other to be fair around the use of the phone and that is an expectation.

4) If, for some reason, a kid is to stay in his room, our practice has been to allow one supervised phone call per shift to or from parents or probation officer. AGAIN, logical exceptions could and should be made where it seems advisable in the judgment of the staff. (This rule does not include the night staff, of course).

The use of the telephone on our unit in particular, and the meaning of the telephone in general to any adolescent exemplifies a good deal about space. On our unit the public pay phone is situated in a corner of the dayroom, close to the TV viewing area and the area where meals are eaten. Consequently, it lies in an interface between private space, as one carries on a personal conversation, and the public space of dayroom and group activities. It is not uncommon to see teenagers swinging back and forth between participating in their own private telephone world and the public interactions of the dayroom; conversely, other teenagers will attempt to interfere with, or participate in, a patient's private conversations. Often, relationships are extended through the telephone into the group or groups at either end of the line. This brings us to the more general meaning of the telephone for the adolescent who is able to extend himself into space while at the same time defining himself in a very localized spot. Talking on the telephone extends his relationships to other people and other places while at the same time helping him remain removed and separated (Pearson, 1958).

The telephone may enable the teenager to extend and enlarge spaces omnipotently, while remaining isolated, or to merge with or relate to others, while remaining differentiated and removed. It is through the telephone that often the space of the family, of the neighborhood, and of outside relationships is brought into the hospital. Disturbing news from home or typically neurotic interactions with a parent impinge upon the treatment process. Attempts to get drugs smuggled into the hospital, or procuring a car or a weapon in order to facilitate an escape plan are vivid reminders of how the telephone extends the space of the treatment unit, just as it extends the personal space of every adolescent. The telephone, thus, cannot be viewed simply as an object of the unit, a "thing" in the environment, but rather as an extender of the environment itself, in much the same way as the television set opens up vistas and extends the limits of the environment in which the adolescent lives.

The important point here is that healthy adult staff members are needed by disturbed teenagers to help them manage their space. Although many adolescents often appear to be without problems, simply in need of forming "good peer relationships" and in need of privacy away from adults, experience has taught us that this is generally not so. Unlike healthier teens, these are still too immature and primitive to use unsupervised peer interactions for growth. The histories of most of our patients show few real friendships or participation in group activities apart from their delinquent behavior. Even the gang delinquents are loners.

The shared space of the day area must be structured in such a way that the adolescent feels safe but not so complacent that he experiences no tension or anxiety necessary to stimulate growth. A delicate balance of regulated ward tensions promotes emotional growth and avoids psychic flooding. The use of space must be regulated according to the needs of each individual. For example, when there is someone whose boundaries and controls are extremely poor, the day area can be used effectively for socialization only when he has a staff member assigned specifically to him as an external support and regulator. When there are two adolescents whose intrapsychic dynamics are complementary and counterproductive to both, they should have limited or supervised contact with each other so that they can be helped to feel and understand what is driving them to seek each other. There may be several who misuse furniture or litter the unit; such are signs of beginning breakdown of controls. Some patients can begin to learn some socialization skills by watching and interacting with a staff member.

In a well-defined milieu with well-defined concepts for the use of space, each patient's deficits and particular areas of difficulty show clearly. Until his problems are highlighted, each adolescent's unacceptable impulses cannot be limited, and treatment opportunities will be lost.

Because the day area can be used for several different activities, such as talking, playing cards, telephoning, and watching TV, it is important that delinquent adolescents receive help in moving from one task to another. Their tendency is to carry tension and stimulation from a previous activity into a new one if there is no time to settle down and plan; this is especially true when the physical space is not changed as the activity changes. The staff member can act here as a "divider," by encouraging and guiding thoughtful planning before changing tasks. At times leaving the setting for several minutes can signal a change in activity and help make this experience more meaningful and demonstrate the distance one needs to engage in a new endeavor with minimal contamination. The day area can become a place for relaxation and enjoyable activities when it is structured in a clear way. This occurs through knowledge of what space in the milieu means and how it affects each adolescent in the presence of a caring, available staff.

*Individual Patient Room**

All teenagers experience many physical and psychological changes and need to maintain themselves as separate and unique, to reflect on their experiences, to dream, to plan, and to fantasize about the future. The individual room provides this privacy and a chance for the patient to be alone. It is territory which can be established as the adolescent's own. It is *mine* as distinct from *yours*. The individual room is the place for rest, for sleep, and for daily renewal. How the staff helps patients use their rooms encourages a growing awareness of self and others, provides a place for self-expression through activities such as study, crafts, and reading, and provides a place for self-expression through

---

* Some of the material presented in this section on the patient's room is derived from "The Therapeutic Use of the Room" by Brenda Hamady and David Swan, presented at the 1973 Illinois State Psychiatric Institute Nursing Conference.

the proper or improper use of furniture and through the presence or absence of decorations.

The importance of a person's room is magnified in the treatment setting. While in the hospital, the patient's assigned room belongs to him. It is home. It is a place where he leaves his personal belongings, where he rests and sleeps. Each adolescent on our treatment unit has a private room, containing a bed, a dresser, a locker for clothes, a desk and chair, and a knickknack shelf. Each room has a window with high tension mesh screening. Personal decorations are encouraged within the limits of safety and fire regulations.

The private space of the individual room, as we have conceptualized it, is a primary tool in treatment. It can become a place for safety and retreat from external stimuli and a safe place for the patient to begin to sort out internal stimuli. It is possible that early differentiation and some level of self-reflection can start in this space for the disturbed adolescent. Because it is the patient's uniquely, it is invaluable for observing, assessing, and treating the adolescent in the hospital.

Easson (1969) has emphasized the importance of the patient's room as a diagnostic tool, as a good indicator of his "level of basic emotional integration."

> A young disturbed teenage girl was experiencing a period of marked confusion. Her room was a mess, and staff would regularly try to help her clean it up. She would become furious, and although the room might get cleaned, later in the day it would be a smelly mess once again. Her room clearly reflected her own inner disorganization, turmoil, and anger. Later, she used her room to demonstrate her extreme ambivalence about everything because even the very basic task of cleaning herself had become a major dilemma. It was an inner struggle of "should I?" or "shouldn't I?" Her room had become a relatively safe place for her, and she used it as a hideout, peeking out of her doorway, deciding whether to come out or not, and then maybe taking a few steps out into the hallway, leaving her door open, and making a fast retreat back into the room. This ambivalent approach-avoidance behavior was repeated time and time again each day. Inside the room, her clothes remained packed in a paperbag and her coat was hung beside the door as she eagerly anticipated the first opportunity to leave.

At the same time, another patient on the unit, a younger male, creatively decorated his room with things he made in the shop. He was controlling and manipulative and became furious when things didn't go his way. The staff could readily anticipate his impending loss of control when he tore down all his decorations, which he had so laborously hung previously, and put away all other belongings he hadn't destroyed, thus leaving the room completely devoid of decoration. He usually behaved this way after being confronted with a piece of behavior or frustrated with getting what he wanted. This denuding of his room was a way of mastering himself and the frustrations and injuries his environment afforded him.

Another girl on the unit was found sleeping on a makeshift bed on the floor, between her bed and the wall. When asked why she was sleeping there, she stated that it was warmer. Her behavior could be regarded as inappropriate and her response evasive. If one moved too quickly to set things "right" again, however, one might fail to recognize what indeed she was saying through her restructuring of her environment, through her creation of a small, enclosed, protected space. She sought warmth and all which that connotes, security and protection from both external and internal threat. Her use of physical space dramatically symbolized her need to be enfolded, held, and reassured by another. Her resources were depleted. She could not soothe herself without some physical evidence of protection. If one is able to read her messages clearly, one can begin to recognize the extent of her fear and proceed, with caution, to reassure her that she will be protected from herself and from others.

The room should be experienced as a safe place by the impulse-disordered adolescent. Single rooms are necessary to avoid constant destructive embroilment in others' boundaries. Peer sharing is a frightening, disruptive activity for the adolescent who constantly externalizes conflict and impulse. Roommates are for healthier egos.

Normal adolescents often use their rooms as a places to entertain friends and talk in secret away from the common "parental" parts of the house. When disturbed adolescents meet in small groups, over-stimulation, and sexual and aggressive acting out almost always result. Disturbed adolescents cannot use space, even their own space away from parental supervision, for productive ends. Instead, for adolescents accustomed to keeping themselves in some sort of crisis state based on external problems, a quiet, safe environment easily becomes another place to "use," to express their conflicts, to find weapon material, to discuss master escape plans, sexual encounters, and destructive behavior toward other patients and staff. Often this talk is mere talk for most of the group, while it becomes a forceful reality for others. Once caught up in these relationships, very few disturbed teenagers can back out, even when they have some partial realization of the destruction and harm to staff and other patients which might result. This has been emphatically confirmed for us several times in ward meetings and individual therapy sessions.

> In the fourth year of the program, six or seven of the adolescents were involved in a plot to help two of the boys run away. The plans included concealing a knife, calling a female staff member to the boys' bathroom, and forcing her to give up her keys. A getaway car had been procured over the phone. As the plans proceeded, all but the two boys involved in the actual plan to run away dropped out. Later, the rest said that while they were aware of the danger of the situation, they remained involved by not telling staff and by keeping secrets. At zero hour, one of the two boys also backed out and then the incident came to staff attention. All the adolescent patients had some knowledge of what was going on, but denied their sporadic insights into the imminent danger. There was also a great deal of confusion about how this plan actually got started, who said what, and whether it would really happen or was "just talk."

Allowing a place for this kind of talk and agitation defeats the purpose of a treatment unit for delinquents. It is no longer psychologically safe for the individual, nor physically safe for the patient group and the staff. When such plotting occurs, it means that alliances with the milieu staff or individual therapists for handling frightening feelings have not been built up or have broken down. If it goes unchecked by staff and therapists, patients may come to question our investment in treatment. A fair chance at treatment for delinquent adolescents means that rooms, doorways, and corridors have to shift from interpersonal space to private space.

Healthy adolescents use their rooms for entertaining but also reserve their own space for privacy, secrecy, and autonomy, needs which disturbed adolescents also display. They can learn to use the room to withdraw so that mastery and growth can occur, and so that problems and conflicts cannot be immediately dissipated. Adolescents can then be given time and both physical and interpersonal space to try to come to grips with what is disturbing them.

> Tom, for instance, had a great deal of difficulty with impulse control. His first reaction when threatened was to hit. One day, another patient sat in Tom's favorite chair in front of the television set, and Tom, feeling angry, walked over and started to provoke him. A staff member intervened and told Tom to come down to his room with her. Once in the room, the staff member pointed out that she had asked him to go to his room because he seemed on the verge of hitting the other person. He was told that he couldn't return to the dayroom until he was able to control himself. In instances such as this, staff may provide the patient an opportunity to express his anger; or it may be advisable to leave the patient, temporarily, alone in his room. How long he stays in his room depends on the severity of his breakdown, and his capacity to examine his behavior, to reintegrate and to tolerate the intervention. Staff must gauge the length of time in order to produce maximum work and benefit for the patient while at the same time avoiding an unnecessary frustrating experience. By sending Tom to his room, the staff member removed him from what seemed to be a threatening situation to a safe place, his room, his own territory, and thereby reduced the stimulation impinging on him from the external environment. As well, when she asked him to examine his behavior, she encouraged him to begin to introspect. But the privacy of his room, its familiarity, and its nurturance support him in this therapeutic process. Certainly, an alliance with the staff member supports this process also, but the safe familiar territory of his room is of inestimable value.

The room becomes an external control for impulsive behavior until the teenager is able to develop his own internalized controls. Sending a patient to his room suppresses an impulse to be destructive, facilitates a process of introspection, and supports a fragile or fragmenting ego. Removing a patient from overwhelming stimulation facilitates his ability to focus on the problem and demonstrates that most problems, even those that seem to be overwhelming, can be managed and understood.

Our use of the room in this manner teaches withdrawal, which, although a somewhat primitive defense, is the first step that many teenagers take in attempting to master their own impulsive styles.

> Jim behaved delinquently in order to avoid feelings of intense pain and depression. He was unable to handle demands for performance or what appeared to him to be excessive external stimulation. While playing a competitive game of cards one day, Jim was accused of cheating and quit, denying hotly that he had done any such thing. He paced around the unit and turned on the stereo full blast. He would not respond to patient or staff requests to turn the volume down. A staff member asked Jim to go to his room, joining him there a few minutes later. She pointed out to him that although he may have been angry, blasting the stereo only worsened things. She suggested that in the future, instead of acting on his anger in this manner, he might go to his room. By sending him to his room, the staff member reduced the amount of external stimulation and provided him with a more controlled environment, his own. As well, Jim was able to distance himself both emotionally and physically from the disturbing situation. Teaching Jim to withdraw by using his room is not a single event, but rather something he learns only after constant repetition of this process. In the beginning, withdrawing to his room was difficult for Jim because while he was there, he became aware of intensely painful depressive feelings which he previously avoided through delinquency. Being in his room uncovered serious suicidal urges which Jim exhibited sporadically prior to admission. In his previous hospitalization, Jim would light fires in his room and on his person when unattended. This again emphasizes the importance of a staff member participating in the process with Jim.

A patient's room, if used properly, can also help him to form boundaries and achieve an emotional separation from the environment.

> Chris was a sporadically withdrawn and highly constricted individual whose serious inhibitions were a way of coping with his tendency to merge with his environment. Chris spent a lot of time with another patient, Bill. Whenever Bill became loud, anxious,

or upset, Chris did the same, even though the situation had no particular meaning for him. Chris would react to Bill's affect, merge with it, and accept it as his own. By taking Chris to his room whenever this happened, a staff member was able to remove him from the emotional confusion to a personalized space. The room served to enhance his own sense of being an individual. The room, although initially an external boundary enforced by staff, eventually can help a patient reestablish and maintain whatever internal boundaries are present and will remain available as a boundary support to which a patient can withdraw. Chris' merging with his environment had a hungry aspect to it. For him, his room served to interrupt more primitive behavior and to block a tendency to demand immediate gratification and merge diffusely with others.

As we better understand these adolescents, we also better understand our responsibilities toward them—to teach each one individually how his room can become a safe place to cool down, a place to begin to look at reasons for disruptive behavior, a place to begin to differentiate, and a place where he can learn to put space, time, thought, and fantasy between impulse and action. Patients, of course, will sometimes protest when asked to go to their rooms. They may feel that staff is unfairly frustrating or blocking direct impulse expression, or they may feel that the expectation to learn to live with internal anxiety is an impossible one. They may react with rage, insults, or demands for civil liberties, but because the staff does not back down, the rules do not change, and patients are helped to carry out what they are asked to do, they finally find some relief.

Though the delinquents are being helped through the environment to grow and live with themselves, they will complain that they are being both deprived and overwhelmed. The decrease in omnipotence and increase in self-other differentiation which are evoked by each encounter with a flexible, but firm, environment may not be evident for months. But eventually most patients learn that going to their rooms is not a punishment—not the end result of a particular intervention. They learn that "good" things can happen there, and that in this quiet, contained, private and personal space, they can, with the help of a staff member, begin to sort out and make sense of their fears, their anxieties, themselves.

In order for the patient's room to remain a safe place, a place where therapeutic interventions can and do occur, it must not be shared. These adolescents, it must be remembered, are engaged in the immediate. They seek pleasurable satisfaction of their impulses and have little knowledge of or capacity to internalize those societal values that embrace controlling ethics and morality. They make little or no attempt to disguise infantile assertiveness or acquisitiveness and, in fact, not unlike a young child who will become angry if he feels his sibling has received a bigger piece of cake, are keenly sensitive to "equal" apportionment of staff "goodies." As well, most of these adolescents have learned not to rely on adults for help, renewal, or growth. They have been forced, through their own sense of abandonment, to depend largely on the improvisation of the peer group. Left without positive ties to mature adults, left without a realistic perspective of their place in the scheme of things, they must, in a sense, pick up disjointed pieces and fashion their lives as best they can, relying on functional alliances with peers. These adolescents, as we have stated, are poorly differentiated and have little recognition of or concern for the other. Their alliances are fleeting and insubstantial, not mutually helpful or encouraging. The consequence of unsupervised peer interaction is often hopeless and destructive embroilment in others' boundaries. Themes of aggression and sexuality very often dominate the interactions, and the results can be disastrous.

The room, a more controlled environment, enables the patient to focus on issues and feelings because staff has defined the room as a place to withdraw and to think. This kind of therapeutic intervention begins with sending or taking the patient to his room, rather than ends with the patient going to his room. This is only the first step in a series of interventions which may need to be repeated, worked with, and modified as the patient grows. During a ward meeting, an adolescent may have difficulty trying to understand what happened with him in an incident presently under discussion by the group—who said what, when, how; when did talking end and action begin, who started it. In the ward meeting, he becomes embroiled with other adolescents and their confused feelings. Yet, later in his room, with staff help, the patient can begin to think, to separate himself, to recall a little more clearly, and to get some relief by finding "himself" without others impinging. The room becomes the place where, when things get confused, a staff member helps the adolescent straighten them out. He realizes that it is safe, that he is not being sent there to be abused by the staff. It is not the room in itself but the quiet, contained, private, and personal space, along with the staff member who helps him to begin to feel in control of what previously eluded him. The staff member helps to develop this aura of safety by being consistent in saying, despite protests, "Let's go to your room now and look at this," or "You need to go to your room now, and I'll be down to look at it with you." Gradually, the adolescent starts to say to the staff member, "I'm going down to my room now." The room has become safe and helpful in itself, and the staff member is not as necessary as before.

As the adolescent learns that some "good" things can happen in his room, the idea of being there is not so frightening and can even become a soothing experience. A striking example of this is an incident that occurred one day during the mid-year school break: Many of the adolescents, some of them with us already for a period of months, went to the zoo with the staff. In the monkey house there were a group of monkeys playing together in a cage. As the monkeys played, the noise level of screaming and yapping among them became very loud. One of the adolescents immediately remarked, "I think they're feeling out of control and need to go to their rooms." The other adolescents agreed. It was a great joke for the adolescents and for the staff, but the truth of the understanding wasn't missed.

Of course, for the room to become a soothing place, time and its dimensions need to be considered. Time spans should be gauged by the staff according to what the individual adolescent can tolerate, and he should be informed of these. He may be told, "Go to your room now, and I'll be down in five minutes; then we'll try to understand what happened," or "You're having a rough time—perhaps you'd better stay in your room except for your regular schedule until you see your therapist and talk about it tomorrow morning. I'll be in each hour to see if you need anything." Each assessment must depend on the amount and kind of contact each patient can tolerate so that the experience will help him grow and not overwhelm or deprive him.

Making the room a private safe retreat for time-limited introspection during the day helps at night when the adolescent must relinquish his vigilant scanning of his environment and fall asleep. A structure and routine must be provided which meet the specific needs of the delinquent adolescent. After a couple of years of observing and with trial and error, the milieu staff developed these outlines:

Bedtime Routine

Bedtime is an extremely difficult period. The adolescent is required to relinquish the controls and defenses built-up during the day which often give way to being flooded by fears and anxieties. The bedtime routine provides the basic structure to enable the patients to quiet down and prepare to sleep. The procedure begins early in the evening shift. The staff encourage a settled atmosphere and attempt to help the adolescents wind down as the evening progresses. Staff members will not discuss personal restrictions or chronic and upsetting anxieties after 9 p.m. (emergency situations are dealt with on a limited basis and referred to the day shift and the therapist).

When dietary provides, staff members make and serve hot chocolate in the winter and lemonade in the summer between 9:45 and 10 p.m. The adolescents are then to start getting ready for bed. A bedtime story is read most evenings about 10:20 p.m. by a staff member. We have found that the story is secondary to the presence and the voice of the staff member during this "try to fall asleep time." To successfully complete the routine, patients are expected to be in bed, in pajamas, and attempting to sleep. There is to be no disruption of patients in bed by those still up. Periodically a patient is allowed to read if it does not appear to be a way to avoid sleep, is not used to excess, and is not an attempt to finish homework. A bedtime restriction is given if the patient is not in his room in pajamas at the designated bedtime. This restriction is removed when the routine is successfully completed.

If a consistent pattern of bedtime restrictions emerges with a patient, the situation is assessed and new ways of helping the adolescent meet the expectation are tried.

Weekend Bedtime: Friday and Saturday nights all patients have a 12:30 a.m. bedtime, at which time they are expected to be in bed trying to sleep. A restriction is given after this time. Sunday night is treated as a regular weekday since there is school again on Monday.

Holiday Bedtime Routine: The night before a holiday, patients are allowed one extra hour.

School Break Routine: Depending on scheduled activities, bedtime is the same as holiday routine.

This routine is modified when it does not sufficiently help the adolescent, and his problems begin to interfere with his everyday responsibilities.

Theresa, 16-years-old, baffled the staff because after a long period of difficulty, she had finally been able to relax and fall asleep. But now, the staff member reading in the hall no longer soothed her, and her disruptive behavior, swearing, standing in her doorway, refusing to settle down, calling out to the other adolescents and provoking them, increased. Going in to sit with her also agitated her. Reading to her from the hall was too distant and impersonal while being in her room with a staff member was too intimate and stimulating. As we understood her increasing need for contact, yet still for distance, we arranged for her foster mother to bring her stuffed teddy bear. It met her new need, and her disruptive behavior around bedtime subsided.

This example from Theresa's treatment demonstrates cogently that although for purposes of discussion we are presenting our treatment philosophy under such topics as framework, time, space, and things, these concepts and parameters of the treatment are of necessity intertwined with each other. We have already discussed both the bedtime and the wakeup routines under our consideration of the framework of the unit. These are also important times of transition in the adolescent's day. How the room can become a source of soothing as well as of anxiety as one separates from or prepares for daytime activities is the focus here. Yet, as this example shows, Theresa's use of things as transitional objects or self-objects to support and nurture her, to make up for psychological deficiencies of her own, and to compensate for or replace personal interactions, is most evident.

Morning wakeup is also a task of everyday living which begins in the room; this supports and fosters the attitude that it is a safe place to be when special help is needed. Again, after some time observing the difficulties our patients had waking up in the morning, the staff developed this working routine:

Wakeup Routine

The purpose of the wakeup routine is to provide the basic structure and contact the patients need to overcome the difficulties and fear of beginning a new day. The night staff calls each patient at 7:45 a.m. for breakfast. Patients are not required to come for the meal, but can use the time to prepare to leave the safety of their beds. Another call is given at 8 a.m., the last call is given at 8:15 a.m. If a patient is not out of bed and dressed by 8:30, he is given a wakeup restriction which can be removed by getting up successfully the next morning. If a consistent pattern of difficulty is observed by the staff with a particular patient, an assessment will be made so that more effective support and intervention can be made.

Weekend Wakeup: Saturday and Sunday mornings, patients are allowed to get up or sleep as they please till noon. Patients are to be up and dressed in street clothes for lunch. If the patients are not up shortly after the noon call, they will receive a wakeup restriction.

Holiday Wakeup: The same as weekend unless there is some planned activity.

School Break Routine: Daily routine is followed except that wakeup is one hour later.

Against the backdrop of a routine, specific problems will become evident and individual, growth-promoting interventions can be made. When morning after morning an adolescent refuses to get out of bed on time despite staff help, it is time to look at the individual more closely in his everyday living. Does he or she have difficulty getting started because of internal confusion and disorganization? If so, chances are that he needs more individualized approaches to waking up such as dividing each activity into separate parts: sitting up in bed, getting out of bed, washing, getting dressed, going out of the room, eating breakfast, putting the tray away, and so forth. With both the routine structure and specialized staff help, he can learn to take small steps at a time, instead of confusing beginnings, middles, and ends, and feeling overwhelmed and refusing to do anything as a result. His refusal and difficulty in following the structure may be a way of testing staff stability and the stability of the milieu. If so, strong consistent stands and expectations by staff will help the adolescent relax and get up and out; warm suggestions helpful to the disorganized adolescent will usually escalate resistance in the defiant adolescent. Resolving these kinds of individual problems and anxieties in the context of the basic structure of the program makes the room feel like an increasingly safe place.

The room has also been used, and often quite effectively, as the only safe and supportive environment for an adolescent when a public area like the dayroom, even with its structure and supervision, is too stimulating and provokes uncontrolled panic. In this type of room use, the adolescent comes out only for necessary scheduled activities. We call this intervention "in room status." This limited space, instead of confining the individual, actually comforts him; he is living only within the areas he can control, albeit with much staff help. He does not feel consistently abandoned to his own impulses, nor does he continually experience failure in planning for, carrying out, and enjoying activities. The adolescent is gradually allowed expansion of his territory once he begins to manage, successfully, aspects of the regular program. Over a period of time, the individual delinquent, in consistent contact with a well-defined and differentiated environment, transmitted by knowledgeable and caring staff, starts to differentiate internally, tempers some of his omnipotence, and begins to internalize some self-control. As he has partial successes in controlling himself with the limited environment of his room, he is gradually given more responsibility and help in areas where he confronts greater external stimulation.

Another type of in room status, "program suspension," permits the patient and the staff to focus on very basic and simple elements of treatment in a consistent and thorough fashion without any program demands such as school or gym being made. In the controlled environment of the room, staff can make more complete assessments of the patient's functioning and begin to proceed methodically to help him achieve increasingly higher levels of functioning. Internal disorganization, lack of social relationships, impaired reality testing, diffuse rage, marked ambivalence, resistance to help, and/or grandiose, omnipotent thinking can be dealt with more thoroughly and consistently without the adolescent being entangled in other less well-understood interactions on the unit. At the same time, the disturbed patient is protected from demands beyond his level of functioning.

After the cloister of the room enables the patient to relate more readily to another individual—the staff member—scheduled times out of the room, and scheduled activity periods can be introduced. During these times, it is essential that a supportive staff member be present. Thus, the staff member becomes a bridge, a "spotter," or a self-object support to help the patient begin to learn interactions in other situations and in other kinds of relationships; the stability of the room is transferred to the larger world of the unit and various activity areas. In this way, room status helps the patient develop to the point where he can function more successfully in the total program.

This treatment approach is a means to an end. It meets the delinquent adolescent, especially the severely impulsive, at a level he can tolerate and use to begin to grow. It takes individual differences in patient needs, dynamics, and structure into account, and shapes the environment accordingly. But, if this is not well understood by the staff, the patient encounters an additional burden. For example, after discharge in a follow-up interview, Theresa, a violently impulsive and depressed adolescent with whom we had worked for two years in the inpatient setting, stated that in our efforts to be fair, we had missed her particular need:

> I would be starting to get agitated on the unit and a ward staff would send me to my room for 15 minutes to settle down. Fifteen minutes was so little time I could never understand how I could settle down—I'd spend the whole time worrying about only having 15 minutes and get more nervous,

The room is also the place adolescents go when the controls of rules and regulations and of staff verbal interventions do not help them. Physical restraints may then be used. The use of physical restraints does not detract from the safe and soothing features of the use of the room, but is indeed an extension and continuation of such efforts. (The use of physical restraints is discussed in Chapter 9).

The room also provides the space for studying; in fact, it was only in defining a specific space and time for this essential adolescent activity that the many deficits in this area showed up. Studying is a task that requires the adolescent to be alone and to concentrate without feeling abandoned to his impulses or his unconscious fantasies. For almost all the adolescents with whom we work, this is too great a task to be carried out without special help and assurance of staff availability. Studying also requires that adolescents immerse themselves in something other than themselves without staff being present, and this provokes in poorly differentiated individuals a sense of loss of the fragile self they try to maintain. Demands for food, water, milk, pencils, and paper may signal such a difficulty. After several different attempts to help our patients with study tasks, we arrived at the following routine:

Study Hour

This hour is set aside in each weekday to provide the adolescents with a setting in which they can learn to study and engage in a constructive activity by themselves. The adolescents are given 10 minutes to acquire the materials they intend to use during the hour, get snacks from the kitchen and go to the bathroom. After this time, all are expected to be in their rooms studying or engaging in some constructive activity. Sleeping, talking with other patients, continually poking head out of door or coming out of room are all grounds for restriction. This restriction may be removed by successfully completing the study hour routine the next day.

Patients may request that staff members bring them things and the staff will judge whether the patient could have obtained the material during the 10 minutes gathering period—the purpose of this is to help the adolescent concentrate on organizing an activity and planning it before beginning.

Patients may request brief help from staff on homework—if a patient shows consistent deficit in some area of (being able to) study, more individual help may be provided by the school or the ward staff depending on the problem area.

Staff encourages studying, but will suggest activities if the adolescent has no homework. Doors may be open during the study hour if the patient can maintain himself without abusing the responsibility.

The room is also a place of respite and planning and can be used as a place of recovery from one activity and preparation for the next. It can be used as a way of concretely separating endings and beginnings so that the internal states and affects of one activity do not interfere with the next, confusing the issues of competence and controls as a result. For example, Bill finishes a class and returns to the unit with 50 minutes until his next scheduled activity. He puts down his books and rushes to play ping-pong until then. If a situation like that is left unchecked, several areas of possible growth for the adolescent may be missed—learning to make internal distinctions between activities, to slow down, to think, and to plan what he wants so that the new activtiy is not just a discharge of tensions from the previous one, but an opportunity to relax and enjoy a skill. Instead, he can be encouraged to go to his room and put away school materials, and then sit there for a few minutes to plan what he'd like to do next. It is important that this be done in his room where he is not overstimulated by table games and other on-going unit activities which may excite immediate action rather than reflection. The game also needs to end early enough for him to return to his own room to wind down, to get supplies for his next activity, and to prepare for it. In fact, it is not enough that the ping-pong stop a little early; the whole pace of the game should shift as the time to end approaches. These are concrete manifestations of the internal divisions that must occur for a sense of self to develop and replace a continuous state of anxiety.

The staff, although allowed access to each room, respect the fact that the room belongs to the individual. They knock before entering, and often respect a "get out of my room." This does not mean that the adolescent controls and terrorizes the staff as he did others on the outside with his omnipotence; the decision to "get out" or stay in the room is made by the staff member based on his assessment of the need for distance and the affective tone of the adolescent's statement in the context of the overall treatment approach for this patient.

Throughout all these interventions, the attitude of the staff is crucial. If the room is viewed as a place to "dump" the patient, or to remove someone who is disturbing, or simply to isolate or quarantine someone, the use of the room becomes a deprivation. However, if the room is viewed as an opportunity to achieve privacy, to decrease overwhelming stimulation, to develop a sense of the self, to begin to establish or re-establish one's own boundaries, and to work with a nurturing staff member to develop various kinds of psychological functions, the room is a useful and powerful adjunct to the therapeutic process.

The Music Room

This small room contains a window with high tension screening, a couple of couches, the piano, and a console stereo built by the patients and a staff member. The use of the equipment in the room is well-defined both as to purpose and care, and operating instructions are explained to each patient. (See discussion in Chapter 7, *Things*.)

The ability to use the music room to socialize, listen to records, or play the piano requires the capacity to share communal space with others. This is one of the developmental tasks of adolescence—learning to use peer relationships constructively in ways different from the contact one had with parents or friends during the latency years. This learning often occurs in just such a social gathering place with music, comfortable seating, and social conversation. For the delinquent adolescent, a social encounter easily becomes another opportunity to express through behavior what cannot be contained or expressed verbally. A group of healthy adolescents might feel stimulated in an intimate setting, yet would use a music room to interact while maintaining interpersonal distance; they would teach and learn new music or a new dance step; they would compare tastes in music. For the hospitalized adolescent, the use of a place for socializing and relaxing has to be facilitated by a staff member's presence, just as in the day area. Interpersonal space for the majority of these boys and girls confuses them at a very basic level—proximity is equivalent to enclosure, and then provocative verbal or physical behavior is often used to differentiate oneself from the others. But with a warm, secure staff member who knows the purpose of the room and the needs of the adolescent, the music room can become a place for tolerable social interaction and personal growth.

When a patient has difficulty in the music room, cannot share space with another, or becomes visibly agitated by the music, he is asked and helped, if necessary, to leave the situation and return to his room. There, the adolescent and the staff member can try to understand what prevents him from using the music room constructively.

Some patients subtly convert the music room into a "special" place for a privileged few, using the space to externalize conflicts rather than to learn to socialize and enjoy music. For instance, Jane asks a staff member to go to the music room for awhile, gets an OK, and then invites one or two others to be with her to listen to the music. Although this seems like a normal, everyday interaction, somehow after awhile, Jane lets it be known that only certain people are welcome, even though others have been assessed by staff as being able to handle the music room. Now, the activity itself stunts, rather than enhances, growth, as it may herald the formation of a delinquent subculture.

The music room can also be a place where unit issues and turmoils get unconsciously "played out." The kind, amount, volume, and the lyrics of the music reflect the status of the unit at any given time. Intervening with the music itself can be a way of dealing with the adolescents at their level of understanding when verbal interactions produce little insight or change. For example, at one point the patients were concerned about closeness and rejection because some therapists were rotating to another service and the chief of the unit was on vacation; they expressed their concern in passing notes, sexual overtures, and provocative behavior. In the midst of this, one adolescent's family brought in, at his request, a record with sexually suggestive lyrics. In view of the great difficulty controlling needy and abused feelings and the pressures to act up sexually, a nurse wisely sent the record back home with his parents, conveying a message as direct and as forceful as the request. Later this was understood in therapy.

Guidelines used for the music room are presented below and, like the others, have been revised as we learn:

Music Room

The music room is a place to socialize and share and to learn the proper use of the specialized equipment (piano and stereo set). We see much deficit in most of the adolescents in the above areas. In order to provide a safe place for learning and enjoying, the following rules have been developed by the staff and patients. They are by no means final and are open to revision.

1) The music room will be supervised at all times by a staff member.

2) The stereo will be signed out by a patient who remains responsible for the stereo till it is signed back in.

3) The music room will be locked at 10 p.m. on weekdays and 11 p.m. on weekends.

4) Patients can only be in the music room either listening to music or playing the piano.

Abuse of any of the above regulations leads to a 24-hour restriction from the privilege of using the music room. Consistent abuse by a patient should be evaluated by the staff and appropriate intervention made.

The Nurses' Station

The nurses' station is a physical extension of the staff; it is a personal work space and symbolizes the corporate staff body. This is an important concept to emphasize when treating delinquents with a poor sense of boundaries, incomplete differentiation, and a faulty concept of what is mine and what is yours. Therefore, the nurses' station ought to be a pleasant, accessible, yet private, space; to make it a public space abandons the delinquents to their identity diffusion. At the same time, it is a semipublic space because it is glassed in and can be viewed from both the day area and the patients' corridor. It is a place for testing the staff boundaries, for finding a constant adult object, and for affirming the veracity of staff attitudes.

Here, staff boundaries are tested—do staff members know their limits, their body space, interpersonal and private space well enough not to allow it to be trespassed? Can staff allow the adolescents to push up against staff boundaries and begin in some way to define and differentiate themselves? The adolescents are told clearly the boundaries of the nurses' station. They are not to have their feet over the doorway or reach in to put something on the desk; all transacting goes on through a staff member. They must learn to stop themselves at a certain point in space and respect definite, but abstractly delineated boundaries; if no one is immediately available to them, they must maintain the boundaries and wait until there is a staff member available. If respecting others' private space is to be a growth experience for the patient, the staff member must learn to respect how much each adolescent can tolerate and, without changing the structures, modify one's response. For example, a nurse might interrupt her work almost immediately to respond to an impulse-ridden adolescent who is just learning to respect the rules and the fairness of someone else's space. In so doing, the staff member is able to demonstrate the existence and functions of the boundaries while simultaneously responding to this adolescent's inability to wait too long. Adolescents must learn that in this defined space the staff performs tasks which ultimately serve them, such as charting, giving reports, and talking with each other.

The constant presence of a staff member in the nursing station is important. Often, the adolescent does not have a firm conviction that someone is available. The adolescent in his room for study hour may, for example, become agitated and unable to contain strong destructive feelings; he may experience these as the room making him nervous, or feeling cooped up and bored, with nothing to do. Just sticking his head out of the door and seeing a staff member in the nurses' station can be reassuring, showing that there is somebody available and that he is not abandoned to deal alone with overwhelming feelings. This kind of reassurance is the fruit of having already "tested" many times and having learned that someone is available who will try to help him understand these experiences, and at the same time will expect him to carry out responsibilities.

The coherence and consistency of staff words and actions provide the adolescent in treatment the trust he needs so that, in changing, he will not lose his sense of himself. The nurses' station becomes the show place of staff values, attitudes, and interactions. How the staff interacts with one another in this space, how time is used, and how material possessions are cared for are all assiduously, though not necessarily consciously, observed by the patients. Can I trust the staff? Do they respect themselves and each other?How do they handle differences? Do they behave in accordance with their expectations of my behavior? Do they take care of possessions and order their space, or are things sloppy and broken? If there is too great or too often a discrepancy between staff life in the nurses' station and patient life on the unit, the purpose and impact of our work can easily be defeated. Staff words can become as empty as the words of the delinquent when, for example, a staff member sits on the nurses' station counter when the patients are expected not to sit on table tops in the dayroom.

SPACE AND VIOLENCE

We were confronted from the very beginning by how essential the type, definition, and use of space are in promoting growth, lessening disorganization, increasing a sense of internal space, and decreasing distorted notions of what space and objects are for. These general treatment goals and their realization in space help us understand how violence occurs and how to respond.

A single expression of violence like hitting another person or destroying property can arise from a different set of causes in different people and at different times and situations. While many causes or motivations may be present in any violent act, their different proportions will be differentially affected by the milieu. Some violence can be avoided through the manipulation and definition of space, while in another situation the same expression of violence cannot be avoided even within a well-defined, modulated, and empathic environment.

One set of causes for violent behavior involves physical and interpersonal disorganization in the environment, resonating with internal overstimulation and weak or primitive defenses in the patient. A second constellation of cause is produced by a break in empathy by the therapist at a time of increasing personal stress.

In any therapeutic milieu, it is important to work with either or both precipitating formulations, but the first job of a good treatment unit is to deal with the violence encouraged and enhanced by external disorganization. As external disorganization is resolved, the incidence of violence will be reduced, and what does occur can be more finely assessed, appreciated, and exploited for individual treatment purposes. Such violence is related to the type, definition, and use of space. For a milieu to work therapeutically with violence, all public and interpersonal space has to be converted to private and/or supervised interpersonal space, and all space has to be defined, clearly and repetitiously, as to its proper function and use.

Reviewing our experiences as the treatment program developed highlights how the concepts of compact space, private space, supervised interpersonal space, and repetitiously defined space evolved. The first examples come from the ward records of the adult/adolescent unit which preceded and precipitated the present all-adolescent unit:

> Tom (15 years old) and Kevin (14 years old) are relating the incident: "Well, we just went into his room and he didn't say anything, just stood there so we initiated him to the unit. One of us got down behind him while the other pushed him over. He still didn't say anything. . . ."

This is the account, after the fact, of how two delinquent boys "initiated" a 22-year-old schizophrenic man to the unit, which at the time was a 30-bed male-female young adult schizophrenic ward with a recent influx of five delinquent adolescents. The incident came to the light several days later when the "initiated" patient was discovered to have a broken jaw, chipped tooth, and a sprained shoulder.

Not long afterwards, another report written by a unit nurse said:

> During report, Jim (a 20-year-old catatonic and mute schizophrenic) came to the nursing station with a very red eye and said

the boys had hit him. Matt (another adult patient) came out too and he was very angry. We all went to Tom's (15 years old) room and Jim said that Mark (14 years old) and Tom had hit him in the face and that Kevin (14 years old) had hit him in the chest. Mark was laughing about it and challenging Matt. Tom was very serious and Kevin denied involvement until Jim said specifically where Kevin had hit him. I restricted all the boys until their doctors lift it and see them. Matt was very upset saying how a man couldn't even be safe sleeping in his bed. Lots of patients in the dayroom expressed anger and fear and several got together with the staff member assigned to the dayroom.

Although the unit was structured, it was becoming evident that the structure necessary for working with delinquent adolescents with severe behavior disorders is different from that helpful to young adult borderline and acutely schizophrenic patients. Now, the challenge of controlling a large and complex environment to assure the safety of all was new and different. Doors that were only seldom locked on the unit were staying locked almost all the time to prevent elopements.

Even with locked doors, the nursing reports ran:

Mark (14 years old) hanging around the door all evening. Looks like he might be planning to take off—sometimes wearing his coat. When asked about it, he says that he's cold and the writer should mind her own business.

Other patients' rooms were boldly taken over and room visiting grossly misused:

At 12:15 a.m., Norman (young adult schizophrenic deaf mute) was making noises so writer went to see what was wrong. Someone had thrown water on him. Boris (16 years old) was found in Norman's washroom. I asked him why he was there. He replied he was urinating and was screaming at the top of his lungs. Told writer she accused him of throwing water on Norman and he didn't (do it). I (had) ask(ed) him what he was doing in Norman's washroom. . . .

Another incident described by a charge nurse:

I caught Olivia (15 years old) in Elmer's (16 years old) room along with Al (16 years old); it looked like Elmer was acting as lookout. I told some of the kids I didn't want them at opposite corridors—later I had to repeat this to Olivia who was with Boris. Boris became verbally abusive. I then intervened in the music room when several couples were too close for comfort—mine anyway. Then all the kids came out of the music room and chairs started flying. Ellen (15 years old) threw chairs around the dayroom and David (young adult, psychotic) threw a table. A special ward meeting was called.

As the above problems in the use of the animate and inanimate environment (space, time, things, persons) multiplied over a period of months, it became more evident that two separate treatment programs had to be developed. The lack of impulse control and misuse of the animate and inanimate environment by the delinquent adolescents could not be managed through the same structures and use of space employed for the adults. The use of time, space, person, and things by the young adults was disorganized to a greater or lesser degree depending on the condition of the patient, but seldom was it overtly consciously destructive.

The treatment staff and all the patients were equally frustrated, as this nurse's report in the eighth month of the combined adolescent and adult unit indicates:

The (ward) meeting was very confronting with both patients and active staff. Ellen (15 years old) got concerned when Rose (a grandmotherly, warm staff member) said she was ready to resign.

Several patients were disruptive throughout the meeting especially Elmer (16 years old), Ellen (15 years old), and Debbie (a young adult). The meeting ended more or less by giving up trying to keep control—Debbie playing piano, ping-pong at intervals; general goofing off.

It seemed that decreasing amounts of space would help us begin to understand more clearly how to help these adolescents toward a healthier use of the human and nonhuman environment. We thought the way to start was to get a unit with a different disposition of space.

The wing opposite the mixed unit on the same floor was empty. It had originally been built in 1959 as a small 15-bed high security unit with glazed brick walls, doors that open out, electric lock main door, all single rooms, one male and one female communal bathroom, and a nurses' station which looked directly out into the dayroom as well as down the corridor of the patients' rooms. There was also a small kitchen and music room at the head of the patients' corridor. It was built for and appeared to be an environment which might be able to provide the kind of control and safety, at least at a physical level, which we felt we needed to begin learning what these adolescents needed and how to provide it.

Besides the corridor which housed the adolescents and included the music room, kitchen, bathrooms, and several staff offices, the only area which was freely accesible to the patients was the dayroom with its TV set, three or four coffee tables, about 10 lounge chairs and 15 straightback chairs, five large tables for playing games and eating and a bumper pool table. The three doors which led onto and off the unit were always locked. It appeared a visually drab, yet compact and safe place.

On moving day, the adolescents apparently felt the impact of the environment and of our thinking, since at the first patient-staff ward meeting, 14-year-old Elsie said, "Don't know if I like this place—anything you do here would bounce off the walls back at you." We had taken a first step in learning how to deal with violence by decreasing space and by eliminating the double rooms and extra bathrooms.

Not long after the move, incident after incident illustrated that the adolescents could not handle even this more limited space. Visiting in each other's rooms was used for all sorts of impulse gratification and proved overwhelming. What often started out as a game or "horseplay" ended up in slapping or hitting; what started out as talking or "rapping" ended up as a plot to get drugs. In trying to sort out with the patients what had happened in these incidents, ambiguity, impulsivity, and confusion were most evident. It was unclear who said what or how the "plan" finally got off the ground. Everyone was amazed that in the end somebody got hurt because "We were just fooling around."

Any and all public and interpersonal space on the unit—corridor, kitchen, music room, dayroom, lavatory—became a site for difficulty and confusion, especially when one or two patients were under some increased stress from individual therapy, family, or the tasks of everyday living. All the possibilities for contact permitted a diffusion and externalization of conflict at about the same rate as or faster than it was being bound by the other aspects of the program structure. Some externalization and diffusion were a replay of what had transpired before admission, and, for many, were the precipitating reasons for admission. As had happened in previous home and school experiences, the patients were being abandoned by the staff to their own poor controls and internal confusion, and were being forced by the demands of so much interaction to fail over and over again. They were not helped by this unregulated use of space to form realistic expectations of themselves, but instead were abandoned to their own fantasies of omnipotence and grandiosity. These false expectations only served again to increase the distance between the actual daily functioning and unrealistic self-ideals. In the end self-esteem dropped even lower, as behavior was not controlled, and failure continued.

Slowly, over the first two years of observation and intervention, we began to see the need to make all public and interpersonal space into private and supervised interpersonal space and so instituted no more room visiting, doorway visiting, or talking in corridors; bathrooms were used one at a time; and all dayroom interactions were with the staff present. We dealt with our own violence—our attitudes and needs —insofar as we could understand them, developed consistent attitudes among the whole staff, kept certain adolescents in their rooms more, forbade contact between certain adolescents or in certain areas, and discharged any adolescent who hit another person. All these interventions were important then, and some are still, but we failed for a long time to grasp the crux of the problem—the need of each one of these hospitalized delinquents for an environment consistent with the limited and primitive level of his object relations.

What were we trying to do in this shift from public and unsupervised to private and supervised space which the adolescents' behavior was telling us was necessary? This further development of the milieu gave each adolescent a chance to struggle continuously with his impulses without being overstimulated by constant close contact with other impulse disordered patients. The chances for further stimulation, disorganization, and failure were decreased, and the experience of internal space was enhanced. Actual expectations of the milieu and the adolescent's potentials were brought into closer proximity. The milieu space, now private and supervised, has lost the heavy social and interpersonal demands which public and interpersonal space make, freeing our patients to work at a level more appropriate to their internal state rather than their chronological age. For the normal adolescent, peer relations, sharing, cooperation, and competition are ways of growing, experimenting, mastering, and comparing new aspects of oneself with others who are similar but different. Hospitalized delinquents are not capable of handling peer relations at this level. Internally, they still struggle with earlier, more primitive issues in almost all aspects of their personality and are almost always forced into useless regression, usually in symptomatic delinquency, when a program demands high level peer interaction.

This reconceptualization of the space of the unit illuminated another aspect of violent delinquents—their lack of relation to the environment as something meaningful in itself and their lack of differentiation in the use of space. Each space was used by delinquents according to their immediate needs for impulse expression and according to unconscious distortions, without much regard for a particular space's function, and so we found trash on the floor, lying around in the day area, writing on doorways, doors, or tables, etc. Above and beyond freeing space from spurious interpersonal contacts, each space and its contents had to be clearly and repetitiously defined; this decreased unconscious distortions in use and counteracted the impulsive expression of internal need without integration and control from external reality. When this kind of distortion of function and use is allowed to continue without intervention in impulse disordered adolescents, there is an easy shift to violence and increasing misuse of the inanimate and animate environment because these adolescents, under stress, show a loss of contact with the reality of others as anything more than vehicles for discharge of feelings.

And so, the consistent definition, and repeated definition, of the use of each space and thing, along with halting its misuse, can, in small but effective ways, increase reality testing and stop the continual distortion of the environment. Although neither the staff nor the adolescent may ever understand the unconscious meaning for each individual for each particular misuse of space and things, the reality definition repeatedly given serves as a barrier to further breakdown and as a backdrop—like the basic structure—for the process of introspection and psychotherapy.

These two movements—from public and unsupervised interpersonal space to private and supervised interpersonal space, and the clear and repetitious definition of function of each space and things—are essential to the milieu treatment of impulse ridden, delinquent adolescents. They can ensure an environment which is not so overstimulating that unnecessary regression occurs.

When spatial and functional disorganization is present in an environment, the second cluster of causes promoting violence—internal disorganization and breaks in empathy—are difficult to delineate. When all space is private or supervised interpersonal and there is a clear definition of space and things, the violence that erupts because of impending psychosis, or overstimulation and trauma, or a failure of the therapist's empathy can be detected, and more precise interventions made. At this level, assessments of the treatability of the adolescent can occur. If the environment is disorganized and ill-defined, the treatment abilities of the staff are more in question than the treatability of the adolescent patients.

Only in a defined and supervised space—a therapeutic milieu—can individual psychotherapy succeed.

7

Things

In infancy the child begins to perceive himself as separate from the things around him and to grasp the human aliveness of himshelf as he differentiates from the animate and inanimate worlds. By playing and experimenting with an array of things, the child develops the capacity to explore wholes and parts, to manipulate and control, and to discover the functions of the things around him. Reciprocally, he comes to define his own capacities and limitations. Searles (1960) has written about the nonhuman environment as a child's "pure culture ground" for practicing more complex human relationships. How a child's parents use things tells the child not only how they view the inanimate world, but also how they relate to him.

In the healthy relationship, the mother provides continuous feedback, allaying the child's anxieties as he attempts to master his object environment; she directs and redirects the child in his exploration, and supports his mastery. For example, a child frustrated with a toy may begin to damage it. His mother may alleviate the frustration by taking the toy and showing the child how it works. This interaction not only helps the child regain mastery of the toy, but provides a soothing experience as well. She tempers the child's many frustrations as he tries to make the external world real and growth producing. Gradually, the child begins to define himself as separate from his material world; the child's separateness from it facilitates a healthy investment in it. Through this process, as well as observing how the mother handles her own things, as well as his, the child, moves from "this is me" or

158

part of me" to "this is mine," and eventually to "my things, our things, and your things," in a continuing process of differentiation.

Utilizing parental feedback, the child develops his own attitudes and internal values toward the material world. He develops closeness to this world and experiences warmth for things in their own right. Stuffed animals and toys come to be loved as he experiences, masters, and integrates new affects and feeling states through play. This mastery with toys and others things is both an expression of and a facilitator for the development of new psychological skills necessary for socialization and interpersonal relating. Things may also become transitional objects, invested with meaning of the child's own creation, part of him, yet not, and serving to allay and master the anxiety he experiences as he separates from the mother. Toys may be objects laden with feelings the child experiences on an interpersonal level, as a refuge or temporary withdrawal, as a displacement, or a projection of feelings and wishes.

Developmental problems may arise when an infant does not separate psychologically from the mother, when the child receives inconsistent mothering which could be either nonstimulating or overstimulating, or when there is severe interference in the affective relationship. Many of the adolescents that we see have been reared by either depressed or unavailable mother figures. The child who does not successfully separate from the mother does not internalize regulatory functions which would ordinarily be provided in a healthy mother-child relationship. The child who is unable to provide these functions for himself will continue to need them to be provided by the external environment. The ability to tolerate frustration, to delay gratification, and to provide self-soothing are all examples of these functions. These intrapsychic disturbances may express themselves in delinquent activity in both the interpersonal and the inanimate environment. When these self-regulating functions are absent, emptiness, boredom, or, frequently, internal tension can result. Many adolescents report that they engage in delinquent activity, not for gain or profit, but because they want "something to do."

Hospitalized adolescents brings with them symptomatic patterns of relating to the material world. These familiar patterns are often laden with their inner turmoil. This turmoil can result in impulsivity, a failure to use the external environment for psychological growth, or a failure to develop or use one's skills to define oneself as separate and unique. For example, Ralph considered himself an avid and highly skilled basketball player; he boasted of how valuable his skills were to the school team. However, he was never allowed to play because he lacked discipline, was constantly late to practice, and sometimes, didn't show up at all.

These symptomatic patterns are diagnostic clues to us. As we carefully observe these patterns, we see evidence that the delinquent adolescent both releases internal tension and expresses his difficulties in regulating tension through his use of his object world. The delinquent frequently has long-standing problems with stealing, property destruction, and misuse of things which play a role in his psychic economy. When we look at these symptoms as diagnostic clues, we realize that the difficulties of these teenagers represent not an inability to adjust to societal norms, but maladaptive behavior indicative of developmental deficit. This crucial distinction helps the delinquent struggle toward maturation in the hospital setting. Once in the hospital, the adolescents may attempt to justify their malignant use of things as a joke, as a result of boredom, or justifiably motivated by their anger. When the staff begins to limit or intervene in their behavior, anxiety emerges and exposes their shaky awareness that they have lost control and are likely to lose control again. Their behavior tells us that they need help in understanding their fears, but to do this, we must first help them to stop, take a look at their behavior, and then assist them in learning how to use their environment in less destructive ways.

The milieu staff, the activity staff, and the psychotherapist must pay close attention to the delinquents' expression of psychopathology in their material world. Their use of things may betray an underlying impulsivity, inner confusion, and chaos, or represent defenses against repressed affect, expressions of grandiosity, or tests of omnipotence. For example, Fred fashioned a rope out of his socks, T-shirts, and pillowcases. He tied them together and stuffed them into his locker. When staff discovered what he had done, he reacted matter-of-factly and then showed the staff how he had begun cutting a hole in his screen. He related his eventual plan to elope from the unit, which is on the sixth floor. Fred seemed surprised that the staff reacted with shock and concern over his plan, as he felt he had thought it out well. For weeks afterwards, Fred maintained the omnipotent fantasy that he could elope from the sixth floor with this rope without getting hurt.

Impulsive adolescents may become frustrated as they try to delay gratification and to establish control of their behavior. The loosening of controls is often exhibited in the use of things about them. As they attempt to deal with frustration, their behavior may escalate to motor discharge. Frequently the delinquent expresses a transient relief of tension through misuse or abuse of things, for he has no alternative methods of controlling his behavior. For example, Yvonne, a bossy and controlling girl, liked to take charge of activities on the unit. During the clean-up after the Thanksgiving dinner, she grabbed some food which another patient was carrying to the refrigerator. Initially, Yvonne could offer no explanation for the irrational act, but later she stated she wanted to be in charge and thought she was really helping out. Her lack of planning or forethought of how this could be accomplished was later understood in her expressing how enraged she felt when, as a youngster abandoned by mother, she often had to take responsibility she felt she could not handle.

Other abuses of inanimate objects may arise from inner confusion and chaos. For example, Fred had written his name with a bar of soap on the mesh screen in the boys' bathroom. When this was explored with him it became clear that, upon rising in the morning, he felt confused and disoriented. Writing his name was an attempt to reinstate autonomy and to define himself.

To assess properly a delinquent's use of things on a hospital unit, one must recognize that the expression of pathology in the inanimate world may manifest itself in both the interpersonal and the intrapsychic spheres. To think of property destruction, stealing, or using things to commit violence only in the interpersonal context, for example, as expressions of rebellion against authority structure is to misunderstand disturbed adolescents and to deprive them of further psychological growth, in that their behavior may arise from more severe psycho-

logical deficits. When Barry broke his clock radio, the staff immediately assumed that he was angry at someone and told him so. This
misunderstanding only increased his sense of isolation. Actually,
Barry's destructiveness reflected not his anger at someone but his sense
of internal desolation, which became clear only after exploration. Breaking his radio was his attempt to ward off impending isolation from the
external world.

The way the delinquent uses certain things often represents an overwhelmed ego state as well as his attempts to relieve internal tension.

> Theresa, a depressed impulsive adolescent, had a severe reaction
> because there was a staff change in covering the unit one afternoon.
> Interdisciplinary staff was assigned to assist the ward staff for
> varying amounts of time on the unit. The patient group was in-
> formed of this change in advance; Theresa reacted with both
> anger and laughter. On the designated afternoon she was described
> as "tenuous." Suddenly she sat on a table in the dayroom, ordering
> the other patients around. After several verbal outbursts and limits
> from staff, she began shooting rubberbands and pencils across the
> room, threatening to hit staff members who came near her. The
> staff intervened and were later able to help her examine the in-
> cident. She was angry and frightened that she had been left in a
> situation in which she did not feel safe. The withdrawal of familiar
> staff and the change in routine was a disruptive experience which
> resulted in equally disruptive and abusive behavior.

Disturbed adolescents perceive the environment as highly unpredictable, and much of their behavior derives from a desperate need to
define predictability. Barry, for example, came out of his room one
day and asked the staff for help in removing gum from his hair. He
had no recollection of how that had occurred and could perceive it
only as a mystery. He often ascribed magical qualities to his nonhuman
environment in which books would disappear, objects would fall from
tables, and other objects would appear in unexpected places.

Even minor changes in the inanimate surroundings can be disruptive.
What adolescents can count on and what is predictable are extremely
important to them. For instance, after the floors were stripped for
waxing, Ned commented plaintively, "Even the floors don't stay the

same." On the other hand, what is most unpredictable is the disturbed adolescents' own response to the environment. Helping them to understand and clarify their use and misuse of that environment, and how this relates to their experiencing it as unpredictable, undependable, and frightening is part of the therapeutic task. Their emotional interplay with the inanimate surroundings can become distorted as they struggle to define what they can expect from their environment.

> On a zoo trip one afternoon, Burton was described as "very loud, agitated, and giggling" before leaving. During the trip the staff had to call him back frequently to remain with the rest of the group. Throughout the trip he tested the staff but responded to limits. After returning from the trip, he moved furniture around, sat on tables, shouted at another patient, and slammed the music room door. He was sent to his room where staff talked with him. What emerged was his attempts to reinstate boundaries between himself and the staff following the trip.

The adolescent may invest in an activity, but inappropriately. Patients who have paper and pencils may write on the walls in their room or scribble on their desk. Ned asked for some magic markers to do some drawing, but got misdirected and began to color in between the ceramic wall tiles in his room. Such violation and testing of unit norms demand a response from the staff. When adolescents do not feel in charge of themselves, when they find their own feelings and wishes unpredictable and their own psychological responses undependable, they are frightened and try to determine who is in charge. Such testing often involves the inappropriate use of things around them. First, the behavior must stop, and the patient needs to restore the damage done. With this progression, we help him make the first step in understanding that his behavior has meaning. At the same time, the behavior needs to be understood in the context of what the adolescent was experiencing at the time and in the circumstances in which it occurred.

Many times adolescents behave as if they are doing whatever they feel like at the time, but this may be only partly true. When the staff helps them to focus not only on the external elements of their interactions with their environment, but also on the inner experience and meaning as well, such behavior often turns out not to be resistance, but reflects a sense of internal disorganization, expressing itself in erratic and destructive behavior as the teenagers attempt to master the increasingly devastating confusion. They try to reconstitute themselves and be in charge. If this is the case, we need to communicate to them that, until they are capable of controlling themselves, we will not allow them or their use of things to get out of control. Disturbed adolescents need help in understanding the meaning of their responses to the inanimate environment. Previously they placed little value on objects or goal directed use of objects. They entered the hospital with a history of destroying games, toys, their own belongings, and the belongings of others as well. As they explore their inner psychological world in psychotherapy, they are also exposed to a consistent and caring staff who help them place value on things in their environment. For example, the staff consider the stereo in the music room to be a valuable piece of equipment, and accordingly, take time to teach each patient its operation and the norms that have been established for its use. In essence, we give them a structure in which to guide their own responses and demonstrate that we not only value things but also care enough for them to spend time with them teaching them about the stereo.

In part, disturbed adolescents find it difficult to value things because of the time and energy they expend in struggling to maintain a balance between external and internal stimulation, and inner psychological organization. Inanimate surroundings may be very stimulating to impulsive adolescents. Sometimes, things in the environment which ordinarily would be a source of gratification may instead become a source of excitement. Beyond understanding and managing their own responses to the environment, adolescents need also to understand the purpose of the inanimate environment itself. Staff support in defining the meaning of the environment is reassuring.

> Early on, the staff believed that the music room should be an open setting for patient use. There was little structure provided as a guideline for playing records or for the social context in which to enjoy music. Patients often played loud games in the room, frequently fought over whose records to play, and argued about unresolved unit issues which had nothing to do with the music. When

records were damaged, the music room would be closed until the patients could resolve the issue. As frequently happens, events like this encouraged staff to explore possible solutions, and at a staff meeting, it was noted: "The ward meeting left the issue of Gary's scratched record unresolved . . . the patients have exhausted themselves in working out how this happened . . . if there were some clear ways of taking care of records in the music room, and if we could emphasize care of each patient's equipment, we could help the patients respect each other's things. This would work except that the music room is not the special place we hoped that it would be. It is a place for fights or a place where there are a few records of interest to more than one person. It is not pleasant looking and neither the staff nor the patients are motivated to dress it up." The patients were unable to enjoy music where these other stimulating activities occurred, and where there was a lack of definition and purpose within the setting.

These perceptions clarified what a music room represented to the patients and what they needed a music room to be. Removing the games, cards and all other stimulating objects that did not relate to music helped achieve a more meaningful enjoyment of music.

As adolescents are helped to master their surrounding, they develop various psychological skills and achieve an integration between themselves and the material world. Now they begin to use things appropriately, learn to plan and anticipate, and recognize that true gratification comes, not from immediacy, but from their behavior being modulated and channeled. Mastering the use of things psychologically enhances intrapsychic skills which subsequently find expression in the interpersonal world. If adolescents are allowed to misuse things, they will experience increased turmoil and their behavior will escalate to more serious breakdowns. Ultimately, they may assault another person. Physical aggression towards others does not promote safety and security on a hospital unit and is not acceptable. Yet, many of our teenagers come into the hospital because they have been violent towards others. A closed hospital unit, in and of itself, does not eliminate opportunities for acting up, including violence. Staff should evaluate the physical setting and recognize that its misuse is indicative of the patient's loose psychological controls. Some tend to look at "minor" aggressive behaviors as only momentarily disruptive. An adolescent who slams the door or breaks a pencil in anger is ignored or considered to be expressing feelings or relieving tension. For the adolescent struggling to maintain controls, this behavior, when minimized, becomes the first in a series of escalating destructive acts. Therefore, from the beginning we try to help impulsive, violent adolescents translate their behavior into thoughtful reflection by teaching them that things have meaning and purpose.

Once in the hospital, disturbed adolescents manifest their intrapsychic and interpersonal problems in concrete ways. A person's possessions always tell something about his definition of himself, his qualities, his likes and dislikes. This is particularly so of the adolescent because he uses belongings such as clothes, radios, and records to differentiate himself from his parents and to define his own tastes, values, and self-image. Our hospital patients through their own tastes, values, and self-image. Our hospital patients through their dress, hygiene, and use of personal belongings express how they see themselves. The kinds of clothes they wear reflect fluctuations in self-esteem and mood, which may shift from hour to hour. Many of our adolescents change clothes three or four times during the course of a day.

> Terry changed outfits several times a day while expressing ambivalence about hospitalization in individual psychotherapy sessions. She angrily stated, "I will change from within and not from without." At times, she said she felt "good" about being in the hospital, and at other times, she feared losing her "identity." In the dayroom, she hung around the nursing station door childishly demanding attention from the staff while at the same time insisting she was completely independent of the staff; during these periods she predictably wore heavy platformed high heeled shoes. Later in the hospitalization, Terry came to understand that she always wore these shoes when her dependency longings were disturbing her.

> For other adolescents, frequently changing clothes indicates attempts to organize themselves. Sporadically, Betty changed clothes when she could not meet her daily responsibilities, felt fragmented, and wanted more staff contact which helped her organize her

thoughts and behavior. Another patient, Karl, had exploded angrily and then went to his room to change clothes; he tried on several combinations of clothes to "see if they matched," and appeared to be trying to reintegrate a disruptive, disorganizing experience.

Clothes represent unconscious communications. An adolescent wearing an outdoor jacket on the unit appears shocked when staff asks whether or not she feels like running away. She is surprised not because the staff caught on to a plan to run, but because she was truly unaware of her impulse to leave. Adolescents are relieved to have these confused feelings clarified. Other communications are apparent in adolescents' clothing, like today's popular T-shirts with pictures and written messages on them. The message of the T-shirt and when it is worn are significant communications. Robert frequently wore a T-shirt with "unemployed" written across the front when he felt uncared for and abandoned; when his therapist was on vacation, Robert wore the shirt daily. Only when this was explored at length was he able to recognize his feelings of loss and loneliness.

How clothes are worn can reflect an impending loss of control. Carl, a violent adolescent, would wear an unbuckled belt on the unit. On the streets he had sometimes used the belt and heavy buckle as a weapon which he would swing like a club. We have seen this behavior in several of our patients and regard it as an urgent communication that needs an immediate staff response to prevent a forthcoming assault. We have observed that when a patient is depressed or dealing with painful issues, he will repeatedly wear the same sweater, sweatshirt, or other distinctive article of clothing, and when he is less depressed or has mastered some of the painful issues, he readily discards the clothing and sometimes even sends it home.

Disturbed adolescents care for their clothes poorly, and many wear torn and soiled clothing regularly. This may be more than a communication, because for many, it represents internal depletion and emptiness. Working empathically with these patients includes helping them to sort clothes and to arrange laundry schedules, and finding the time to bring out the unit sewing basket and sitting with them while they repair their clothes.

How adolescents dress may also reflect their relationship with parental figures. Parents who bring to the hospital inappropriate clothing or clothes that are too small or too large for their children demonstrate how they distort or depersonalize the patient, and often the adolescent has introjected these distortions. Many patients have no sense of their body configuration and have not integrated any sense of size, taste, or appropriateness in dress. Rebecca's mother, for example, periodically brought her shopping bags full of clothes of various sizes and styles, frequently soiled and stained. Rebecca accepted these clothes because they manifested outwardly how she felt inside—dirty, bad, and worthless. As these adolescents progress in treatment, they show changes in their choice and range of clothing as well as show increased bodily awareness. Now they can conceptualize size, color, style, likes and dislikes.

Clothes represent the patient's relationship with staff as well. At one point in therapy, Anne reported "feeling better about myself," and referred to her therapist as a "lifeline." As she expressed her infantile strivings openly, she dressed in short skirts and knee-high socks, with bows in her hair: "I like little girl clothes now." A more consolidated sense of self and more stable self-esteem are expressed through clothing as well. As Yvonne's treatment began to remove some of her deficits, her appearance changed from disheveled, thrown together, and careless, to more organized, age appropriate, and neater.

Healthy adolescents often share and exchange clothing, reflecting increasing ties and loyalties to a peer group. However, among disturbed adolescents, this behavior may indicate boundary breakdown and ego diffusion. Generally speaking, clothing exchange on the unit tends to be indiscriminate, asexual, and frequently impersonal. Because this behavior contributes to further personality disorganization, we discourage this practice to help patients preserve their identity and separateness. One day the staff discovered that Burton had been wearing Frank's clothes, Theresa was wearing Burton's pants, and Frank was wearing Burton's jacket, representing a three-way psychological merger.

Other possessions adolescents bring with them to the hospital are invested with meaning and feelings and express many of their inner experiences. Many are not their possessions at all, but have been stolen, borrowed, or misappropriated. It takes a great deal of staff intervention to help the patients sort out what belongs to them and what belongs to others. The whole concept of private ownership is vague and ambiguous for many of our patients because they come from homes where belongings were never treated as one's own. For example, after Ernie had come to the hospital, he asked his mother to bring two of his books, but discovered that she had thrown the books and other possessions away. On the unit, his persistent demands for things to read or work on in part reflected his fear that supplies would not be predictably available.

Other experiences with personal possessions tell us of the stresses and turmoils of our patients. Lost or misplaced possessions are a frequent occurrence, indicating poor self-awareness and inner disorganization. Leaving personal belongings in an inappropriate place on the unit is not necessarily a classical act of forgetfulness, symbolic of unconscious meaning. Often it is the staff that discover that an object has been misplaced, and when the adolescent is informed, he is often surprised that it was missing in the first place. This often represents serious psychological deficit rather than a symptomatic act or slip. They are generally unaware of how their belongings get to certain places and cannot establish cause and effect patterns in their behavior. They may not be distorting when they strongly affirm that losing something has "nothing to do with me." The staff feels that we're talking about a mystery because we are dealing with teenagers who do not see themselves as independent sources of initiative from whom thoughts and actions flow. Pursuing the incident promotes growth because it helps the adolescents recognize that there are causal relationships between their feelings and their subsequent behavior.

Adolescents who used drugs or alcohol extensively in the past to "feel good" or "have fun" do not readily give up such familiar ways of dealing with painful feelings like loneliness, depression, or fragmentation. They may try to get drugs or alcohol to the unit even though it is clear that unprescribed drugs are forbidden, or they may employ objects reflecting the drug culture to soothe themselves or resist engagement in treatment. A drug poster on the wall may be an attempt to define or calm themselves, to determine whether or not the staff is sensitive to the meaning drugs have for them. Although their talk, possessions, clothes, posters, music, and reading materials indicate that the drug culture still has great importance for them, they may affirm that drugs are not a problem, a clear demonstration of their need to externalize. They see drug usage, not as the resolution or attempted resolution of an internal problem, but rather as no problem at all. If they can begin to explore the relationship between their feelings and drug behavior, they are much more likely to develop a treatment alliance with us.

Disturbed adolescents misuse and abuse their own belongings. An adolescent who throws his books, radio, or other personal items during a period of disorganization or rage may be demonstrating not a lack of investment in his belongings, but a temporary sense of detachment and disequilibrium; he lacks the capacity to distinguish, label, and verbalize feeling states. Personal belongings are also objects which can provide the disturbed adolescent with emotional comfort, nurturance, and soothing. For this reason, we avoid isolating or secluding a patient from his personal effects. Ernie would play his recorder when he felt lonely and isolated, especially when he could not tolerate human contact. Paul requested a guitar from home, and although he could only play a few chords, he valued having it with him and insisted on it having a special place in his room where he could "look at it." We understood the guitar as an organizing object for him.

In addition to his own, the belongings we as staff provide the adolescent have special significance. Each patient's room is a combination of his possessions and the belongings we furnish, including a bed, locker, desk, chairs, lamp, curtains, and bookcase. Complaints about the bed being too hard or the chairs not comfortable may point overtly to some of the drawbacks of institutional living, but our attitudes need not convey an institutionalized atmosphere. Furniture in good condition conveys an important message about how we care. Worn or damaged furniture is repaired or replaced quickly. Such an intervention has various meanings. Because many of our adolescents come into the hospital with extensive histories of property abuse, damaged furniture would suggest that we do not expect them to master their own impulses and would confront them with a confusing message about managing their behavior. Furthermore, if something doesn't work properly and we permit its continued use, in a sense we tell the adolescents not to rely on our taking care of them or their environment. Most subtly, damaged furniture communicates to the adolescents ambivalence about responding to their needs. Adolescents who don't expect much from us will tolerate things that don't work right, and consequently, their belief that no one cares is reinforced. If we have not noticed the damage, they may surmise that we don't notice them or their deficits. The whole notion of being damaged threatens adolescents who experience themselves as deficient. Patients frequently describe themselves as feeling like things, having become dehumanized by their experiences of emotional deprivation and physical abuse. Many are shocked and amazed that we believe that things should work properly and that we monitor the way in which their living environment is maintained until they are able to do this for themselves. Delinquents have no reason to believe that our milieu is benign and that our communications will be direct; they need a while to begin to trust us. Our attitude towards the material world is an integral part of this process.

Patients' rooms and what they do with them represent quite directly how they are getting along with us. For the newly admitted teenager, shocked and frightened by being removed from a familiar environment, the room is usually quite empty. A newly admitted girl was quiet and withdrawn for several weeks; she was unknown to us, and we to her. One day a staff member visited her in her room and found that she had very neatly and precisely blocked out her name in pencil across the security screen of her window. Up to this point she had done nothing to personalize her room, and the staff described it as being barren and empty of definition. As she wrote her name on the screen, she was, though not constructively, attempting to bring some definition to a situation in which she felt out of touch and confused.

It may be a matter of weeks before newly admitted patients begin to add things to their rooms. They may have such difficulty coming to terms with their new environment; the idea of their room being "theirs" is much too threatening. For instance, Karl had been in the hospital several weeks, the first few weeks of which he spent describing his stay as "just a few days." One morning he came to the Occupational Therapy shop and commented about the "nice plants in here." This was the first time he even noticed them as part of the room. After he asked if there were more plants and it was suggested that he could get a plant for his room, he added, "Yeah, I could do that, couldn't I?" When adolescents begin decorating their rooms, we know that the unit has become familiar and they have accepted hospitalization.

We stress the privacy of each room for all our patients. Each room's door was originally installed with a small window for observing the patient; however, each patient usually covers it immediately. A newly admitted patient's room is easily recognized by a blank piece of paper covering the window, but later most patients replace it with a picture, print, or drawing. During the course of hospitalization a patient may change this several times, and often there is an implicit message. One of our patients would hang up geometric drawings when he felt out of touch and disconnected. At other times, when he would try to reach out to others, he would insert drawings of animals, houses, or outdoor scenes.

Karl had installed in his window a small poster of an almost human dog wearing a hat and scarf. When he felt frightened and attacked, he would say that he was "treated like a dog" and that "dogs need protection from being mistreated."

Once adolescents have been with us for awhile, they begin to personalize their rooms. Sometimes, this occurs so gradually that it may go unnoticed. Some adolescents are more comfortable with fewer things because they provide a less stimulating environment. Fred, for example, had very few personal belongings. The furniture in his room was often a source of overstimulation; he would threaten to throw it and, once it was removed from his room, verbalized a great sense of relief.

Other adolescents show their lack of self-awareness in the barren atmosphere of their rooms. Progress in therapy will become evident not only in the increasing richness of their interpersonal relationships, but also in how their rooms change. Diane, for instance, was initially described by staff as empty and distant. As she began to make internal changes, she also developed a greater capacity for self-expression as she decorated and arranged her room.

Some adolescents never personalize their rooms because they never adjust to the newness of the hospital, or because in their serious pathology they cannot establish attachments to things or people. To invest is too threatening. Adolescents may go through the day "putting on" the ideas of others and "acting on" the involvement of others; or they may invest their rooms with things which do not reflect a self or define a personality, but are copies of others, or stereotypes, rather than creative efforts. There must be a self before one can express it, and so it may be difficult at times to recognize that the rooms of some teenagers, though busy and complex, are void of a real sense of one's self.

Some adolescents leave their rooms untouched to convey that their stay will be brief; bringing things of their own to the room would violate their refusal to make a commitment to treatment. Other adolescents who have been in the hospital for a long time and have not added things of their own to the room demonstrate an absence of attachment which is startling. When one formulates their early childhood experiences, one might discover that their external environment was not without material possessions, but was devoid of mothering. They had limited play experiences with mother, which interfered with their ability to recognize and invest in their environment and prevents them from placing the special mark of their personality onto their surroundings. An interactive hospital milieu can provide a corrective affective relationship for these adolescents and encourage involvement with their surroundings.

How adolescents arrange their rooms tells staff about their mood and emotions. Where they place their furniture depends on how threatening they perceive the environment. If the furniture closes off open communication, the patient may be feeling so intruded upon that contact is intolerable, and the furniture serves as a protective barrier between himself and the staff. Kent had been threatening to hit the staff and placed his chair at the doorway of his room. For Kent, this was a step forward because previously he would have assaulted someone to protect himself from intrusion or closeness. Other patients may modify and arrange their rooms not to eliminate contact, but to control the amount and intensity of interactions. At one point in her hospitalization, Rebecca redesigned her room and told staff that the area next to the door was "my office" for interviews and the rear part was "my space."

Some adolescents arrange and rearrange their rooms frequently. While describing feelings of intense loneliness and depression, Veronica related how she arranged her room so that she was in the center with all her furniture surrounding her; if she needed anything, all she had to do was reach a short distance in any direction to get it. Other adolescents will rearrange their rooms frequently as they attempt to master feelings of disorganization, confusion, or isolation. Fred drew pictures in therapy sessions of a new and different way he had arranged his room. He drew the precise details of where his locker was placed in relation to his bed, desk, dresser, and other items.

Some patients express deeply disturbing feeling states in bizarre arrangements of their rooms. Edward, paranoid and withdrawn, placed his clothes locker sideways behind his bed and curled up inside of it. He experienced safety and security in the confined, definite space of the locker after experiences he described as overstimulating. At other times he would experience himself as dead, lying in a casket (Kayton, 1972). Chuck learned of his therapist's vacation, gorged himself with food, and hung belt strips and ribbons from his ceiling, conveying a sense of impending fragmentation. The staff's observation of how the adolescent patient arranges his room leads to a greater understanding of his internal psychological world and his attempts to communicate.

Shared property is an integral part of the daily community life of the hospitalized adolescent. The TV, unit stereo, games, daily newspaper, books, plants, and furniture are shared by all. Community property may appear less important to each individual because of the ambiguity in shared ownership, but a community develops a sense of ownership as relationships with each other become meaningful. Since our adolescents have difficulty sorting out what is a relationship and where the sense of one's self fits in that relationship, staff and patients must work diligently to form a community with norms and standards of dependability and consistency in the use and care of community property.

Staff involvement is graphically demonstrated when they attend closely to how the unit looks and how shared belongings are cared for and used. In the early days of our program, the dayroom was messy and cluttered, and the staff would enter in and put things in order. Our patients did not seem to notice the empty milk cartons, the popcorn on the floor, or the disarray of furniture in the dayroom, especially on Monday mornings. The weekend means fewer staff, no individual therapists, and a few days away from the structure of the school and activities. These circumstances combine to threaten the stability of many of our patients, and may manifest itself in a "who cares?" attitude about the unit.

In order to share belongings, adolescents must be able to compromise without losing their self-esteem.

> Fred's participation in deciding which TV program to watch was a passive, "I'll go along with whatever everyone else wants." Rarely in the group would he give a definite opinion, but in individual therapy sessions he boasted that he could run the unit better than the staff. As he began to deal with the discrepancy between his attitude and his observable behavior, he expressed how often he wanted to listen to a particular record, or watch a certain TV program, or share his ideas with others about possible group activities, but he thought that his ideas would not be duly considered or gain approval. In order to preserve his own self-esteem he utilized passive approval as a controlling maneuver. He felt himself the silent leader of the group, "allowing" decisions to be made from a position of grandiose control.

Our adolescents find it difficult to realize that all needs cannot be met at the same time, all the time. Someone may want to watch a particular television program or play a special record, but somebody else might already be using the equipment. The easiest solution offered, "We should each have a TV set and a record player in our rooms," may not be an expression of selfishness, but a communication that the patients' feelings are stimulated, perhaps traumatically, when they are asked to share, compromise, or delay gratification. The sought-after object becomes a focal point for teaching teenage patients that their needs cannot always be met immediately. They become anxious when they feel gratification is thwarted, but lump together all their perceived feelings and unconsciously held fantasies in, "I don't get my needs met," and find themselves burdened by intense feelings out of proportion to the current situation, by past situations as well, and by transferences. The patient experiences not only the disappointment of the present situation, but the burden of responding inappropriately. Here and now, adolescents may not be able to find another way of getting their wishes met, and we must gauge their ability to utilize our psychological supports, perhaps in redirecting their activity, or in helping them get out of the situation which is momentarily intolerable.

> Rebecca, who had been talking with the staff about feeling "immature and silly" on the unit, rushed out of her room after study hour before anyone else could come to the dayroom in order to watch a particular TV program. She was shocked when staff reminded her that she would need to work this out with other patients who wanted to watch television. Moments later, she snapped at a patient who was going through the TV guide, "I hope you can read what's in it." After exploration with staff, Rebecca expressed hopelessness that she wouldn't get a chance to watch what she wanted.

Our adolescents' inability to show concern for others often shows itself in an apparent lack of investment in their shared environment.

> After finishing a card game, Sol took the score sheet, rolled it up into a ball, and threw it over his shoulder onto the floor. This habit went without notice for sometime, but one day someone asked who had thrown the paper onto the floor, and Sol spoke up and said that he had done it. In a community meeting following this incident, staff and patients talked about the issue, and Sol said that he had done this several times and didn't think it important. He was matter-of-fact, and didn't seem conflicted or uncomfortable in the confrontation. The patient group began challenging him and asking him why he had done this; he said he felt it was all right not to take the trouble to carry through on every small task. In therapy sessions, he denied anxiety about this because he felt that his behavior had no impact on what he perceived as an unimportant environment. He often treated the other patients and staff as if they too were unimportant. It was only through constant confrontation by staff and patients that Sol began

to experience some anxiety about his behavior. Because the patient group persisted, he began to understand that his misuse of their common environment was a misuse of them as well, and affected how they felt about themselves.

Deterioration of, lack of concern for, or misuse of shared belongings indicates faulty group cohesion and problematic group relationships, often resulting from the development of delinquent subcultures.

For awhile, several mysteries occurred on the unit. Games were left lying about, and no one knew who left them. Apple cores were discovered behind doors, and other unit items were found in inappropriate places. While trying to solve these mysteries in a ward meeting, Ernie said, "The unit is like a garbage truck going uphill with the back open, and all the garbage is falling out." After persistent exploration, the patients began to reveal that there had been covert threats made among the patients to each other, as well as outbursts of aggressive behavior between them. By trying to understand the deterioration of the nonhuman environment, the patients revealed the deterioration in group relationships.

Other mysteries arise when patients have unresolved issues with each other or with the staff that cannot be expressed, when the feelings involved are not available to awareness and verbal expression, or when expressing feelings may be too risky. Then, emotions and fantasies show up in overt behaviors like the mysterious disappearance or destruction of property, community or others'. For instance, feelings about the admission of several new patients and simultaneous staff changes emerged in defacing and ripping pages out of magazines that belonged to the unit. Admission of new patients may disrupt the group homeostasis and stimulate feelings of abandonment by the older patients which may be expressed initially in destruction of property.

To summarize, furniture, clothes, decorations, records, stereo, TV, games—things—are important clues to the adolescent's psychological world, to the interventions he needs, and to how successful we are in intervening. To ignore the material world would be to conduct treatment in a vacuum and to deny an important reality of the adolescent's existence.

8

Work with Families

Erikson (1950) describes adolescence as "the age of the final establishment of a dominant positive ego identity. It is then that a future within reach becomes part of the conscious life span. It is then that the question arises whether or not the future was anticipated in earlier expectations" (p. 306). These expectations are generally held by the distraught parents of hospitalized adolescents, who often see their hopes and dreams for their child's future in terrible jeopardy. Therefore, there is a quality of "last chance" desperation that seems to surround the hospitalization of an adolescent. Everyone feels it—the youngster who may realize on some level that if he doesn't make it here, he may never make it; the staff who often feel, and correctly so, that the proper intervention (if only we knew what that intervention should be!) is the single factor that will change the patient's life; and the family whose effort to get the adolescent hospitalized was indeed an act of last chance desperation. The desperation, the urgency, the "grasping at straws" not only doubles all bets, but raises the stakes of psychiatric hospitalization to "double or nothing."

Our work with families bears this out. As Sklansky, Silverman, and Rabichow (1969) describe, "Adolescence is an age of anxiety for parents as well as for the adolescent. Even parents of normal adolescents often feel bewildered, attacked, rebelled against, insecure in their authority, worried about the present and fearful of the future" (p. 184).

The burden of an emotionally disturbed youngster is generally catastrophic for families. The need for hospitalization, the kind of hospitalization, and the kind of setting and program orientation most beneficial can become overwhelming questions. Easson (1969) has said, "More than any other age group, the growing adolescent is vulnerable and may be handicapped emotionally and intellectually by unnecessary or badly planned hospital placement" (p. 1). The decision to proceed with a psychiatric hospitalization is an emotionally charged event for the adolescent and his family. It has been our experience that careful attention to and planning for treatment of the family must be part of the patient's hospitalization.

Families are involved from the very beginning. Before a patient is accepted into the program, the entire family is screened. This is done primarily for diagnostic purposes, but also serves as a means of getting a family commitment to the treatment program. In addition, it proclaims that the symptomatic behavior of one member of a family generally reflects pathological factors in the entire family constellation.

Families of patients are worked with on several levels. They are expected to attend a weekly Parents' Group, as well as have a weekly session with the social worker. The Parents' Group consists of all the parents of the hospitalized patients and a male and a female co-therapist. The group serves several purposes. First of all, it helps each parent realize that there are others with the same problems. Since there generally is so much guilt about having a child "sick" enough to require hospitalization, there is comfort in sharing experiences with others, and indeed, many of the sessions are concerned with guilt and with the loss of self-esteem that accompanies guilt.

The group also educates, in that the philosophy of the treatment program is discussed and distortions and misconceptions are corrected. For instance, parents who, for whatever reason, are not allowed to visit their child for awhile invariably assume that it is because they are "bad" for their child and their presence somehow harms the adolescent. In the Parents' Group they learn about overstimulation and the need to minimize it for certain adolescents. They also learn that an adolescent who has difficulty forming a relationship with his therapist may need to cut down on the people he has to relate to and that the restriction against visiting is not an indictment of their parenting.

We have also discovered that the Parents' Group has been an invaluable tool when the teenager signs a release request and demands to be discharged. Because many of the parents have been manipulated and intimidated by their adolescent in the past, they frequently feel impotent rage when the patient signs the release request. In the group they get support and encouragement from others to take a strong and firm stand against taking the patient home under these circumstances. Frequently, this is all that's been necessary to elicit a retraction, because the patient is usually shocked and amazed at the determined and unswerving attitude now exhibited by a parent who previously gave in to protests and threats. We have discovered that in many instances the group serves a social function as well, although that was not our purpose when we started it. Parents become friendly with other parents and for some couples this is their night out together; in some instances it is the only time they spend together.

For conventional group therapy, the ideal group therapy situation involves a specified number of people, generally eight to 10 who are motivated to seek some sort of help for themselves. A therapist generally assesses what these needs are and comes to the conclusion that group therapy is the treatment of choice. Often members of groups are very carefully selected. Some therapists seek homogeneity in age, sex, type of problems, etc. Other group therapists prefer to mix young and old, single and married, psychotic and neurotic. The composition of the group is planned and arranged according to a particular theory and a preconceived plan of who should be included in order to meet the goals of the individual members as well as the goals of the group. Groups of drug addicts, for instance, serve specific purposes of confronting and breaking down defenses, and generally the focus is on the group process itself and how the members interact with one another. In contrast, a group of unwed pregnant teenagers might be more supportive in nature and focus on problem-solving and decision-making. Questions of coping with young children can be mutually explored and information can be shared. Sensitivity groups have still another focus, and "consciousness raising" groups of feminists, homosexuals, and others have still another purpose. However, membership in all the above groups is generally voluntary, and usually the participant is expecting some sort of gain from that membership.

In actual practice, the Parents' Group breaks all the rules for conventional group therapy. Membership in our Parents' Group is not voluntary in the usual sense of the word. The expectation is that unless the parents participate, we cannot treat the child. Some parents translate this to mean that participation is the price they pay for the hospitalization. Reactions to this expectation vary considerably and have to do with each parent's own pathology and the dynamics of the total family constellation. For some parents, the expectation is seen as a totally unreasonable demand. One parent wailed, "but that's my bowling night . . ." and indeed her feeling of deprivation pervaded her total group experience while her daughter was in the program. These parents generally have already experienced great distress because of the mischief of their children. Many have been called to school numerous times, often missing work because of it. Many have had to go to court repeatedly and they describe feelings of anger, inconvenience, humiliation, and financial loss. One parent reported that she slept in her girdle every night because she always expected a call from the police saying that her son was in trouble again. When these parents make the decision to seek hospitalization for their children, it generally represents some sort of resolution for them, and the painful agonizing over that decision is often accompanied by a feeling of relief and a hope that now that the decision has been made, no additional sacrifices will be asked. Therefore, when they are told that we will work intensively with them in the Parents' Group as well as in individual sessions with the social worker, their feelings of being overwhelmed often get displaced onto their child.

Parents talk about the great deal of time, effort and money lost on their delinquent child, often, they feel, at the expense of their other children. They say this very directly to the patient who, in turn, is made to feel guilty and "unworthy" of receiving help because it causes his parents so much distress. Many of these patients request release from the hospital as a symbolic sacrifice in hopes of placating the angry parents. It is often difficult for these parents to see the bind in which they set themselves. On the one hand, they want help for their child —yet on the other hand, their unwillingness to participate will make it impossible to receive that help. The feeling they present is one of

". . . if you only knew how much I've suffered in the past, you would not ask this of me."

Fortunately, many such parents can be helped with a great deal of support. Other group members share their feelings of sacrifice, and simply exchanging experiences can be very beneficial. One common resolution to this dilemma seems to be an attitude of "OK, I'll comply with your unreasonable demands—then if he doesn't straighten out, nobody can say I haven't done everything I could. So therefore, I don't have to feel guilty." Successful outcomes with this kind of resistance occur when later the parents actually perceive that in their participation they are getting something for themselves. Generally when their claim of sacrifice is dropped, their attendance becomes extremely productive, and the patient becomes very invested in the parents' participation in the group—seeing it as their expression of care and concern. Some patients have reported that when their parents do not attend the group, they fear abandonment.

Not all parents resist group involvement. Some parents welcome the opportunity to participate in a group situation. These people have generally felt isolated and alone. Often their child's acting out has been a deep and painful secret from other family members, and their guilt and shame over having a troublesome adolescent have kept them from receiving support from their relatives and friends. Participation in the group offers an opportunity to unburden themselves and get the support and comfort they so desperately need.

One of the questions frequently posed by these parents is ". . . what do you tell relatives and friends about where the child is. . . .?" One set of parents was so afraid of the paternal grandparents' finding out their son was hospitalized that they went to elaborate and exhausting extremes to maintain the shameful secret. When the grandparents came by, they were always told Ned was at the library, or playing baseball, or with a friend. In the meantime, Christmas gifts and birthday cards were produced as having come from Ned at the appropriate times. This particular couple spent an enormous amount of time on this deception, elaborating even more complex schemes. This went on for the entire length of their son's hospitalization, a period of some six months. One set of parents, when their son was close to discharge, asked if they could bring in a sun lamp. It seems that they had told some relatives that the boy had been in Florida all those months! One parent handled the situation by telling relatives and friends that his son was in jail! He found this more acceptable than the possible fantasies about a mental hospital. Other parents say that their child is in boarding school. The need to deceive is frequently aroused by the guilt and shame of hospitalization. The feelings of relief that some parents report are also generally accompanied by feelings of having "put the child away." Some parents have reported intense and angry reactions on the part of siblings, other relatives, and often their own parents. Separating the child from the family disturbs the entire family homeostasis, and ordinary ways of relating to one another of necessity must be changed. If the hospitalized adolescent played a particular role in that family—scapegoat, or provocateur, or the "crazy" one—other family members may fear that someone else will now have to assume that role or that all family roles will be changed, or that shameful family secrets will be found out, and all the family defenses will be torn asunder.

A very real consequence of hospitalizing a disturbed adolescent is the change that occurs in the parents' marital situation. Often the hospitalization removes the symptom bearer from a highly pathological family situation. When parents resists involvement in the program because they don't have any problems, only "the child" has problems, we can point out that any family that has a delinquent living with them, of necessity, must have difficulty coping with the problems his behavior causes. For many parents, the way they have related to one another has been through their adolescent's delinquent behavior. With their child's hospitalization, they are forced to relate to one another in different and sometimes very uncomfortable ways. Marriages that were unstable to begin with generally suffer the most during the adolescent's hospitalization. Difficulties with one another can now no longer be diffused through or blamed upon the adolescent. The marriage of Tammy's parents, for instance, was a highly pathological one. When Tammy was hospitalized, they resisted participating in the program. They felt "forced" to comply by attending the Parents' Group and having individual sessions with the social worker, and their anger and hostility over this arrangement were quite apparent. Gradually, patterns began to emerge. Father began to use the treatment and became invested in the program. Mother became more angry and bitter. Unresolved sexual problems were, as mother put it, "dredged up" and verbalized. Although hotly denied later, it became clearer that the family was having trouble with the other siblings as well. There was talk of divorce and suicide as the marriage deteriorated further. Mother, who was the most threatened by the change in the family homeostasis, declared that if they got divorced, it would be the fault of the hospital staff. The push to regain the old way of relating to one another was so strong in this woman that she threatened to pull her daughter out of the program, although there was clear evidence that the patient was doing well. This was acted out around the issue of the patient not receiving a home pass at Christmas. The mother came to the Parents' Group enraged over this and demanded to know how we dared to ruin Christmas for their entire family which consisted of the two parents, a grandmother, and nine siblings as well as the patient. When we explored this in terms of the patient's progress on the unit and her overall treatment plan, the mother was deaf to any rational explanation and ended her tirade with a poignant ". . . but I have needs too." It was father who adamantly refused to take their daughter out. Later on, when individual sessions with the social worker focused on the marital situation rather than on the patient—and there was some evidence that their relationship could be improved—the need to restore the old pathological homeostasis was lessened and Tammy was permitted to continue with her own badly needed treatment.

The change in the family homeostasis very strongly affects the patient's siblings as well, and many times they fight the hospitalization, sometimes even threatening the parents in the process. Siblings of hospitalized adolescents are affected on many levels. Generally, there is guilt because of past squabbles and the usual unpleasantness most siblings inflict on one another. Sometimes a sibling is even more delinquent than the one hospitalized. The hospitalized sibling is the one who generally gets caught in his delinquency and the nonhospitalized one has a feeling, on an unconscious level usually, that he is the one who needs the treatment. Another common fear is that the hospitalization means that one is mentally ill, and if one family member has been identified as "crazy," that may mean that others might be just as disturbed. Some see the hospitalization of their sibling as an abandonment by the parents, and they experience a combination of fear of their own abandonment, of relief that someone else was the victim and that they were spared, and at the same time, of guilt for having survived at the expense of someone else. Any, all, or a combination of these feelings can be traumatizing for the siblings of the hospitalized adolescent, and we frequently work with siblings in family sessions, or individually if necessary.

Parents often incur the wrath of their own parents as well, and, as has been described earlier, often go to great lengths to hide the hospitalization. Frequently, the delinquency has been kept secret, so that grandparents often have an unusually rosy, if unrealistic, view of their adolescent grandchild. When the hospitalization occurs and has not been kept a secret from them, a common reaction is shock, disbelief, and often anger at the parents. Many grandparents see the hospitalization as an indictment of their own parenting efforts and react as if the hospitalization represents some sort of betrayal of the family image. Unresolved parent-child conflicts between parent and grandparent emerge during this crisis period, and the hospitalized adolescent is the arena where these battles are fought. One extreme example involves Billy.

> Billy's grandmother was born in a small, rural, impoverished village in Puerto Rico. After having a child out of wedlock (Billy's mother), she left home to seek domestic work. She and her daughter lived in the house where she was employed. When the daughter was seven years old, the mother became pregnant again, and, because her employer would not accept two children in the home, Billy's mother was sent to live in a church-run boarding school. The mother and second daughter eventually were able to establish their own home, and Billy's mother was sent for. She was 15 years old when the family was reunited, and they eventually came to Chicago to seek a better life.

> Billy's mother still experienced the boarding school as an abandonment, even though intellectually she recognized the reasons for it. She suffered greatly during those years, and described the school

as an oppressive and repressive place where she often knew hunger, cold, and unreasonable punishment. She rebelled against her tormenters by becoming delinquent and sexually promiscuous. When she was reunited with her mother, this behavior continued. Her mother's experience was recreated when the daughter became pregnant with Billy. When he was born, they decided to give him up for adoption, and he was turned over to an agency. They heard nothing further about it until Billy was four months old. At that time they received a letter from the agency stating that Billy had not been adopted and requesting money for his continued care. The grandmother then made the decision that they would take the baby home. She describes going to the agency and "falling in love" with this beautiful baby. Billy thus came home to grandmother and her two daughters, and all three women cared for him.

Shortly afterward, as the girls became increasingly involved with jobs and boyfriends, the mothering tasks became clearly defined as grandmother's. As Billy grew, he called grandmother, "Mother," and he called his mother by her given name, even though he knew what the real relationships were. Billy's mother, who could never forget or forgive her mother for the earlier abandonment, grew less and less invested in Billy. As she dated and partied more, her relationship with her mother became increasingly tumultuous and had many aspects of adolescent rebellion about it. She eventually left the house to marry, divorce, have another son, and marry again. She left Billy behind as a "gift" to her mother. Grandmother proceeded to pamper, coddle, and overprotect him, to fulfill her own need to mother as well as to show her daughter what a "bad mother" she was. On the one hand, she fiercely clung to the child, and yet when he became obstreperous or difficult to control, she would call mother and demand that she do something with "her" child. As Billy grew, the relationship between the mother and grandmother continued to be stormy and conflictual. At the same time, there were strong ties and positive feelings. There were times when the grandmother refused to let the mother participate in decisions about Billy and then there were other times when she demanded money and participation from the mother.

This pathological situation continued all during Billy's latency and until he reached puberty. To complicate matters, Billy was left with a series of babysitters as grandmother had to continue working as a domestic. At no time was there a stable male figure around, and at no time was there any mention of who Billy's father might be or what had happened to him. When Billy reached adolescence, he became preoccupied with violence and would make up gory stories about bloody events he swore he witnessed. In addition, he became more withdrawn, did poorly in school and on several occasions, urinated in glass jars which he kept stored in his room. He became overly aggressive toward his half-brother and on several occasions had menaced grandmother by shoving her and physically restraining her when she attempted to hit him. The mother became increasingly alarmed by his behavior and the fact that he had flunked the test for the high school they had hoped he would attend. When his "play" with brother included poking his fingers in his eyes and holding a pillow over his face for a dangerously long period of time, his mother decided that something had to be done. Against the grandmother's wishes, she had Billy tested at an outpatient clinic. The testing indicated that Billy was a very disturbed boy who potentially could act out his murderous and sadistic impulses unless a therapeutic intervention was made. They recommended long-term hospitalization and referred him to our program.

When, on the day of the screening, our diagnosis confirmed the original findings, we offered to take Billy into our program. The mother was the natural mother and legal guardian so she had to be the one to sign Billy in. The grandmother was furious and fought desperately against the admission, insisting that there was nothing the matter with the boy. When Billy was hospitalized, the homeostasis in the family was forever altered. We even changed the way we usually worked with families in this situation. Ordinarily, one social worker is in charge and sees whatever necessary relatives need to be seen in each individual family. However, the conflict between mother and grandmother was so great that we had one social worker work with the mother and another social worker work with the grandmother who remained adamantly opposed to the entire proceedings.

For years prior to the hospitalization, the mother and grandmother had participated in a love-hate relationship. For instance, if the grandmother disapproved of anything, she would open the kitchen drawer, take out a knife, hand it to the mother and invite her to stab her to death, because her behavior was killing her anyway. At the same time, the mother was a constant visitor to the house, took grandmother shopping and on other errands and celebrated all holidays with mother. Billy's hospitalization now changed all that. His mother and grandmother became completely estranged from one another, although they both attended the Parents' Group. Their behavior there had a war game quality about it. If the mother mentioned something that indicated that Billy had pathology, grandmother would counter-attack with a comment on the mother's disinterest in mothering because of her sexual promiscuity. If the grandmother commented that Billy did not need to be in the hospital, mother would attack grandmother's mothering and overprotectiveness. Both combatants felt free to comment about other patients or other aspects of the program without inviting hostility from the other.

In their individual sessions with their social workers, their negative feelings towards one another were verbalized freely. The mother constantly referred back to her mother's abandonment of her and was aware on some level of repeating the patterns with Billy. She constantly referred to him as a "stranger" to her, and saw the hospitalization as the last concrete thing she would do for him. She saw herself as withdrawing from him even further after he was discharged, leaving him completely to his grandmother. The mother was actually using the hospitalization to separate completely from the grandmother—a process she had attempted to master before, but had never adequately resolved. The grandmother sensed that her family was "falling apart" and that she was losing mother and especially her domination of the mother. However, rather than face the mother's growing autonomy which was the real issue, she insisted on blaming the hospitalization itself. As her anger at the mother grew, she came to the totally unrealistic conclusion that the mother put Billy into the hospital solely to punish her.

There was a change in her other daughter as well. She had always been the "good" daughter, compliant, and passive. Moreover, she had taken on many of the household chores and mothering of Billy when he was small. Even though she was now out of the home, Billy's hospitalization triggered some unresolved parent-child conflicts between her and her mother. When the grandmother, in her attempt to gain sympathy for her feelings about the hospital, sought to make an ally of her second daughter, she was shocked and dismayed to learn that she had feelings of her own. Not only did she support the hospitalization, she confronted the grandmother with having been "robbed of my childhood" by fulfilling parenting tasks when very young.

Although this case represents an extreme example of how the hospitalization affects the family homeostasis, all families are affected in one degree or another by the separation of one of its members. The degree of disruption generated is almost directly correlated with the degree of pathology already existing in the family. The entire family needs a great deal of support during this very stressful period. We have found the Parents' Group to be an invaluable tool in helping to provide for that support.

The Parents' Group does not conform to the ideal group therapy model in that we take involuntary members as they come, with no attempt at matching any variable. The members of the group share in common only the fact that their adolescent is presently an inpatient in our program. Our members are of different races, ages, education, and socioeconomic classes. They differ in their desire to be part of the group. We accept new members upon admission of their adolescent into the program without regard to whether or not their entry at this time would further or impede the work of the group. Moreover, we can lose members precipitously and abruptly if their child signs himself out of the hospital, or for some reason, is discharged administratively. In situations like this, often there is little time to work through adequately a proper termination process, and once again these parents have to suffer because of the behavior of their acting out adolescent.

At one time, early in the program, we attempted to keep parents in the group even though their child was no longer a patient in the program. Theresa's mother was enraged when Theresa was given an administrative discharge because of repeated acts of violence. We invited the mother to continue in the group for awhile to help her ventilate some of these feelings. Theresa, in the meantime, began to regret leaving the hospital and three months later asked for a screening for readmission. She was readmitted possibly because she was influenced by seeing her mother continue in the group. Although letting a parent stay after the adolescent was discharged worked extremely well in this instance, it soon became apparent that our group was becoming much too large and unwieldy. We then began a Parents' Alumni Group for the parents of discharged patients, for, just as the hospitalization was one part of a continuum for the ongoing psychotherapy of the disturbed adolescent, the inpatient Parents' Group represented only one aspect of the support system needed for the family of the disturbed adolescent.

Although we have continually referred to our group as a Parents' Group, there have been times when nonparents became members, too. For instance, Edith, whose mother was dead and whose father was an invalid, lived with her sister, who had just married for the second time, bringing Edith as well as her own four-year-old child from her previous marriage into this second marriage. When Edith was hospitalized, her bewildered young brother-in-law, who was attempting to adjust to being married, suddenly found himself a member of our group. His willingness to participate, as confusing as he found all of this to be, helped to ease Edith's return to their home upon discharge. We have also integrated fiancés into our group, as the patient would have these people as stepparents upon discharge. One mother, who was somewhat ambivalent about whether or not she really wanted to marry a particular man, used the group as a testing ground. If he were willing to participate and come to the group, she would marry him. She saw this as a real test of his motivation to marry her.

On the other side of the spectrum, Carol's parents were involved in deep conflict at the time of Carol's admission to the program. During the course of her hospitalization, the parents decided they would divorce. They announced this to the group, and week after week fought so bitterly during the group session that we had to set strong limits on their behavior. Finally, we had to make a decision because their open conflicts were monopolizing the sessions; since Carol would be returning home to her mother, who was obtaining custody of her from the Court, we asked father to leave the group. Each situation is different, however, and must be handled on an individual basis. During the course of Chuck's hospitalization, his parents came to the group representing themselves as the ideal married couple. Gradually, they began to air their differences, finally announced their separation, their impending divorce, and then their reconciliation. However, during this whole process they never missed a group session, nor was there any reason to ask anyone to leave because their behavior was entirely appropriate and their use of the group was clearly therapeutic during this very trying time.

In the case of divorced parents, certainly the parent that has the legal custody is expected to become a member of Parents' Group. The involvement in the program of the other spouse has to be assessed on an individual basis. If the other spouse, usually the father, has been out of the picture for a long time and has not had much contact with the patient, then usually there is no problem. However, in many cases the mother may not have had contact with her divorced husband but the patient has. In these cases, the father has to be involved in the program, but the Parents' Group is not recommended, as the divorced pair would be too uncomfortable with one another. However, it is important that the father be in contact with the social worker during the course of the hospitalization; we have had many patients who have idealized the missing father and have grandiose fantasies about the father rescuing them even though the reality may be that the patient has had only minimal and superficial contact with the father. These fantasies have to be explored, of course, in the patient's therapy sessions, but the parents also need to understand this oftentime bewildering phenomenon.

> Sherm's mother was enraged when Sherm spoke longingly of his absent father who had brutalized both Sherm and his mother. Sherm was a ward of the State at the time of his admission and had not lived with either parent for several years prior to his admission to the program. Because of Sherm's previous violent behavior, his mother determined that he could never again live at home. However, she could never convey this directly, and because she felt guilty about her decision, she handled it by becoming vigorously involved in the program. She attended every Parents' Group session and every session with the social worker. At the same time she became very seductive with Sherm during her visits with him. This behavior evoked in him the longing to be reunited with his mother, while at the same time he knew at some level that she would never actually permit this. So he punished her by praising the father who had abandoned the family years earlier. Unfortunately, there was no way to reach or work with this father, and so Sherm had no opportunity to explore and test out his fantasies. However, he continued to improve in the pro-

gram and continued to express the desire to return home to mother. When it came time to consider seriously discharge planning for Sherm, the mother became increasingly fearful and handled the situation in the same way the idealized father did. She announced to the group and to the social worker that she was leaving and promptly dropped out of sight. When that happened, painful as it was, Sherm worked in therapy to accept the fact that he could not be reunited with his mother and became much more amenable to placement in the foster home which was eventually arranged for him.

In addition to working with fiancés, divorced parents, idealized absent parents, sisters and brothers-in-law, and grandmothers, the Parents' Group has, on occasion, absorbed other nonparents as well. When Kent was admitted to the program, the social worker made her first diagnostic appointment with his mother. The mother, an extremely limited and dependent woman, brought her friend, Mary, to that appointment. She insisted that Mary be present during her interview. It soon became apparent that this was not simply a willful or capricious request on mother's part. Mary actually was the missing part of mother's own ego and her presence was actually quite necessary to mother's being able to function at all. Therefore, Mary was allowed to visit Kent, although we usually allow only parents to visit when patients are first hospitalized, and naturally Mary became a member of the Parents' Group, where the two of them functioned very capably as one.

We have found the Parents' Group to be a valuable and important adjunct to our Adolescent Program. It offers familiarity with the program, support, opportunities to ventilate, to work on problems, and to socialize. Although parents do not volunteer to become group members, we have not seen this as too serious an obstacle in eventually gaining their complete support for the program. Flexibility in working with divorced spouses, parent surrogates, and other types of nonparent members is invaluable. When in doubt, we recommend including the potential member rather than risk losing a significant other to the total treatment program.

However, we learned that we had to work with families on another level as well. We discovered that when we first started out, there was a great deal of hostility between the milieu staff and the patients' parents. We found that social workers during team meetings would try to explain a parent's point of view to an unsympathetic milieu staff; at the same time the Parents' Group therapists were trying to explain the milieu philosophy to angry parents. Visiting hours were deteriorating into a battle ground. Frequently, parents were restricted from visiting which often provoked them to miss Parents' Group and/or their weekly sessions with the social worker. In addition, there was increased staff resistance to granting home passes, and when discharge planning began, the staff resisted letting these adolescents go home to those "horrible people."

What we did to ameliorate this situation was to evolve a philosophy about visiting hours and to formulate the role that milieu staff play during that time. We first expanded the idea of "milieu." Generally, when we talk about the milieu, we refer to the culture and atmosphere of the hospital. However, patients also come from a milieu where they lived with their parents. Hospitalization represents not only a separation, but a transfer as well, from one milieu to another. Patients are separated from their families because a person or agency decided that help was needed: the school principal, the police, the Court, a social agency, a private therapist, the patient's family, or even the patient himself. The patient disturbed someone in his milieu by his behavior that was offensive, illegal, rebellious, or contrary to the norms of society. When the situation is evaluated at screening, removal may be the only solution. And so, for some, hospitalization represents not only an environment supportive to psychotherapy, but also separation and removal.

We learned that most staff who work with adolescents on an inpatient service have some stereotyped notions about the milieu from which the patient comes, even prior to the patient's admission: the adolescent's mother and father are "rotten" parents; the patient comes from a malignant, "bad" environment into our therapeutic, "good" milieu. These parents are so destructive to their child that we must staff a hospital 24 hours-a-day, seven-days-a-week, in order to keep that patient away from the "bad" family. Then we do a very curious thing

—we decide that there should be visiting hours, time when we turn over the disturbed adolescent to this family or other equally "bad" visitors for several uninterrupted hours at a time. Frequently, the next day, we hear that the patient is "off a wall," or that he wound up in restraints, or behaved in some destructive way. Sometimes the solution is to restrict the visiting, but even when we don't, the notion of families being the "bad guys" and hospital staff the "good guys" is reinforced. Reports of verbal hostility between staff and visitor is often heard, generally to the patient's delight and often with the patient aiding and abetting the situation. Some especially manipulative patients recreate in the hospital the splitting of parental objects, exactly as was done in the home, thus meeting the same pathological needs in the same way he did on the outside. Friedlander (1960) points out, ". . . the disturbance which under certain environmental and psychological conditions leads to antisocial behavior, is a very deep-rooted one. It is not an illness, inflicted upon a healthy personality, but a character-disturbance rooted in experiences during the first years of life" (p. 199).

Once we identified this problem, we exposed the staff to new and different ways of thinking about the parents of the hospitalized adolescent. To begin with, no one sets out to be a bad parent. Many parents have had inadequate parenting themselves and have had no experience in a healthy parent-child relationship. Furthermore, often the identified patient is not the sickest member of the family, but rather the symptom bearer of the family's disturbance. Most often, the basic conflict is between the marital pair; in many instances a child becomes a delinquent or lapses into psychosis to keep the marriage intact. On an unconscious level, a child, at a very early age, can sense that when the parents are focusing or him and his "bad" or "sick" behavior, they don't have to deal with each other or with the problems they are having as husband and wife. We helped our staff to see that regardless of how poorly parents raised their child, bringing that child into a psychiatric hospital is very difficult. These are people under stress, people who hurt, regardless of how well defended they are. Also, regardless of how poorly they raised that child, bringing that child into a psychiatric hospital is an extremely positive bit of parenting. They are seeking help, and seeking help when needed is good parenting, and should be acknowledged as such.

Regardless of how defended they are, these parents feel guilt and shame; even when they project all the "badness" on to the patient, their image of themselves suffers great damage. A hospital admission for their child is an admission of defeat for their parenting efforts. In effect, they are saying, "I've failed, and so now I must turn to you to be a better parent than I am." This admission puts them in a terrible bind: on the one hand, they want help for their child; on the other hand, staff's success proves how "bad" they are. The patient enters into this situation and gleefully exploits and exacerbates it. We hear many reports of patients telling staff horror stories about the home situation; at the same time, they are telling parents horror stories about how badly they are treated in the hospital. If staff perceives parents as hostile and guilty of sabotaging treatment, which may happen, it may be due to the bind the parents find themselves in when they seek hospitalization for their child.

We attempt to cut through this bind by integrating families into the milieu. Most basic is the conviction that total milieu treatment includes visiting hours. Nursing personnel who have clearly defined tasks during the other parts of the patient's day can also have clearly defined functions when visitors come onto the unit. Here, we do not mean "supervised visiting," which we sometimes initiate for various reasons, and in which the staff member's role is basically to observe and ensure that no drugs are passed or there is no sexual or violent behavior. Integrating families into the milieu does not require that nursing staff be present during the entire visit, except in unusual situations when that is prescribed. We do not want to intrude upon the privacy of patients and their families, nor do we expect nursing staff to become family therapists. We try to help staff develop an attitude of helping parents as well as patients. This evolves in a gradual and casual way. A staff member joins the patient and his visitors briefly, introduces himself and makes small talk for as long as he and the visitors are comfortable and then just as casually leaves. We have learned a lot from these brief interactions. Even normal adolescents and their parents can rarely tolerate a two-hour "rap" session together, and our disturbed adolescents usually welcome the inclusion of a third party. As staff participated in visits, parents began to see them as human beings rather than as supermen who knew all the answers and could do no wrong or as sadistic jailors who mistreated and punished their precious child. Staff began to see parents as real people, too, with problems of their own. In many instances, they even began to like each other! Distortions about the program were reduced. If Johnny wound up in restraints the previous night, an explanation by a staff member, especially if he was the one on duty at the time, was extremely helpful. Frequently the staff member could provide information the family knew nothing about because the patients had told their parents little or nothing about school, O.T., field trips, recreational programs, or their therapy sessions two or three times a week.

Ideally, a partnership between staff and parents should evolve. Family members gradually should feel free to seek out a staff member if there is anything puzzling or bothering them, and ideally the staff member would be able to interact with the family in a free and honest manner. This atmosphere could provide new, creative, and innovative ways of working together. If this atmosphere of partnership has developed, when a staff member hears quarreling between patients and their visitors, he could enter the situation simply by asking, "Can I help?" Formerly, this type of intervention was perceived as protecting the patient regardless of how the situation arose or who was provoking whom. In this newly created atmosphere, the staff member can truly be of help because an atmosphere of trust between all parties has been established. Similarly, a staff member might comment to a parent that Johnny has a great deal of difficulty getting up in the morning and asks if this has been a problem at home. This not only encourages a freer flow of information and facilitates communication, but it also gives the patient an opportunity to see this partnership in action and to see parents as well as staff demonstrate their concerns for him. This further solidifies the union between parents and staff so that the patients are unable to use their pathological mechanisms of "divide and conquer." In addition, the staff member, in feeding this information to the team, provides diagnostic information to the team, and helps in formulating treatment plans.

There is room for innovations and variations. A female patient was visited regularly by her parents. Her mother was an active, aggressive, nonstop talker who dominated the entire family visit. The father, a quiet, passive, chronically depressed man, looked as though he was suffering untold agonies during the visit. He had never fully accepted the need for the patient's hospitalization, and there was serious concern that he might sabotage treatment. The staff member who chose to work with this family was concerned about these visits, and with consultation, determined that the father was being shut out by the talkative females and needed something for himself. The staff member then sought out the father, removed him from the family group, and they began having casual "man-to-man" chats about sports, business, world events, and the like. Although the stratagem, all by itself, does not suggest anything dramatic, the psychological effect was powerful; visits became more enjoyable for father because he had someone who would listen to him for a change, and a subtle change in attitude toward the hospital and the hospitalization began to emerge.

Although certain other factors are also present, it can be taught and demonstrated that ward staff's attitudes and interactions with family members play a vital and integral part in making a milieu viable. We emphasize to staff that we are caretakers in an ongoing milieu program which must include visiting hours as an all-important part of that milieu. Furthermore, we are temporary caretakers because the adolescents we care for usually return to these families. The hospitalization, although separating the adolescents from their families, must provide some benefits to both if the return to home is to be workable. On the unit, our plan started out modestly. It was simply to help ward staff intervene in destructive visits. Not only did we accomplish this goal, we discovered a great change in staff's attitude toward parents. Hostility and mistrust in many cases gave way to understanding and compassion. We almost never consider placement outside the home any more because staff more often see the family as less malignant and more workable than formerly. When parents feel less guilt-ridden and more understood, this attitude is not lost on the patient. When parents feel more sure of themselves and the rightness of the hospitalization, the patient's anxiety lessens.

Work with families must be a vital and ongoing part of our total treatment approach. The more successful we are in integrating families into our milieu, the more benign will be the milieu to which the patient will return.

9

Specialized Modalities
of Intervention

In any hospital program for adolescents, each aspect of that program should be designed to provide psychological supports and challenges consistent with each teenager's level of development. Consequently, regardless of where in the program a teenager is at the moment involved, he can trust that he will not be expected to master tasks that exceed his ability. Staff must work together to understand and agree upon what parts of the program can be considered routine. School, activities, ward meetings, therapy sessions, and certain ward routines are tasks which everyone attends, but the degree of challenge within these areas will vary greatly depending upon individual treatment goals.

There are a number of activities, tasks, or routines which cannot be understood as part of the process of psychotherapy or as delimited by the parameters of person, time, space, or things. These interventions occur in different localities such as the school hall, or the school classroom, the Occupational Therapy shop, the dayroom, the patient's own room, a specialized conference area, or a state park. These interventions may have important time components, such as the length of a class period, or revolve around the use of things such as the Occupational Therapy shop or the role of games and leisure time activity. In all instances, the personal interventions of the staff are crucial, whether it be the teacher's ability to convey to her students during a crisis how they need to distinguish their personal problems from their academic tasks, or the decisive and caring stand the nurse makes when she decides to place a patient in physical restraints.

These specialized modalities of intervention—intervening in violent behavior, the use of physical restraints, the Adolescent Progress Review, the school, the Occupational Therapy shop, games and leisure time activities, camping and the Thanksgiving Dinner—embrace many of the principles that we have already described and need to be understood as an integration of these viewpoints.

PROGRESSIVE INTERVENTIONS INTO
VIOLENT BEHAVIOR*

The most important single element in controlling patient violence is the skill and expertise of the ward staff in recognizing and dealing with the cues that a breakdown is imminent. It is rare that violence occurs in the hospital unit without the patient's having sent several signals in advance, in the form of physical or verbal behavior, that he is beginning to lose control. In order for ward staff to recognize breakdowns before the patient begins to strike out, ward staff must share observations, make assessments, and maintain a high level of knowledge about an individual patient's responses and how patients react to one another in a group situation. In this way, staff begins to work as a team and develops consistency in handling aggressive behavior. Such team work depends not only on the individual adolescent's history, psychodynamics, and therapeutic progress, but also on an understanding and skillful use of the interventions available to ward staff members in the particular milieu.

Our purpose is not simply to control the patient externally, but to help the teenager regain and/or utilize his own self-control. An initial intervention usually involves a staff member's saying something to the teenager. The staff member may limit the adolescent's behavior by telling him what he may or may not do; or the staff member may try to help him find acceptable alternatives in order to cope with the feelings he is experiencing. With a psychotic patient, for example,

---

* This section is a revised version of a paper presented by Lita Simpson Sabonis at the Illinois State Psychiatric Institute Nursing Conference in January, 1974.

the staff member may attempt to define what is and what is not reality and help the patient to test reality or at least help him act in accordance with reality if he is having difficulty defining it for himself. The staff member might sit down and talk with the teenager, attempting to provide an ally in the situation as they then attempt together to find out what is happening. The mere knowledge that staff is aware of the patient's difficulties may help the patient regain controls. Sometimes, two staff members may be more helpful by diffusing the intense paranoia and antagonism that some teenage patients feel toward a specific staff member. The youth can also profit from watching how two other people converse and communicate with each other. This way of operating also enables the ward staff members to provide balance and perspective for each other while increasing their flexibility in dealing with a troublesome situation. The staff may also involve the patient in the decision-making process and try to help him generate some ideas and decisions about what can best help him settle down at the moment. In this way, the patient can begin to learn how to get what he needs even if he can't always get what he wants. Sometimes it is helpful to have a more or less "neutral" person such as the nursing supervisor or a psychiatrist on duty meet with the patient. This new person may enable the teenager to save face, and both staff and patient may profit from the assessment of an outside, more or less objective observer.

These are examples of how talking with and to a patient can be helpful, but in some situations it may be more appropriate for the ward staff not to talk a great deal, but to interact with a disturbed teenager nonverbally. A patient who has difficulty verbalizing his own feelings may not respond to talking, but may feel a considerable amount of support by interacting with ward staff nonverbally. Doing something together can redirect destructive behavior and channel a teenager's energy into activities that may be more healthy and ultimately more gratifying. Engaging in an activity can cut through destructive plans and teach teenagers that it is not always necessary for them to act on exactly what they feel at the moment—that they can function appropriately despite their disturbing feelings. In order to use these activities successfully as interventions, the staff has to know the patient's skills and the requirements of a particular activity. A patient, for example, who is a skilled ping-pong player and needs a "work out" to channel some of his angry feelings might benefit from a few good games. On the other hand, someone who is very agitated and already having trouble coping with a wish to hit somebody might become frustrated in an attempt at playing the game and might escalate further. The simple fact of rapid activity and gross physical movement might accelerate an already agitated patient. For this patient a quieter game such as cards might help to focus energy and provide some inherent physical restrictions by engaging in a game sitting in a chair at a table. Of course, verbal activity can be integrated with nonverbal activity as a staff member converses with the patient about these feelings and difficulties while at the same time carrying on some kind of game.

However, there are times when neither verbal nor nonverbal behavior help calm a patient because either would be too stimulating. At other times, patients may be unable to stop and are compelled to continue their destructiveness in the presence of others. At these times, ward staff may decide to exert greater control and send the patients to their rooms. This maneuver can lessen external stimulation, provide a familiar environment, and help patients feel better being "held" in a smaller, more manageable space. Again, then, the ward staff might be able to interact verbally or nonverbally more therapeutically once the patient is removed from the stimulation of the group. Some teenagers can also "save face" by not having to perform in front of other patients while trying to recover themselves and by not being forced to handle the added burden of other patients' teasing or encouraging them to act out. Of course, some of the encouragement may exist in the teenagers' mind and fantasy as they project onto their peers what they expect of themselves in defying authority. The room can become a safe and private place for teenagers to save face.

However, if it seems that a particular patient is overwhelmed and unable to regain control, it may be necessary to use a quiet room, a room locked and bare of all furnishings so that the patient is provided no objects to hurt himself or someone else. This intervention requires a psychiatrist's order, and constant or frequent contact with staff members. Yet, our own preference when a patient is escalating too rapidly, is unable to respond to other less drastic interventions, or is exhibiting behavior which is too unpredictable and dangerous, is to use full leather restraints. Whenever possible, the patient needs to be interviewed first by a psychiatrist, but sometimes on an emergency basis, that is not possible.

After it has been decided that the patient needs to go into restraints plans are made to prevent injury to other patients, the staff, and the agitated patient. Consequently, it is important that the decision for restraints be made before the patient has lost all control and is already striking out. Sometimes, of course, this is not possible. When the staff plans to intervene with this degree of control there should always be enough staff members available to handle whatever situation may arise. Usually ward staff from other units are called, taking into consideration the sex of the patient and which and how many staff members will be needed. It may be necessary to prevent the patient from acquiring potential weapons by removing furniture from the room, locking the patient kitchen or other areas, or having the staff stay with the patient until the rest of the staff arrives to put the patient in restraints. The rest of the patient group must be taken into consideration also. If the patient in question is agitating or threatening others, the staff needs to move much more quickly. Sometimes the patients will feed into each other's agitation and the scene is set for a riot. If it seems that such a situation is incipient, more ward staff are alerted and the hospital security force is asked to stand by.

Once the patient is in full leather restraints, his safety and the safety of others is guaranteed, and the ward staff can begin to help the patient regain personal controls. This might involve using medication, but more often than not involves personal interactions with staff members present in the room. The patient may need restraints in order to begin experiencing the depth and intensity of his anger safely. Once the patient has experienced this rage, the patient may be able to begin to examine ways of channeling feelings constructively. It is quite therapeutic for a staff member to be able to sit with the patient even in the midst of the most terrible and terrifying feelings as both staff and patient recognize that, at the moment at least, no one will get hurt (Fromm-Reichmann, 1959). It may be during this time that the teenager has some chance to understand his behavior, which later on he might not be able to recover once the intensity of his feelings is past.

Restraints can also provide for a teenager's contradictory needs for being held in the middle of violent feelings while at the same time needing physical distance from others, so characteristic of the growth dilemma of adolescence.

With psychotic or near-psychotic patients who are out of touch with realtiy, or with patients who are so overwhelmed by feelings that they cannot interact with staff, a long time is required before the patient is able to regain control and the ward staff can again use themselves therapeutically.

Ideally, staff can intervene in an escalating situation before a breakdown has actually occurred, and some form of verbal intervention is all that is required. This depends, of course, on accurate and precise assessment of a patient's pathology. However, in situations where rapid escalation is taking place, less drastic controls are not sufficient and restraints need to be used immediately. Other factors that need to be taken into consideration are the patient's likelihood to agitate others, a patient's ability to plan an attack and set up a battle, how well a particular shift is staffed, and whether or not the patient is able to be removed from the group to lessen the likelihood of contagion.

Even on well-staffed units, staff concern for their own safety and concern about their own anger towards patients can affect how violent behavior is handled. At these times it is important that ward staff be able to confront and talk with each other so that the intervention made is the best one possible. A nursing supervisor can be a very important help as he has the distance to be objective, but at the same time knows staff's strengths and weaknesses.

At some point in treatment, a teenager is able to take more responsibility for his own behavior and may on occasion anticipate a breakdown and ask for restraints, medication, or an opportunity to be with a staff member. The patient's greater ability to control himself must be respected, but at the same time staff continues to make its own assessment and decides whether, indeed, the patient needs the particular intervention he is seeking. Certainly restraints can become a comfortable maneuver for both patients and staff, and at some point in the patient's treatment may actually interfere with further psychological growth and mastery.

As long as we work with people who need hospitalization, we will probably be confronted with violence. The anxiety a patient feels that may provoke violence can be a useful lever in therapy as long as it is not overwhelming. Above all, treatment must be a safe experience for patients and staff. Although some would say that the use of medication, a quiet room, or physical restraints seem to be contrary to humanitarian purposes and patients' rights, in order for treatment to occur, the unit must be a safe environment, free from serious disruption and threat.

The Therapeutic Use of Physical Restraints

Current clinical practice suggests that the use of physical restraints is falling out of favor. Restraints, considered antiquated remnants of punitive confinement and viewed by many as "cruel and unusual punishment," seem to have been replaced by tranquilizing medication. Prior to the introduction of phenothiazine medication, hydrotherapy, wet packs, seclusion, isolation, and physical restraints were all therapeutic modalities used to prevent injury to the self or to others, and to soothe and calm an agitated and destructive patient.

Wexler (1951) describes the use of force in the psychoanalytic treatment of a violent, schizophrenic patient. He describes the difficulty in discussing this openly with other professionals; his justification for the use of physical force is that a behavioral response is necessary to prevent a patient's omnipotence from running amok, and he suggests that the patient cannot tolerate the unprecedented power she would have been given had he not responded. He suggests that it is not love, but rather fear and hatred, that causes a therapist to abandon a patient to his own emotional vicissitudes.

As with the growing child, it is sometimes necessary to hold a patient, and hold him tightly, so that he will not be overwhelmed by his own rage and urges. This attitude places the restraining process within the context of an overall treatment milieu, as do Holmes and Werner

(1966) when they describe restraining a patient within the context of other therapeutic interactions with the milieu staff. Lion, Levenberg, and Strange (1972) give practical recommendations for the therapeutic use of restraints and indicate that while verbal interactions and limit-setting should be tried first, it is frequently necessary to help a violent patient (whether the patient be an adolescent testing limits or a delusional psychotic patient) deal with the fears of his own destructiveness and his yearning, overtly or covertly, for limits on his own urges. Goldberg and Rubin (1970) note that patients use various aspects of the hospital experience as transitional objects to pacify themselves, and the interventions used are themselves repetitions of the patients' early childhood experiences; in other words, the kinds of interactions that patients utilize with staff to calm and soothe themselves replicate ways in which their parents soothed and calmed them, or failed to soothe and calm them. Consequently, a variety of therapeutic interventions need to be available on the unit to help patients who are struggling with violent urges and are becoming increasingly fragmented and out of control.

In this neuroleptic era, many psychiatrists believe that tranquilizing medication has replaced physical restraints in the therapeutic armamentarium, that restraints should be used only as a last resort with dangerous or violent patients, and that when restraints are used, it is only because of deficiencies in the quality or quantity of ward personnel. We believe that the use of physical restraints becomes a symbolic extension of a nurturing parent holding a child and should not be viewed as a "last resort," but rather as the treatment of choice with certain kinds of patients in certain situations. Staff should be able to diagnose and anticipate incipient fragmentation and intervene quickly and should also be adept at other kinds of interventions such as spending time with patients or talking with the patients, or helping patients remove themselves from a stimulating situation. To view restraints as a punitive or sadistic intervention or as an indication of serious staff deficiency misses the point and may only inhibit staff and prevent patients from receiving the very kind of control that they need.

With the advent of behavior modification approaches, with increasingly legal definitions of therapy, and greater emphasis on patients' rights, physical restraints are seen as the consequences of certain behavior and justified or not justified as appropriate punitive responses, like sentences handed down in court with the punishment fitting the crime. The patient has the right to refuse this aspect of treatment and to demand due process. This again misses the point; physical restraining of a patient is definitive treatment and is part of the psychiatric armamentarium of diagnosing a disturbance and prescribing the appropriate treatment.

Verbal abuse, threats, and damage to property often precede violence to person, with patients quickly escalating to such violence. This violence, however, is not to be equated with hostility, rage, or anger; some violence arises from psychic disorganization and is massive random motor discharge resulting from traumatic overstimulation and fragmentation (Marohn, 1974; Marohn, Dalle-Molle, Offer, and Ostrov, 1973). Prompt and appropriate staff interventions are crucial in preventing or treating escalating or disintegrating behavior. Medication may decrease internal stimulation and paranoia, but may also interfere with certain aspects of patient-staff contact. Personal verbal responses by staff may provide direction, limit-setting, and comfort to disturbed patients. Removing a patient from a stimulating situation may eliminate contagion and peer stimulation. We do not use a quiet room, but rather help the patient remove himself from a stimulating experience to his own room where he is reassured by such familiar surroundings as his radio, posters, books, stuffed animals, and the like.

Holding the patient as a parent holds a child may restrain the patient from hurting himself or others, may soothe and reassure him, may provide external ego controls, may help establish body ego boundaries, and may provide organization and structure for a fragmented self. The use of physical restraints also accomplishes these ends. Tammy, a 15-year-old girl, returned several months after her discharge from the hospital to report that she continued to experience some anxiety attending school on the outside. She stated that the first time in her life that she had felt calm was when she was in restraints and that she had never before experienced such comfort. Now when she becomes frightened, she remembers what it was like to be placed in restraints, and is able to calm herself down. This suggests an internalization of a therapeutic modality, not yet operating silently, but somewhat akin to the child having begun the process of internalizing an object representation and moving in the direction of performing such functions for herself as she progresses psychologically.

However, with adolescent and adult patients, their physical size and the very real possibilities of homosexual or heterosexual stimulation create problems with staff holding patients. Physical restraints correspond with adolescent patients' contradictory needs for being held while experiencing violent feelings and for needing physical distance from others. Physical restraints, when used in conjunction with staff's affective, verbal interventions, serve as extensions of and substitutions for holding; this must be done within the total treatment context, with policies and procedures clearly and mutually understood. Thus, on our unit, patients are informed why restraints are used, how they are applied, and what happens when the patient is in restraints. If the situation permits, patients are informed that they will be placed in restraints. Both of these steps are aimed at helping the patient integrate and cooperate with the experience.

The most important factor in helping patients deal with their own violent propensities is the attitude towards physical violence that develops among the staff; this, above all else, establishes a unit culture. Illustrative of the work we do in establishing this culture are the following several sections taken from the current staff policy manual of the Delinquency Treatment Unit:

Threatening

Threatening is an unacceptable behavior which indicates loss of control or potential violent behavior. It is taken seriously and requires staff response. Determining the appropriate behavioral response requires careful consideration.

If we always use the Adolescent Progress Review (A.P.R.) restriction as a response to a verbal threat we undercut the seriousness of the A.P.R., but also the effectiveness of the individual staff member's restriction or ability to deal with the situation.

We must assess the seriousness of the threatening that has taken place and determine what, if any, behavior accompanied the threat. If a patient, angry and in an impulsive manner, states "I'll get you," this is a threat but doesn't call for an A.P.R. restriction. However, if a patient comes at you or picks up an object while stating "I'll get you," there is a much different quality about that and indeed may warrant a behavioral intervention as well as an A.P.R. restriction.

We must use our common sense and depend on each other to assess and decide on what threat requires an A.P.R. restriction, and what doesn't.

Physical Contact

The following attitudes have been established to provide controls around merging, seductiveness, setting up to hit, and other forms of destructive contact.

Contact with staff members: There is no reason for a patient to be touching or hanging onto a staff member except for the touching that takes place in a structured activity such as recreation. All incidents are brought to the attention of the patient. Unless the staff judge otherwise, he is helped to see that this is a breakdown of boundaries. If a staff member touches a patient it is never without warning, even if the patient is going in to full leather restraints. A patient should not be touched without specific reason.

Contact with patients: Contact between patients is not allowed. Patients are not allowed to lean on each other in chairs, hold hands, neck, pet, etc. Shoving, slapping, etc. is considered serious aggressive behavior and is covered by the violence policy.

Violence

Realizing that as we try to prevent violent behavior it still occurs, we need a unified and consistent attitude, policy, and procedure for dealing with it. This lowers the probability that property will be damaged or that someone will be hurt or killed through thoughtless, haphazard, and disorganized responses to violent behavior. This program admits patients who are unable to control their own violent urges without help. It is expected that the entire staff will make a serious attempt to provide this help.

It is felt that there is no stronger agent of intervention than the unified staff attitude. The present staff attitude toward violence is that it is extremely serious even in its least aggressive-looking forms and that it is not expected to happen. Our response starts with seriously setting limits on any kind of verbal threatening, or misuse of physical objects in the environment. Violence, verbal or physical, against person or things is not to occur. Questions regarding motivations for such behaviors or declarations that the patient needs help are important, but often dangerous if posed during the ongoing situation. They often serve as aggravations. Dealing directly with the behavior is far more important until the behavior stops. Our experience shows that to attempt to do anything not aimed at stopping the behavior is to invite trouble. Explanations, bargains, reevaluations, justifications or anything that delays control over the situation should never be explored during or prior to stopping the violent behavior. It is useful, however, to assure the adolescent that he will have a chance to air his grievance once management is no longer an issue.

There are two policies that deal with violence on 6 West. One deals with verbal aggression and aggressive agitation, the other deals with physical aggression. All staff members should be well acquainted with these.

Verbal aggression and aggressive agitation are a probable starting place for physical aggression. Therefore, this is an important behavior to be aware of and limit. The recommended response is a firm limit on the behavior followed by sending the patient to his room to consider the meaning of the verbal abuse.

There are times when the patient can do this without the isolation of the room, but these times are rare and we need to teach such verbally aggressive adolescents the value of using their rooms when the environment (internal or external) becomes so threatening or frightening that they must threaten back.

The purpose of taking physical aggression seriously is to protect all patients and staff from physical injury, to prevent destruction to property, to prevent escalation of violent urges and panic among patients, beginning at their earliest manifestations.

Procedure: 1. Know the program's policy on violence

2. Be aware of outstanding incidents of:

a. verbal abuse—direct and indirect
b. misuse and disrespect for community property

    c. abuse toward own property and room
    d. abuse toward other patients and their property
    e. abuse toward staff
    f. abuse toward other persons

Response to any of the above behaviors is to be direct, predictable, and immediate.

If their level of agitation is high during verbal abuse patients are to be sent to their room to calm down and to provide them with some distance from the immediate situation, as well as an opportunity for one to one contact with staff.

6 West Policy Re: Physical Violence

Definition: Any physical aggression directed against property, against self, or against another person.

Placement in room is the immediate response to any physical aggression against person or property.

Physical aggression directed against another person or against property will result in in-room status and immediate suspension of all program activities. The chief or acting chief should then be notified and make a decision if Special A.P.R. will meet. If the decision is for the Special A.P.R. to meet, then the in-room status continues as long as ward staff deems necessary.

Suspension of program activities includes:

1. No School
2. No O.T., R.T.
3. No special activity meetings
4. Meals in room
5. Ward meeting participation will be decided by ward meeting leader and ward staff charge person
6. Individual sessions will be decided by therapist and ward staff.

Special A.P.R. usually meet when necessary at 2 p.m. the next working day. All people necessary for understanding the incident will be interviewed by the Special A.P.R. to determine whether modifications in the patient's treatment program are indicated. If discharge of the patient is necessary, evaluation is made regarding transfer to another facility or discharge to home.

Changes in the patient's privileges on the unit and recommenda-
tion to the team of possible changes in the treatment plan will also
be made by the Special A.P.R.

Physical Control of Patients

This unit's policies on the use of Full Leather Restraints (F.L.R.)
have been developed over a period of years. The policies and
attitude concerning F.L.R. have evolved as the staff has worked
with and observed the needs of disturbed adolescent patients. The
use of F.L.R. must be understood in the context of the total
program.

The majority of patients on our unit constantly live with an
impulse control problem—they have the strong tendency to act
before thinking about the consequences of their actions. A good
part of treatment in the milieu consists of helping these patients
in controlling and managing their impulses. We are continually
striving to help disturbed adolescents realize and accept the consequences of their behavior. We help them to learn that they can
control their own behavior, and then help them select and use
alternative ways of dealing with their feelings.

Over a period of time this staff has noticed that before patients
totally lose control of their impulses, they more often than not
give many indications that this is about to happen. For example,
a patient may spit on the floor or damage a chair; next he may
verbally threaten someone; next, he may strike out and hit (totally losing control). Our job as milieu therapist is to confront the
slightest case of an impulse problem—in the above example, that
was spitting on the floor. This behavior would be confronted and
the patient helped to accept responsibility for spitting on the floor;
for instance by cleaning the floor, talking with staff, spending time
in his room, receiving a restriction, or some other behavioral
response.

By a close observation of the behavior of adolescent patients we
should have a good indication of the control that patients have
over themselves. By intervening early in a behavior that indicates
a beginning of loss of control, we prevent the escalation which
results in total loss of control, such as hitting. Using these principles the milieu staff has become quite skilled in dealing with
adolescent patients with impulse control problems, and has come
a long way towards preventing patients from totally losing control.

F.L.R. is one of the tools our staff uses in helping adolescents to learn to control themselves. If behaviorally an adolescent patient indicates to us that he is approaching being out of control, and other interventions have failed, we feel F.L.R. is essential in helping that patient control himself. This avoids putting the patient in a position where he does lose control to the point of striking someone. In other words, in keeping with our practice in dealing with impulse control problems, we will use F.L.R. *before* a patient has totally lost control.

F.L.R. is based on the immediate need of the adolescent patient, not as punishment or the result of staff frustration. As an example, suppose an adolescent patient was continually talking loudly in the dayroom, and in doing so disturbing other patients and staff. Assuming the patient was not responding to verbal limits to quiet down, our response would be to send that patient to his room, a tool often used in helping adolescents control their behavior. Alone, perhaps talking with staff, the patient has time to calm down and give some thought to his behavior. After a period of time (the length depending on a number of factors) the patient is allowed to return to the dayroom when a staff member feels he has enough control to interact appropriately in the dayroom with other patients and staff.

Suppose, however, the adolescent patient goes to the room but does not stay there, coming out without first having dealt with a staff member. At this point, a clear limit is set, letting the patient know that we clearly expect him to return to the room. We have learned that adolescent patients can use time and distance (often to save face in front of peers), and in this regard, a time limit may be set on the patient (two to three minutes) and staff may give the patient distance by going into the nursing station. All activities in the dayroom (cards, TV, etc.) may be stopped to stress the importance of the patient returning to his room. If the patient does not return to his room, this behavior tells us he is experiencing a possible loss of control and may need help before further loss occurs. The individual's past behavior and pathology are also considered. The patient may appear calm and relaxed, but his behavior suggests something entirely the opposite. If it is evaluated that F.L.R. is indicated, the patient is informed he is going into restraints; our staff will then use male help to physically carry (if necessary) the patient to his room and place him in F.L.R. This is actually meeting the needs of the disturbed adolescent and is not punitive.

Our patients need to know the milieu is a safe environment; they need to know that if they can't control themselves, the staff can and will. These adolescents have had trouble throughout their lives dealing with their anger and impulses; they are frightened of what anger will force them to do. To a disturbed adolescent about to lose control, words and rationale mean very little—he needs a behavioral response that will help him deal with the extreme fear, anger, and anxiety he is experiencing. In this regard, for the adolescent in the above example, the message we give him by using F.L.R. is extremely important; namely, that we have the ability to control and deal with his impulses. At some level it is a relief for that patient to know that we will take over the job of controlling his unruly impulses. Treatment cannot take place on our unit unless these disturbed adolescents feel secure in knowing that we can control their angry behavior. F.L.R. is a tool which helps us to do this.

Our adolescent patients are fully aware of our attitude concerning restraints. Except in cases of extreme emergency, patients are informed prior to going into F.L.R. Also, once a patient is told he is going to be placed in restraints, we never back down on this. The patients also know that they, themselves, may ask for the use of F.L.R. if they feel they are getting out of control, something which several patients have done; then the staff make an assessment to determine if the patient actually is in need of F.L.R.

Staff members who administer F.L.R. have been trained in hospital courses in which they have mastered techniques in how to apply F.L.R. in a manner which is safe for both patients and staff.

In the course of each patient's hospitalization, we would expect that the need for restraints would decrease as the patient begins to internalize controls and develop the capacity to soothe himself. With some patients we see utilization of restraints shifting from the patients' being restrained against their will, to being restrained without opposition, to requesting restraints, as they begin to internalize treatment interventions and develops an increased capacity to modulate their own behavior, although not yet autonomously. In response to such a request, staff members need to assess whether or not restraints should be used or whether other kinds of interventions should be attempted. Additionally, as staff develop skills in preventing acts of violence through increased knowledge of each patient and early diagnosis and intervention, the use of restraints with each patient should decrease.

The use of restraints needs to be conceptualized as part of the therapeutic armamentarium, a continuum of therapeutic responses that are available to staff to deal with a myriad of behaviors which may eventually escalate to violence. To dismiss this intervention as old-fashioned sadism or countertransference problems suggests a superficial approach to the treatment of the violent delinquent.

In a situation where physical restraints are appropriate treatment, to withhold them is nontherapeutic and may indeed be a violation of the patient's right to treatment.

ADOLESCENT PROGRESS REVIEW (A.P.R.)

The Adolescent Progress Review is a weekly meeting of the administrative staff of the unit—the chief of the unit, the milieu supervisor, the activity supervisor, the school principal, and the social work supervisor—who, along with the psychotherapist, meet to review each patient's progress or lack of progress during the previous week, discuss any management decisions such as changes in privileges, and/or grant passes that are consistent both with the behavior and the understanding of the patient's dynamics and treatment plan as derived in separate treatment team meetings. On this unit, authority is shared authority in which the therapist participates. The purpose of the treatment team meetings is to assess, infer, and prescribe treatment; it is an opportunity for all the disciplines to integrate their understanding of the patient and his behavior, and for the psychotherapist to integrate the clinical transference with the behaviors observed elsewhere in the program. This team makes major management decisions such as when the patient is ready for his first home visit and when a patient is ready for discharge; other management decisions are made by the A.P.R. The patient meets with the A.P.R. and gets feedback about his work in activities, in school, his behavior on the unit, his family, and, particularly from the chief of the unit, what further work needs to be done in psychotherapy and in other aspects of his program.

Changes in privileges are then mentioned and discussed and patients have an opportunity to question, seek clarification, and respond to various aspects of his particular program.

The A.P.R. serves to highlight the kind of psychological support and structure that is available externally to the disturbed adolescent. It reinforces the primary value in our treatment culture, namely the importance of self-observation and understanding, and the idea that behavior flows from an internal psychological world, an understanding of which can be integrated into one's personality. It demonstrates rather clearly for the teenager how the team works together, and how all aspects of the hospital program are integrated with each other and with the work of psychotherapy. It respects the patients' ideas and feelings by providing them an opportunity to discuss these with the administrative staff, without implying that the patients are in control of their own treatment.

The A.P.R., like the ward meeting, is one of those opportunities for each patient to have personal contact with the chief of the unit. The role and person of the chief of the unit in the A.P.R. is crucial. We have already emphasized the importance of the chief in maintaining the authority structure of the unit. There is considerable evidence in the treatment of delinquent adolescents that idealization of the therapist is a crucial factor in a successful outcome (Marohn, 1977). An indecisive and uncertain therapist cannot convey to the adolescent a sense of security and confidence, and this may interfere with the unfolding of an idealizing transference. An adolescent's ability to idealize is an important sign in determining a favorable or unfavorable prognosis. At the same time, it may very well be that patients may show their capacity to idealize a therapist through the mode of habitual deidealization and depreciation.

In a similar vein, the chief of the unit, like the therapist, must be firm, consistent, principled, and decisive. The chief must feel comfortable in saying no and setting limits, and willing to frustrate the urgent demands of patients and staff when necessary. Such leadership by the chief provides not only the organization which the social system of the treatment unit requires, but also further opportunities for the emergence of idealizing transferences. Such idealizations are closely related to the kind of working or therapeutic alliance that occurs in treatment, and is certainly the basis for group formation and cohesion (Freud, 1921; Kohut, 1976).

This phenomenon is often reflected in the charismatic personality of many individuals who run adolescent treatment units. Such charisma may be particularly appealing to adolescents, especially behaviorally disordered adolescents. We suspect, however, that charisma may have its limitations. If the success of the treatment program depends solely on the idealization or overidealization of its leader, the program will eventually flounder, just as therapy will flounder when its success depends solely upon the idealization or overidealization of a particularly gifted therapist. Certain ideal relationships are successful as long as contact is maintained, but they fail because in many instances, the staff of the program or the patients have failed to internalize the ideas, indeed the functions, which must ultimately replace the attachment to attractive personal attributes of a leader or therapist. If treatment means incorporating highly personalized and exciting qualities of the leader, the staff and patients are crippled because they are dependent on the chief's idiosyncrasies and have become members of a cult. Certain principles and beliefs of the chief or therapist will become the patient's and influence his attitudes about himself and his ways of relating to others. Relationships with persons are changed into functions and become part of the psychological structure of the staff and the patient. Such transmuting internalizations (Kohut, 1971) are much more likely to guarantee the ultimate survival of a change process, in contrast to therapeutic efforts which are comparable to exciting infatuations or dramatic religious conversions. Change, internal change, after all, is a slow and laborious process and is not to be equated with a love affair.

SCHOOL*

Although student-patients have been hospitalized for psychiatric in-

---

* This section is based in part on the paper "Integrating Psychotherapy and Academic Functioning—Use of the Crisis Teacher in a Hospital School" presented by Judith Kahn Marohn, M.A., Principal, Adolescent School, at the Annual Meeting of the American Society for Adolescent Psychiatry, Toronto, Canada, April 29, 1977.

dications, many have learning deficits or problems; some, however, function at, near, or above expected grade level. Most patients in the program are expected to attend school as an age-appropriate task; other goals for their in-hospital education are individualized and may include remedial work in specific subject areas, grade-level work to maintain academic functioning, and the accumulation of credits to be added to those already earned and used toward eighth grade or high school graduation. From time to time some patients have remained in the school following discharge from the unit for specific treatment reasons related to discharge plans.

The school staff meets regularly to consider students' progress, to review new patients' school histories and academic achievement test results, to determine educational plans best suited to each one's needs, to participate in in-service training, and to discuss the day's work. It is important that the school staffing be provided not by an outside agency organization such as a school district, but rather that the educators be employed by, salaried by, and under the administrative control of the program director. Too often, if separate school funding is provided as an economy measure and lines of school authority are distinct from the treatment program, the school exists in a vacuum and there is no integration of academic goals with treatment goals. On the other hand, a danger at the opposite end of the spectrum is that educators are judged and judge themselves by the standards of mental health professionals, and derive their sense of competence not from the dictates of their own profession, but rather by standards of therapeutic efficacy. We want the work of our educators to be integrated with the work of the treatment program, but not immersed in it, nor separate and distinct from it. The principal, educators, and the educational diagnostician participate actively in the deliberations of the inpatient unit: screen prospective and new patients and contact home schools to obtain past school histories; participate in discharge planning, sometimes traveling to schools for consultation with or without the student, and frequently making arrangements by phone; communicate with home schools about discharged patients; participate in all treatment teams of each student-patient, sharing observations made in school and integrating team discussions and formulations with academic planning as appropriate; and attend and participate in the weekly staff meeting of the unit, program case conferences, work conferences, and in-service training classes.

Classes on several academic levels are provided in English, social studies, science, and math to accommodate the differing abilities and needs of students, in addition to classes in consumer education, typing, shorthand, and drafting. All courses are designed to meet the needs of individual students and/or the group, and, consequently, may change over a semester as student-patients are discharged and new ones are enrolled in school. Homework is assigned as the lesson plans necessitate for the group and/or individuals. The teachers use standard textbooks, teacher-developed lessons, a variety of audio-visual equipment, and public library books in their curricula. When appropriate for the class and not contraindicated by individual treatment plans, field trips are conducted. Class enrollments, with the exception of some physical education classes, range from one to six students, depending on the numbers of students in need of a class as well as the need for individualized instruction and support.

Physical education classes are coeducational and required for all patient-students unless medically contraindicated. The classes meet three times a week for 50 minutes and consist of units of activity and a regular exercise program, which is different for boys and girls. The instructors, one male and one female, are activity therapists. The units of activity are aimed at physical skill building and sportsmanship/team cooperation, and include tennis, tumbling, volleyball, track and field, and basketball.

Books, both hardcover and paperback, at various levels of reading difficulty and ranges of interest, are available for students to check out from the school on a weekly basis with options for renewal; current periodicals are also available on the same basis.

Severely disturbed adolescents can separate their personal conflicts and deficits from day-to-day tasks and can fully participate in school classes, while elsewhere focusing on their personal problems. The educators' main function is to work with students in a structured academic atmosphere on behavior related to the mastery of learning skills and academic material. Therefore, students should be prepared for classes each day with required materials and completed homework, reasonable school dress and appearance, and appropriate academic and school behavior with teachers and peers. Built into the school program and the school-unit working relationships are support systems for students unable to meet these general expectations.

Grades are given in all classes, and report cards are issued every half-semester and at the end of summer school. Students are responsible for having their card signed by their therapist and a parent or guardian, unless contraindicated in terms of treatment, and returning it to the school. We do not offer General Educational Development Test (GED) preparation because we feel that our classrooms provide, above and beyond the academic material, ingredients important to patients' progress. We want our patients to learn that gains come from personal involvement and that developing skills and abilities necessary for future success is more important than passing a test.

Individual tutoring for patients who are too regressed for classroom involvement is not available because we make clear distinctions between the role of the educator and that of other staff members who interact with patients around issues of psychotherapy on a daily basis. In individual tutoring for such patients, the educator's role becomes that of a therapist as well. Patients not yet ready for academics make important and necessary gains interacting with staff in therapeutic areas of the structured daily program before they are ready to begin classes. Similarly, we do not ask home schools to send work for patients to complete independently or in tutoring. The classroom experience is of great importance to our patients, most of whom have had academic and/or behavioral problems in school in the past, and we believe that they need to be involved here, not have one foot here and another outside.

All students are tested with academic achievement tests prior to enrollment; students' assets and deficits are examined, their placement and progress in school prior to hospitalization considered, and recommendations about class enrollment made to the entire treatment team where final decisions are reached. Specific academic and behavioral goals are determined by the school staff for each student for each class to which he is assigned. Initial and annual educational conferences with the parents and social worker are part of this planning process. In general, students begin with one or two classes, adding others up to a total of four (excluding physical education), as deemed appropriate by the school staff in conjunction with the treatment planning team.

School is the "work" of adolescents. Here, conflict-free spheres or areas of their personality are called into play; even the most disturbed delinquent adolescents are capable of functioning at some level of competence in a classroom situation, but this may require support from the ward staff and therapist before it can happen and to compromise or shorten that process is to cheat the teenagers.

In emphasizing academics rather than therapeutics, we try to help the students develop, as elsewhere in the program, internalized skills like studying, dissecting problems, planning how to tackle a school task, and the like. We want our students to learn how to learn, just as in other aspects of the program we try to teach them how to introspect. In both instances, we attempt to provide models and functions for them, which eventually we expect they will internalize and be able to perform for themselves.

The classroom experience is of great importance for our students, and we try to help them separate out the classroom experience from other aspects of their therapy. For example, we encourage them to separate the work done in the classroom from the turmoil or conflicts they experience in their treatment sessions, family visits, or interactions with the ward staff. Although we recognize that such experiences may tax them, we have a treatment program which will help them work on those difficulties, yet provide for and protect those intact areas of the personality which can approach, understand, and master academic material. Our emphasis on learning may help the adolescent to achieve formal or abstract thinking (Dulit, 1972), an achievement of academic, and some therapeutic importance. Our students should be properly prepared every day with the required materials and completed homework so that they can engage in class as required by each teacher and by the dictates of the subject material. Their performance will be affected by their educational levels and abilities, and not necessarily disrupted by emotionally stressful experiences elsewhere in the treatment program. The teachers work not to provide psychotherapy, but to help students master learning skills and the material itself.

A "crisis teacher" is available and can provide a "time out" period from the actual classroom, during which the student is helped to refocus and return to the learning task (Morse, 1965). When a student is having difficulty, the teacher calls the crisis teacher and explains, in the presence of the student, the nature of the difficulty. The crisis teacher then works with the student and reviews the events with him attempting to separate the academic tasks from personal problems. Sometimes, if this fails, the student will be returned to the unit, but in most instances, the intervention is successful for various reasons. The student is removed from the pressure of peer group influence, and may "save face." He is removed from whatever narcissistic injuries might have been experienced in the transference with the teacher in the classroom and is provided another opportunity to work out the difficulties. The student is helped to exercise further the capacity to observe oneself, a function encouraged and fostered elsewhere in the program as well, and so this intervention is consistent with other aspects of the therapeutic milieu. The intervention of the crisis teacher occurs in an open and confronting way, minimizing and eliminating secrets. Providing such external structure and limits gives many students the freedom to perform; the consistency, predictability, and availability of the crisis teacher echoes the responsiveness of the entire program.

OCCUPATIONAL THERAPY SHOP

Occupational Therapy is a predictable structure within the program. Attendance in shop is routine, and each adolescent participates at a specific time each day. This regularity is important for several reasons. Many of our adolescents lack the skills and controls to be self-motivating. This inability can be attributed to a lack of internal structure evident in debilitating feelings of apathy and boredom. Unlike healthy teenagers who show an ever increasing capacity for pursuing interests and enjoying their growing competence in them, our adolescents become distressed when confronted with organizing time around the pursuit of an interest and defining what these interests might be. The regularity of the O.T. hour provides the external framework in which the adolescent can more freely address the task of definition.

The shop setting is also predictable. The physical space defines the work which takes place there, and the mode of expression is recognized as "doing." The shop has a wide range of activities in which the adolescent can engage while staff assess how much and what kind of involvement, the degree of complexity, time limits, and the essential skill factors that will be required in order to complete a project sucessfully. Shop activities can be a source of growth, provided that the complexity of the tasks as well as the adolescent's deficits are assessed. One of the first tasks the adolescent faces in shop is to choose a project. This initial step already tells us a great deal about the disturbed adolescent. Impulsive patients are easily overstimulated in shop because the physical setting itself communicates "action" and the impulsive adolescent cannot explore the environment, but is impelled to react to it. The impulsive adolescent reacts to numerous stimuli in the shop as well as his own internal disorganization, and he has great difficulty making an appropriate choice. For instance, Paul would become increasingly agitated when he had to select a new project. He would scan shop samples or project cabinets and decide quickly on a project without any consideration of the work involved. His selection was based on "that looks like fun," but he would be relieved when choices were limited for him. Through repeated and predictable external structuring, Paul began to monitor his own ability to choose, and delayed himself by looking through craft books before making a decision.

The way other adolescents choose projects reflects their difficulty in maintaining a sense of self as differentiated from others. They are so merged with the therapist or other patients in shop that their choices are governed by their perceptions of how others react. For example, Olivia would point to another patient's work and say "I'll make one of those," or she would observe her therapist looking at a project and immediately choose that, and was also so undifferentiated from "things" in the shop that she would make detailed copies. Only later could she seek out projects which expressed her own sense of autonomy and individuality.

Adolescents who are more aware of and conflicted about their lack of separateness may become intensely anxious and frightened when experimenting with choices of projects. They go to great lengths to choose something "different" in an attempt to master feelings of confusion about their own uniqueness and find it too threatening to use samples, books, or suggestions as guides in making choices. Diane, who in individual therapy had been struggling to separate from the hospital, wanted to make a leather purse in shop. She insisted on making her own pattern for the purse and had drawn out a picture of it; she was aware of a file containing a variety of basic purse patterns but disdained using the file. By making her own pattern, she derived satisfaction that it was "my own" pattern, even though, once completed, she amusedly commented, "It looks a lot like the patterns in the file cabinet, doesn't it?"

Human deprivation and neediness overshadow choosing a project for some adolescents. Alice, for example, chose a preassembled wood box for a project, but was not interested in painting, staining, or putting a design on it because she said that she liked it the way it was. Such lack of adornment typified the impoverishment of her relationships, and satisfied her need for immediate gratification. With some encouragement, she decided that she would paint the box but then wanted six more boxes to paint, just as she would frequently take samples from the shelves, say how she liked them, and ask to keep them. She, like others, could not distinguish something to do and choosing something to have. Margaret, similarly, had stolen several articles from other patients. When staff went to her room to help her sort out which articles belonged to others, they discovered numerous scraps of craft materials that she had pilfered from the shop. When confronted, Margaret told staff "These are my projects."

Adolescents who exaggerate their abilities show their difficulty in choosing a project by being unable to communicate their ideas and by distorting what might be realistically possible, especially as their grandiosity is stimulated by success. Nancy, for example, had completed several decoupage projects, gradually needing less assistance with her work. One morning, however, she came into shop and presented her idea of making a miniature house with partitioned rooms, furniture, and windows, along with various other trimmings. As she described her plan, her thoughts became more confused, and she began rambling diffusely about how her idea would work. As she began to realize the disorganized content of her communications, she ended in an enraged outburst, "I know it can work; I saw one before." A patient's grandiosity can be expressed in other ways as well, as when Ned was told that his choice of a project was completely unworkable, and he retorted, "What would have happened if everyone told Columbus his ideas wouldn't work?" Others have referred to their ideas as "masterpieces," "Picasso like," or "works of art to be treasured in the Art Institute." At times these statements were not meant to be humorous. Fourteen-year-old Alice sincerely believed that her scribbles made when very young were beautiful and artistic because her mother had saved them. She believed that her work was admired by all.

Other patients may symbolize their feelings of detachment and of being distorted and different in a choice of projects. For months Ernie wanted to make high-heeled black boots, a huge black cape that reached to the ground, and a black wide-rimmed hat to "wear down the streets." As Ernie gradually began to experience more realistic achievements, these fantasies subsided and he showed great delight in doing projects similar to those of other patients. At one point, while showing another adolescent his decoupage work, he said how much he liked his own project and, "Remember how nice yours looked? I can't believe it; these things really come out nice, don't they?"

The process of choosing a project is greatly influenced by how the adolescent organizes his world. Many of our teenagers cannot integrate various life experiences into their personalities. By building on interest and skills, they begin to develop inner resources and actualize their own potentials, implying both self-awareness and separateness from others. Such growth is concretely expressed in shop when adolescents begin to choose projects which have more personal meaning for them based on either likes or an increased differentiation from others. Early in treatment, patients may choose to make projects for family members and describe their selection as "something to do." Robert wanted to make the same ceramic mold for several relatives, varying only the colors of the glaze. When asked what a specific relative might prefer, he could not offer a physical description of that person, much less his likes, tastes, or individual qualities. Once increased differentiation occurs, the patient can choose projects that are specifically designed for distinct persons.

Many of our patients have difficulty thinking in terms of consequences; they do not anticipate, for example, the short-term or long-range results of a burglary and even deny that consequences are important. They approach the concrete task of planning in shop in a similar way. While planning to put a design he had made onto a wood backing, Kirk was reluctant to use a ruler to insure uniformity in placing the design. When asked what would happen to the design if he did not use the ruler, he responded "Well, how am I supposed to know?" Our patients with severe ego deficits do not experience planning as a guideline for directing their work. Since our patients have difficulty in imagining or projecting into the future, they react with discouragement, hopelessness, and withdrawal. At these times, the occupational therapist can provide the support to separate feelings of hopelessness from the task itself.

> Cal would usually have constructive and potentially workable ideas about what projects to do, but when he needed to initiate concrete plans, he would become increasingly distant and passive. Once he interrupted his withdrawal by inserting a joke into a conversation across the room; this elicited laughter and more joking throughout the group. The joke was an attempt to establish contact rather than an attempt at humor. When Cal had to make plans, he felt isolated and unable to organize his thinking. When the occupational therapist recognized this pattern, she spent time with Cal, helping him to think through a workable plan and to assuage feelings of hopelessness.

Planning, by its very nature, demands a postponement of action. Impulsive adolescents cannot delay gratification and may experience intolerable frustration when even limited delay might be required to plan. Sometimes, planning, as a necessary step, is not even considered. Theresa, for example, showed some capacity for delay when she would call out to the occupational therapist, "What should I do next?" If help was not immediately forthcoming, she would revert to disorganized and often destructive behavior. Once, while waiting for help with a color arrangement, Theresa found the wait intolerable and proceeded to paint on her own, but the resultant smearing of colors enraged her. While reflecting on this experience, she said "I thought you weren't going to come." When an adolescent cannot tolerate frustration, modulate feelings, and postpone action, the staff must be available. Through repeated experiences of real and predictable staff availability, the patient will gradually develop a greater tolerance for delay. Betty had progressed to this point; while waiting for assistance, she went to her project box and busied herself by cleaning it out. At other times she might "fill the time" by washing the shop sink, watering the plants, or watching the fish in the aquarium. Other waiting adolescents progress beyond "keeping busy" and begin to organize their thoughts about how to proceed. When the adolescent sees that a successful outcome is due in part to thoughtful and purposeful planning, he enjoys the process itself.

Thoughtful planning is different from "over planning" which is obsessive and constricting and results in unnecessary delay. Such "planning" represents a need to control everything, a fear of inner imperfection, or a fear of inner disintegration. Ernie would spend many shop hours obsessively going over a project plan and would repeat the same plan in different forms making minute changes over and over again. Although each plan was feasible, he felt the need to remeasure and rework it constantly. Ernie sought perfection in order to gain control over his perception of himself as very damaged.

Completing a project, like planning, is a clearly defined concrete shop task through which adolescents develop skills in predicting and guiding their own actions. How adolescents approach this task reflects concerns about their competency, expressed in erratic fluctuations in their daily performance. Disturbed adolescents with no sense of continuity cannot follow through on even short-lived commitments, and cannot sustain involvement in their project. Many of our teenagers who attend shop daily "forget" what work they had done the previous day, and even "forget" the very project on which they were working.

Although adolescents might enjoy the work they are doing, this feeling may last only for the duration of the shop hour. Paul would come to shop and wonder what he should do. One day, when he was asked what he had done the day before, he thought for a moment, smiled, and said "O yeah, my belt." Such adolescents benefits from a structured time at the beginning and end of each hour in which to reflect on and integrate their ongoing work.

The inability to appraise work because of unrealistic goals may cause adolescents to lose interest in a project. Ernie so closely evaluated each step of his project that he took a long time to complete his work. He struggled with various solutions to make his work look better. He could not readily trust others' assessments, more benign and less rigid than his, but as he sought outside opinions, he greeted the occupational therapist's approval of his work with "Well, if you say so." Such harshness with oneself can have other causes as well. Carla repeated projects she had done at the hospital from which she had been recently transferred. She complained that her work was not right and became so exasperated that she pushed the project away and demanded to leave. As she discussed this further she said "I've done this before. Sometimes, I think there is something wrong with the tools, but maybe it's me." She was relieved when she expressed the fear that she had "lost abilities" gained during her previous hospitalization. This fear was kindled by her transfer and caused her to minimize her work in shop. She, like other adolescents, needed the presence of another person to help her reflect on and assess and appraise her work. Generally, our adolescents have a limited capacity for self-reflection because they do not integrate actions with thoughts, feelings, and intentions. Paul responded to the occupational therapist's compliments with, "You helped me a lot," by which he meant "You did it; I would have messed it up." He agreed that it was helpful that the occupational therapist encouraged him to slow down and concentrate, but only when she confirmed that he had actually slowed down and followed through was he able to acknowledge his own efforts.

Staff members often need to help our adolescents identify and differentiate feelings and responses, and shop tasks help to develop such awareness since projects make emotional demands and stimulate feelings. For example, an adolescent can become easily discouraged when the work is boring, frustrating, or difficult. While filing two pieces of metal which he was preparing to solder, Kirk called for assistance several times. He was unaware that his impatience was in part due to a realistically frustrating task. Other tasks may be difficult because they require control of threatening feelings. For example, when Paul needed to use the electric saw to cut a piece of wood, he took no precautions; but when the occupational therapist expressed her concerns about using power equipment, Paul related his fears of "not stopping" and cutting right through the work bench. Often, concrete tasks in the shop are more helpful than interpersonal experiences in helping an adolescent examine his affective responses and manage his emotions.

Following through with shop tasks may be disrupted by fears of failure, real or imagined. These fears are validated when an adolescent makes a mistake, but another may completely disregard errors and continue working without any concern about the eventual outcome. Such may reflect impaired reality testing or lack of investment. Another may disclaim the concrete and visible reality of an error just as he disowns other "bad and unacceptable" behavior elsewhere on the unit. When confronted with a mistake, Kirk would become enraged and disorganized. He would minimize his own responsibility for the error, often faulting materials, tools, and even others. Kirk could assume responsibility for his own actions when helped to alleviate the feeling of being "attacked." Later, he would acknowledge a mistake with "That's simple to fix." Some mistakes represent unresolved and serious interpersonal conflicts. Yvonne had a long-standing history of destroying her and others' belongings. She was very angry about her discharge, feeling that it was too soon. One morning, while working on a hooked rug, she damaged the backing which required extensive repairs. Exploration in her individual sessions unravelled the meaning of this behavior.

Shop activities are highly structured, growth-producing experiences. Searles (1960) emphasizes material objects as a practice ground for complex interpersonal relationships, the "pure culture" for becoming aware of one's capacities and limitations. Certainly the staff must assess the adolescent's ego strengths, deficits, and readiness to master tasks, but his success with projects also depends on assessing the inherent characteristics of the activity. The makeup of the activity affects the adolescent's ability to respond to the demands of the work. Activities vary in the gradation of structure, that is the range of restraints and controls the activity affords, the degree of constraints in individual expression, the nature of this expression, the extent of predictability, and the potential for reality testing. For instance, free-form clay sculpture is a highly unstructured activity because it lends itself to symbolic expression with minimal limits imposed by the material. In contrast, pouring clay into a plaster mold is highly structured because expression is guided, the outcome is highly predictable, and the source of control is contained within the activity itself. Our adolescents often respond diffusely to nonstructured activities because they are apprehensive about their own lack of controls, and cannot gauge their emotional reactions to unstructured activities. When he saw another patient preparing some clay for work on a potter's wheel, Jerry frantically exclaimed, "Oh, let me do that; I'll take that clay and smash it on the wall." On the other hand, Jerry's destructive impulses were less likely to emerge when channelled through the molding of a clay pot, planned and formed with the guidance of a template which helps to shape it. Because the outcome of structured activities is highly predictable, concurrent success and gratification are ensured. Using a prepatterned design to complete a colorful poster can provide an adolescent the assurance he seeks.

An activity is also of variable complexity, depending on the numbers and kinds of directions, the numbers and clarity of procedures, the degree of repetition, the amount and kind of equipment and materials needed, and the degree of competence required. A highly complex activity is characterized by varied and complicated directions, a series of involved, difficult, and accurately executed procedures, precision in the use of materials and equipment, and requires considerable skill and competence. Cutting, carving, stamping, and assembling a leather purse requires attention to detail, accurate and coordinated movements, uninterrupted concentration for lengthy periods, and controlled and skilled use of tools and equipment. In comparison, a leather wrist band, cut and stamped with a simple design, is much less complex.

Our adolescents' lack of skills, concentration, and attention are no match for the demands of highly complex activities, especially when they are unaware of their limitations. Beth asked if she could glaze detailed figures and scenery on a mug, even though she had difficulty handling less complex tasks; however, she was content to highlight the figures by glazing only a background color, a more clear-cut and simple task.

Activities are of short or long duration, require few or many sessions to complete the activity, involve various and different delays and task sequences, and differ in the specificity of the end product. In general, our adolescents choose activities which promise quick results, rather than long-term projects which require several sessions to complete, are repetitive and unexciting, and depend on assessment, planning, tolerance for delay, and a high level of motivation. Cutting out a metal form or a piece of wood is gratifying because it takes only a short time to accomplish, but when this task is combined with filing or sanding, delay is introduced, which becomes extremely difficult for an adolescent whose sense of well-being depends upon immediate and tangible results. The intrinsic satisfaction derived from mastering progressively longer-term activities does not come early or easily.

> Paul was working on a project that took him several weeks to complete. He had gradually developed some tolerance for completing projects which required more time and detail and was beginning to say he felt "a lot better" about leaving his project in the shop from day to day, knowing he would eventually be able to take it with him. As he nearly completed a metal sculpture, his excitement became anxiety when he thought he wouldn't be able to take it with him that day. The last step was simply to attach the sculpture to a base, and he tried to get the sculpture to stand without its base and became disorganized and panicked when he couldn't. His anxiety and panic decreased when he was assured that he did have the time to finish the task that hour.

The space required for activities must be assessed, including the type and nature of physical motions involved, the amount and kinds of material and equipment required, the organization and arrangement of the materials, and the extent of private and shared space. For instance, the constricting motions involved in painting an intricate design contrast with those involved in the wide, more sweeping motions of weaving fabric on a loom. The space needed for the materials and equipment to embroider contrasts with the making of a ceramic pot. By arranging activity areas ordered around specific crafts, the shop setting itself can encourage the freedom to master these skills. Ordered surroundings enhance one's sense of control and boundaries. Donna became anxious when people or things intruded into her work space, and she often organized her work area with "my boundary," an imaginary line she drew in space. When weaving on the loom situated in a demarcated and isolated location in the shop, Evelyn complained that she didn't like the work because she felt "out of touch," pointing to her need for increased contact. Other adolescents, impulsive and easily disorganized when stimulated, can work productively only when tools, materials, and equipment are sharply delimited. For instance, Robert worked quickly and could complete many steps in a project during one O.T. period, but could maintain his orientation only when staff helped him to plan what materials, equipment, and tools would be needed for each step.

Structure, complexity, time, and space are essential characteristics combined in any activity. Assessing these, as well as the needs and skills of a particular adolescent at a particular time, will provide him with an opportunity for independent assertion and mastery. In addition, any of these combined elements can be restructured to meet the patient's level of interest or skill. For example, the high levels of skill and motivation required for leather design can be made less complex and demanding when the leather is imprinted with a stamping tool rather than a carving tool, substituting some certainty for variability.

The goals of the occupational therapist include assessing both the activity and the patient, as well as using herself to provide functions and support for the adolescent's individual achievement. The gains an adolescent makes in shop show elsewhere in other aspects of the treatment program in a greater capacity for self-awareness and skill development.

GAMES AND LEISURE TIME ACTIVITIES

Although occupational therapy is a specific aspect of our program, participation in activities in general fills a considerable portion of the adolescent's free time on the unit, and these activities and games can become useful therapeutic tools within the milieu. If, for instance, games and other activities are considered as ways to pacify disturbed teenagers, their behavior will soon let us know that an important link in the therapeutic chain has given way. Free time endeavors need to be understood in terms of their purposes, how they promote mastery, and how activities become part of life on the unit.

We try to understand the kinds of gratification disturbed youngsters derive from involvement in games and activities. Redl (1972) emphasizes that game structure has an impact on disturbed youngsters. Specifically, games have intrinsic built-in ego supports as well as opportunities for impulse gratification. A game is exciting and gratifying when it includes limits of clearly defined procedures and rules. When these elements are mixed judiciously, the adolescent is more apt to call the game "fun."

Often, adolescents talks about "games" they have played in which there were no limits within the "game" itself, and consequently, no source of ego controls. Such games can be too exciting for some teenagers, especially when they provide no built-in controls for handling feelings. One patient described a game of throwing snowballs at cars with a group of friends. At the time he described the event, the patient and staff group were planning a winter outdoor activity. He suggested that this would be a "fun" activity and that "whamming" snowballs at each other would be the most fun, especially if teams were divided as patients against staff. He eagerly anticipated the gratification of his aggressive impulses, so much so that it was not easy to refocus him on group activity.

Game participation provides useful outlets for feelings and for sublimation of impulses, but Redl (1972) adds that constructive participation in games involves more than discharge and sublimation. For example, Fred and his mother played cards during their weekly visiting hours. These games were quiet and seemed to be going along well until we discovered that they both cheated and enjoyed it, and never defined any finish to the card games, but added one score after another from week to week. They also threatened each other; mother would say, "I've got a play that will get you next week," telling Fred that he would never be able to figure out the "secret" play by the following visit. We discovered this when Fred would be found cheating openly in card games with the staff. His orientation to games was like keeping or discovering family secrets, and then making subtle threats to expose them just as his family did in relating to one another.

The intrinsic factors of a game must be assessed, as well as the adolescent's current functioning. As we have described in the analysis of activities in the shop, the elements of games also need to be considered when working with disturbed adolescents. A game's complexity depends on the numbers, types, and difficulty of rules, commands and directions, the amount and kinds of equipment involved, the number and clarity of steps, the frequency and sequence of taking turns, and the importance of chance as opposed to skill or strategy. Any or all of these may range from simple to complex within a game, and different games will have various combinations which define them as simple or highly complex. Along these lines, a game of "Simon Says" is much less complex than a game of chess.

If a game depends on strategy, it demands of the player the ability to outsmart an opponent and be comfortable as an aggressor, as well as being able to problem-solve spontaneously, think things through sequentially, keep attention focused on the game's progression, prepare for the unexpected, speculate and anticipate the other player's game plan without losing face when one misjudges, and tolerate the resulting frustration. This is all done within the context of well-defined procedures, rules, and regulations. Some adolescents cannot contend with such game complexity when one considers their skills and the intense issues they deal with in treatment. This dictates not that staff should protect the adolescent from playing these games, but rather that they be aware of those situations which are rough spots and respond to them supportively and empathically.

A game is defined temporally by whether its ending is specific or nonspecific, depending on what determines the ending: points, participant consensus, the clock, etc. The end of a rummy card game is more absolute than the agreement of participants required to end a game of Monopoly. A game which ends when a player attains a certain number of points can be less specific than one which ends with a clear cutoff of the clock. Some games can have a specific ending, but can be played over and over again, so that the ending is determined by participant consensus; ping-pong is such a game played frequently on the unit, and a match can be developed around the best of a certain number of games. Sometimes the adolescents will play games like this and fail to decide, agree upon, or even consider that first a decision needs to be made about what constitutes a contest.

> Once, several boys on the unit started a Monopoly game which went on for several days. When all the play money ran out, Fred, the banker in the game, made more money out of his notebook paper. There was a lot of tension among the boys—bickering over TV programs, arguing who was first in line to go to school—and the staff was dimly aware that the Monopoly game lay on the table in the corner of the dayroom for several days. When the boys began giving each other dirty looks and subtly threatening each other, the staff intervened to sort out the cause of the tension. As it turned out, the Monopoly game was a tremendous source of tension because none of them had any idea how long it would go on and because they competed over who was winning at any given time in terms of money, property, etc. The game got out of hand, partly because of its undefined ending.

In addition to the nature of the ending, the pace and the length of the game are important. Many adolescents have such a vague sense of their continuity in time that they cannot respond appropriately to the time demands of games. Some games, or movements within games, go very fast and little time elapses between beginning and end; such is the case in ping-pong or tennis. The pace of action oriented relays is different from the quiet, rhythmic progression of quiet group games. The excitement of fast paced progressions is difficult for our adolescents because they cannot stop themselves, and staff members must facilitate the transition to an ending, as when a quiet game is introduced at the end of a series of relays, or when well-spaced breaks are pro-

vided between games. Eventually, the adolescent will be able to modulate the feelings he experiences in such pressured situations.

The space required for games also needs to be considered. Many
hospitals are not set up to accommodate the space demands of various
daily activities. For instance, the unit ping-pong table fits fairly comfortably in a section of the large dayroom, but its placement there was,
nevertheless, a nuisance both to the players and to those walking back
and forth. It was difficult to play while trying to "tune out" other
activities going on at the same time. Games would frequently end up
with the adolescents hyperstimulated. Some adolescents felt on display,
and so a special room, adjacent to the unit, was set aside for ping-
pong. Certain tasks, specifically games, require special kinds of space.
Many adolescents need quiet surroundings. A staff member playing a
table game in the quiet of the patient's room, as opposed to the dayroom, may make the experience more fun.

Some games allow for the expression of physical aggression, either
directly or symbolically, and can be a threatening experience for some.
In a game called "Maze," one player chases another through lines of
people who make up the maze. On one occasion, a girl who was being
chased ran outside of the maze, causing everyone to scream at her.
Later, she laughed about how anxious the game made her feel, as she
was unsure if the "chaser" would catch up to her and attack her.
Although games have rules for dealing with boundary breakdowns
and for controlling aggression, some adolescents cannot distinguish
between attacking the other player's zone or token or property and
attacking the player himself. Yet, other adolescents may find the same
game a safe expression of and way of mastering aggressive impulses.

Games will also vary according to their mental, physical, and social
demands. Many of our adolescents are not aware of their bodies or
their skills, or social abilities, and they cannot appraise these capacities
realistically.

Physical change and development are an ever-present issue in an adolescent treatment program which should help the adolescent adjust to
body changes and develop physical skills. Disturbed adolescents have
all kinds of changing notions about their bodies, a poorly integrated
awareness of their bodies, and an unrealistic appraisal of their physical

capacities. It is not uncommon for a patient to tell the group about athletic feats which defy sound judgment and reality. They struggle with many insecurities and feel frightened and exposed when physical performance is at stake.

Many games call for physical skills such as rhythm, balance, coordinated movements, and integrated body awareness. Such highly skilled and complex activities as volleyball and tennis are sports which the recreational staff teaches in a sequential skill-building program. Some of the more active games played on the unit or in the gym, which are usually considered leisure activities, involve varying degrees of skill. For example, tic-tac-toe played with bean bags thrown at a floor board calls for skills in directionality, distance-judgment, and body tone. An adolescent whose emotional development is much like that of a four-year-old, who knows he can balance on a tightrope because he saw someone do it at a circus, may be at a disadvantage from the start. It would be helpful for this teenager to try out the game with an understanding staff member before being exposed to the critical eyes of his peers.

Many games are exciting because they challenge our thinking abilities in the presence of an element of chance. They are simple or complex depending on first, the nature and extent of skill/knowledge vs. chance, second, the degree of imagination and creativity vs. repetition, and third, the complexity of plays and moves and whether they are concrete or demand more abstract planning and reasoning. These factors of the game build expectations which not all adolescents will be able to meet with the same degree of follow-through and motivation. Even the time of day a "thinking" game is played alters its outcome. Playing "Concentration" in a break between two classes might be overtaxing.

Disturbed adolescents become easily overwhelmed when participation in games threatens their self-esteem by exposing their lack of skills. Easily threatened in most social interactions, Ned would become extremely grandiose when participating in games. He would deny his poor performance in competitive games by expounding on his unique "style." Adolescents like Ned can often make great strides in modulating self-esteem by participating in games with an understanding staff member rather than with peers.

Social interactions and various roles emerge in games. Players may assume a role, perhaps hold onto it, then assume an opposite role in the same game. Players must be able to give up one role for another, such as changing from winner to loser in one game. They must also handle the feelings that go with this. There can be positions of leader-follower, offensive-defensive, individual-partner-team, winner-loser, or pursuer-victim. Playing a role may depend on cooperation or competition within the game and this will affect the players also.

In order to help the adolescent find leisure time activities more gratifying and fulfilling, staff must recognize the interplay between the adolescent and the environment. Activity analysis is essential to this recognition and includes investigating the game elements because any breakdown of a game derives from an admixture of these elements, and because they are useful guidelines to understand and determine what will allow an adolescent to enjoy a game, especially when the adolescent's developmental level is matched with a challenge he can master.

Trieschman, Whittaker, and Brendtro (1969) describe a wide range of activities for milieu work which can be blended with the level of each patient's functioning. They stress the importance of assessing the complexity of the elements of the activities in relationship to the adolescent's skill level, ability to maintain controls, and level of motivation. Additionally, some consideration should be given to the intrinsic nature of the activity, above and beyond who the participants will be at any given time. The staff needs to have adequate knowledge of the game structure so that patients can successfully participate. Understanding the makeup of the game and game progression permits the staff to modify and restructure the game as needed. Thus, the adolescent with limited skills is not denied successful participation. For example, a game that permits four players may be limited to two in order to avoid or reduce overstimulation for some patients, or games may be adapted or restructured to provide increased ego supports for growth. A snowball "fight," for instance, restructured into a game in which a well-spaced target is hit, provides sublimation of aggression without the intent to hurt.

Any analysis of activities will encompass all these elements: space, complexity, time, body awareness, thought, chance, and social interaction. These are useful guidelines in understanding and determining what kinds of game compositions will allow adolescents to derive the most enjoyment. When the staff develop an awareness of game and activity structure, games can have a more purposeful function. A new staff member may complain "Games are supposed to be fun, so why take the fun out of them by analyzing them?" Sometimes staff's desire to have fun, or to see the patients as normal, are roadblocks to realizing that disturbed adolescents don't necessarily experience a game the way we think they do, or should. When staff understand the elements and purpose of games, they can then help the patients enjoy and learn from them. One major purpose of games is to have fun, but there is no guarantee that the patient will have fun simply because he is involved in a game or activity. Players react not only to each other, but also to the game elements. Games that are age appropriate presuppose certain psychological and cognitive skills which our patients often lack, and so they may be unable to master certain games and activities or to tolerate their reactions to them. Awareness of game structure enables the staff to intervene in rough spots as the game progresses, instead of simply observing that "something" has gone wrong, thus leaving the patients in the lurch.

Adolescents will enjoy games, especially when there is some challenge and hope of mastery. This might necessitate adapting or restructuring games to provide ego supports. Games, as diversions, serve as outlets for energy and feelings; games may help to relieve boredom and the low self-esteem which nondefined free hours may produce; but we must stress the differences between games that divert tension and help channel energy and games that are ineffective in handling impulses. An adolescent whose behavior has been escalating may already be overtaxed when confronted at a particular time with a game in an attempt to limit his behavior. The staff can teach adolescents when games or activities serve as opportunities for self-assertion. When we work with disturbed adolescents, we modify and restructure games to meet their needs. This demands much more than simply observing or stopping a game because things are out of hand; it demands thoughtful, therapeutic participation.

CAMPING

Twice a year, at the end of the regular school year in June and at the end of summer school in September, the unit is closed for four full days, and all the adolescents, activity staff, milieu staff, and some interdisciplinary staff camp at a state park several hours' distance from the hospital. Our first two trips involved enormous difficulties because of staff inexperience with "open spaces." We failed to define the environment clearly and aggravated most of our patients' sense of little control and of poor differentiation. As we recognized this, we started to "plan" the environment of the camp; we staked out territory and made visible limits—the stream on this side, the hills to the back, the cook tent on the other side, etc. Within the planned territory we defined spaces for activities, for eating and for sleeping. Once the staff learned this basic planning and structuring, it was awhile before we realized that the patients had not, that they were simply lost in the openness and lack of concrete definition.

Tents served as private hospital rooms, especially during the day when an adolescent needed the "safety" of a tent to calm down. Separate assessments were made in regard to who could and who could not leave the camping area and participate, with a staff member, in gathering wood or water, or other activities. Each teenager was provided the freedom he could handle with the help of an adult.

As space became defined and differentiated, the camping trips also became growth experiences—successes in the use of the environment never before experienced.

Camping has become an integral part of our program, and the entire staff has come to realize that camping is an extended therapeutic experience which involves several phases and levels of work. Camping has required a considerable investment as we have attempted to integrate it into the overall treatment program. Despite the fact that the activity staff and the milieu staff are usually designated campers, the involvement of the entire staff, including social workers and therapists, helps define camping as part of the total treatment experience. It is no longer a disjointed aspect of milieu treatment, but rather is clearly related to the kinds of growth-producing experiences we provide elsewhere in the program. And so, staff needs to focus on the principles of evaluation and treatment by which we operate in the daily milieu and attempt to apply these in a camping structure. Camping is generally viewed as an opportunity to "get away from it all." In our therapeutic camping we don't get away from it all. Many, if not all, of the treatment principles remain the same as we attempt to transpose the hospital milieu to the outdoors.

In part, the closed hospital unit is a safe place because teenagers have little opportunity to decide whether or not they are going to stay. The locked door is protection against poor impulse control and a reassuring message that staff assume a good measure of responsibility for their treatment. The fact that camping may be fun or recreational does not at all eliminate a patient's potential for disruption or internal upheaval; impulses are not wiped away by fun. We attempt to provide in our campsite some of the same security of the unit. A wide open area, which conveys a feeling of undefined space, can only add to the confusion experienced by teenagers who have difficulty determining definite boundaries. On the other hand, a campsite which is defined by natural surroundings of trees, creeks, and hills allows the teenagers to root themselves more securely at the campsite and begin defining their boundaries and the boundaries of the staff. Campsites that are near well-traveled roads or areas populated with many other campers are less desirable because staff and patients have difficulty under these conditions developing a sense of community and physical links within the surroundings. Smaller defined spaces within the overall campsite are preferable, such as places for cooking, eating, and activities. Giving consideration to choosing the physical space is part of assessing what the adolescents need. A poorly chosen physical space has resulted in patients' experiencing internal disruption, leading to running away, rock throwing, animal mutilation, and sex play.

Just as in the hospital setting, where staff has fairly well-defined roles and functions and designated time away from patients in order to confront and work out staff problems, so, too, these are important features of a camping experience. Time needs to be set aside for staff to be alone with each other and talk about the progress of their work. A daily all-staff meeting before patients wake up is particularly useful. Such meetings not only provide opportunities for communication and support, but also help define and redefine staff roles and functions and prevent diffusion and isolation. We learned this only after several outbursts of violent behavior which occurred on an earlier campout; they resulted from dissension among the staff with no adequate opportunity to resolve the difficulties. For instance, on one campout Sam began to mutilate a frog and one of the camp leaders thought that engaging him and the rest of the group in a baseball game would be a suitable diversion. Others felt, however, that the experience would be too stimulating and only serve to escalate propensity for violence. The campers played baseball, and Sam's violent behavior increased. The issue was poorly resolved because the staff had not worked out ways to meet and discuss such issues and come to common understandings of what behaviors mean and how to respond.

The fun of camping is so tantalizing that staff have difficulty maintaining their ability to assess patients appropriately and correctly. The staff begins to view themselves as having less impact on the teenagers as camping becomes a leveling, communal experience. It is not uncommon for a staff member to think that the teenager who, just yesterday, needed considerable support in making it to and from school, is now a normal teenager who can have fun camping. It is not unusual for staff to want to have their own fun on the campout, and for example, exclude the patient group during the evening campfire and turn it into a staff party. Staff members must continue to act as healthy role models and keep in mind that when we gratify our own needs primarily, we abandon the disturbed adolescent.

Camping has value in and of itself by providing a sense of communion with the natural environment, demonstrating the value of community living, providing opportunities to learn through direct observation and experience, and adding depth to previous learning by providing actual experience. Disturbed adolescents have new opportunities to test out their psychological capabilities and gains made in treatment through their use of leisure time and their participation in peer group activities.

Many of our teenagers who have camped before coming to the hospital have described prior camping experiences as devoid of warmth and human contact. Ernie described his camping experience as part of runaways in which he would pack up and take off to a County Forest Preserve to live by himself for a few days. For other teenagers, camping represented a hoped-for warm family reunion which was usually thwarted by family deficiencies and problems which could not be dispelled even by a new environment. A hospital camping program cannot undo previous deficiencies, but it can provide a positive experience of discovering and investigating the environment and offer some personal gratification.

A meaningful camping experience begins and ends in the hospital. In advance, much time is spent planning the trip, allowing ample opportunity to explore feelings and fantasies of what the experience might be like. Staff and patients work together to delineate the structure and schedule of camp days: the menu, the activities, the assignments, various tasks. It is important to go over some of the basic structure, such as wakeup and bedtime, and to define times for leaving the hospital and returning. All campers are provided with a written schedule that they can carry with them.

Many teenagers are quite unfamiliar with camping equipment, and so part of the precamp experience involves staff spending time with the teenagers individually and in small groups explaining the use of and importance of various kinds of camp equipment. At our institution, a large recreation area adjacent to the hospital provides staff and teenagers opportunities to practice pitching tents and handling the equipment. Thus, the camp experience begins to become a concrete reality.

Again, our assessment of how patients will participate while camping must involve careful scrutiny of what we can expect of each adolescent—at what level he can participate and with what degree of motivation or with what potential disruption. Individual treatment plans on the unit are, for the most part, maintained during camping. We have found that providing each patient-camper with an individual staff relationship is particularly useful in maintaining this therapeutic stance. The nature of this one-to-one relationship will, of course, vary according to the adolescent's ability to tolerate the camping experience; it depends on how much the staff member needs to provide externally to compensate for those functions that the patient lacks internally.

Martha, a 16-year-old depressed borderline girl who had limited awareness of her inner psychological world, required a one-to-one staff relationship and constant monitoring of her impulses and levels of controls. On one campout, Martha looked well put together, but she could not tolerate activities and pleaded to be excused or complained of being ill. She anxiously talked about things going on outside of the campout. When she saw a man on a motorcycle, she said, "Gee I'd like to be riding on a motorcycle." Her participation deteriorated rapidly, and later she wandered in and out of a baseball game. That night she burned a hole in her tent and ran away. Poor staff assessment of and planning for her psychological deficits made it difficult for her to master and integrate the camping experience. In a later campout, she did better. We provided her with a close one-to-one staff relationship which diminished the intensity of the demands placed upon her, gave her little opportunity to leave the campsite, and provided a much more secure and controlled environment wherein she experienced freedom to achieve and master.

The one-to-one is not meant to encourage special relationships or foster isolation. Some teenagers experience the one-to-one as an opportunity for unlimited mothering; the intense involvement of staff only increases their longings for nurturing. Consequently, we have several staff members on duty who serve as "floaters" and can replace or relieve the one-to-one or serve as additional buffers to dilute a particularly intense relationship. The one-to-one staff member must know when the teenager needs to be encouraged to function independently, when he needs an exclusive period of time with staff, or when he needs staff support and collegial participation in an activity. On one camping trip, Terry approached his one-to-one prior to a group activity and told him that he had a fool-proof plan to take off from the campsite if he felt like it. He went on to describe an elaborate and rather fantastic plan, and when the staff member pointed out it was time to get ready for the baseball game, Terry stated that he could not play even though he might like to. Whatever his fears were about participating in the game, they were certainly complicated by his fears of running away. Increasingly, he felt unprotected, convinced that his runaway effort would not be stopped. Later, staff decided that he should go to bed early; he was told to get into his sleeping bag, was "tucked in" and shortly afterwards he fell asleep with the staff member next to him to provide the kind of soothing and calming he was not able to provide for himself.

Just as the patients' rooms on the unit serve as home base from which they venture forth to master new experiences and into which they retreat to contemplate their psychological world, so, too, can the campsite serve as a similar home base. Our teenagers need to touch home base and get some distance from the stimulation of various activities. It is not uncommon for teenagers to refer to the campsite as the "unit," and other kinds of experiences such as baseball games or hikes as "trips." And so the campsite is the working milieu where feelings can be sorted out and anxieties faced without having to "go it alone." As on the unit, time is provided for the teenagers to make transitions from one event to the next, as they attempt to achieve some kind of sensible balance between active and passive activity, to decelerate, and to rest. In all phases the staff play an important role.

The intense experiences of a campout stimulates fantasies about staff and patients becoming members of a family. On return to the unit, there sometimes are attempts to recreate those fantasies in the hospital, while at the same time defending against the concomitant fears. The staff is no longer accessible on a one-to-one basis 24 hours a day. The ending of the camp experience begins tangibly when the food supply begins to run low, when gathering wood is no longer a high priority item, and when there are many other reminders. It is to these concrete realities that teenagers begin attaching their feelings of winding down and returning to the hospital. The last evening campfire carries with it a sense of aloneness, shorter attention spans, and increased irritability, and many teenagers begin to complain about and depreciate the whole experience. This can be the first opportunity for the group to talk together about the problems of reentry, work which must continue on return to the hospital in individual therapy sessions, ward meetings, and a number of informal interactions on the hospital unit.

Even when the campout has been a growth-producing experience, it will stir up many intense feelings and longings which need to be addressed. Breaking up camp and returning to the unit is only a concrete ending. Just as the precamping experience was important, the postcamp phase directly relates to how well teenagers are able to integrate the experience as part of their treatment. After the group has returned to the hospital, there is usually some depression or at least a readjustment to the now less intense and less exclusive relationships with staff. If staff-patient roles were blurred during the campout, serious confusion can result (Marohn, Dalle-Molle, Offer, and Ostrov, 1973). The closeness of camping is often threatening to disturbed teenagers who associate warmth and closeness with being exploited or with losing boundaries and controls. They may behave delinquently in an attempt to separate and establish distance. Providing too much closeness on the campout can complicate life on the unit on return. In any event, a considerable amount of work is required to help the teenager recognize that closeness and warmth do not mean blurring and disintegration. A period of postcamping depression or an episode of contagion and acting out several weeks after returning from a camping trip is not uncommon. Staff, too, need time to integrate and learn from the camping experience. Usually we meet for an hour or two several days after the trip to "de-brief" or talk about and learn from the camping experience.

THANKSGIVING DINNER

The annual patient-staff Thanksgiving dinner has evolved into one of the major holiday events of our unit. However, its beginnings were modest and initially we were unaware that we were establishing a tradition. Once the unit had opened, and staff and patients alike were beginning to feel comfortable with each other, we focused on what our approach would be toward predictable annual events like patients' birthdays and holidays, events based in reality and unchanging from one year to the next. Planning for the celebration of patients' birthdays is relatively easy. Usually parents bring in a cake and the patient shares it with the rest of the group while everyone sings "Happy Birthday." As simple as this seems, some patients regard this as the happiest birthday they have ever celebrated, a suggestion of how impoverished and unnurturing their environments have been.

Christmas is the most difficult holiday because the myths and the fantasies of giving and receiving create impossible expectations that are doomed to bitter disappointment. Commercials and ads depict unbelievably wholesome families who smile and show their love for one another by giving beautiful and expensive gifts which the recipient responds to by showing great appreciation and being demonstratively affectionate. Moreover, Santa Claus is loving and generous and rewards good behavior. Often, a patient needs to cling to such fantasies even when past Christmases have been depressing, conflictual, or crisis-ridden. Although we celebrate Christmas on the unit with a tree and decorations, we choose not to attempt to create a family atmosphere.

Many of our delinquents cannot tolerate and need to defend against their own dependency longings. To try to provide these youngsters with what their parents should have supplied frequently results in rage reactions. For instance, during the first Christmas holiday on the unit, the staff planned several events, including decorations, meals, caroling, and other social activities. The staff was dedicated to making the holiday joyful and the activities occurred on schedule with enthusiastic participation. As the holiday season closed, there was a noticeable increase in restlessness, anger, and open defiance of unit norms. To counteract this trend, the staff planned still another activity on New Year's Eve in an attempt to stem this rise of negative behavior. Patients were encouraged to participate in the games and activities with the limited number of staff available, but the result was a continued escalation of the same behavior—refusals to cooperate, belittling the staff, and near open rebellion. Later, the staff assessed that in their wish to make this a "good experience," they failed to recognize the distinction of each individual's psychological problems and felt guilty that the adolescents were in the hospital instead of at home with their families. There are still many activities planned for the holiday season, but a patient's level of development is acknowledged. Limiting a patient's participation in the holiday programming is seen not as depriving but rather as freeing him to participate at his level of tolerance and mastery.

The Christmas myths and the emotions evoked could be an overwhelmingly negative experience for our patients in whom most feeling states are conflictual. The Thanksgiving holiday, on the other hand, has many elements that can contribute to a growth experience, although we must admit that our first Thanksgiving expressed thanks for finally getting our program started, as well as a wish for staff and patients to engage in a social activity apart from the day to day life of the psychiatric hospital. The celebration of the holiday is the meal itself. Many of the deficits in our patients are deeply rooted in disturbances of an oral nature, such as dysfunctional eating habits ranging from anorexia to compulsive gorging. In addition to eating disturbance, many patients have distorted fantasies and wishes about mealtime. Some patients deprive themselves of food masochistically; some attempt to resolve an interpersonal conflict by offering or receiving food; others relate to their parents only around what food they will bring during visiting hours. Many patients ask for a diet tray as an external control over their intake of food, while others ask for a double tray, often expressing their emotional neediness in physical hunger. Some patients dawdle over their food and are finicky and picky, while others grab their trays and retreat to a corner of the dayroom to gulp down the meal. Oral disturbances are expressed in many ways, but mealtimes and eating are highly charged emotional events for many of our patients, and how they approach food reflects their unresolved conflicts in this area. The Thanksgiving dinner can provide patients an opportunity to think about, plan for, and prepare a sumptuous meal which commemorates a national holiday. This patient-staff project is not something that staff either imposes on the patients or does for the patients.

Of course, all holidays are noted on the unit in appropriate fashion. After the Halloween party is over and the decorations taken down, we explore what the unit celebration of Thanksgiving might be. Now, we discover that some patients have never participated in a Thanksgiving dinner and that in some households no time is set aside for planned preparation of a meal, nor do family members sit down with one another to eat at a specific time. For some, discussing whether or not to arrange for a special kind of meal is even more helpful when in therapy sessions they compare this experience with their past experiences at home.

Although the process varies each year, the group eventually decides to celebrate with a dinner, usually the Wednesday before Thanksgiving. This gives the entire staff group a chance to participate as well as include those patients who are going home for Thanksgiving. Once the group decides to have the dinner, they must choose the menu. Some patients suggest that we send out for a pizza, others hamburgers and french fries. Cal, for instance, persisted in his choice of hamburgers and eventually described how the previous Thanksgiving he had run away from home and had stopped in a restaurant on Thanksgiving Day to eat a hamburger. His persistence could then be viewed, not only as the exploration of an appropriate menu, but also as an attempt to share and master feelings of loneliness and depletion.

Although it sometimes takes awhile, the patient group usually winds up selecting a fairly traditional Thanksgiving dinner with turkey (and sometimes ham as well) as the entree. Associating a particular kind of food with a particular kind of meal for a particular kind of day is a new experience for many of our patients. Evelyn, for instance, went home on a holiday pass. On returning, she described the family meal as her mother cooking one item while various relatives brought other items; she described the meal as "good" but disorganized and "thrown together," because the various selections were not well planned or arranged to go with one another, suggesting mealtime disorganization. In contrast, we try to achieve consistency and predictability; every item on the menu is discussed at length, which gives the patients an opportunity to verbalize their likes and dislikes and to recall anecdotes about particular kinds of food or experiences with food in the past. Some patients have never tasted cranberry sauce; others have never tasted soul food. These long discussions about the menu provide opportunities for compromise and for considering others.

The safe atmosphere of the community meeting helps to channel one's oral needs and dependency wishes appropriately. After the menu has been decided upon, staff-patient committees are chosen for shopping, setting up, decorating, arranging tables and chairs, cooking, cleaning up, etc. Here, even the most disorganized patients participate in making up lists, setting times for specified activities, and formulating plans and following through on them. For patients who never know what they might do in the next two minutes this can be a maturing experience. For many patients this is the first time they have ever had to concern themselves with pots and pans, silverware, decorations, borrowing chairs, and how many cans of cherries are needed to make eight pies. For many, this is a first chance to practice skills learned in arithmetic and consumer education classes; for others, the first time they have experienced group problem-solving.

The nature of the staff involvement is crucial to the task becoming a cooperative effort rather than an imposed assignment. Staff help the patient think about the task, plan and organize the task in its entirety, and fantasize what it might be like.

> Jack had signed up on the schedule to make the fruit punch. A few days before the dinner, a staff member went down to his room to help prepare him for his job. As soon as "fruit punch" was mentioned, Jack jumped up in a panic saying, "I don't know how to do this—Paul isn't here, we're supposed to do it together. . . ." The staff member assured him that everything would be all right. She left the room to get the cookbook and returned, and the two of them read through the recipe. With great relief, he stated ". . . Wow, does this sound good." The staff member also explained where all the ingredients were as well as reassured Jack that the other staff member who would work with him to make the fruit punch would arrange a specific time for them to do it.

As preparations proceed, it becomes evident that there is something very special about this coming event, and this produces many fears and anxieties. Many patients begin to bring into their therapy sessions their discomfort about sitting down with "so many people." A common concern is table manners, fear that they will gorge their food, or act silly or inappropriately. Sally feared that her "finicky" eating habits would invite disapproval and that she would be forced to eat everything that was passed because she did not have the social skills necessary to refuse food politely. Some fear their own reactions when confronted with unfamiliar food or food cooked differently from at home. Ernie said that he could not eat the prepared dressing because his grandmother would make oyster dressing and he wanted only that kind. Ernie had pleasant memories about the oyster dressing and being with his grandmother on Thanksgiving; when he talked about these, he could likewise express his concerns about not being gratified now. He tried the new dressing, and found some enjoyment in mastering the unfamiliar. On the other hand, Alice was a newcomer to the unit, and as preparations for the dinner went forward, she said that she would not eat and that the only Thanksgiving dinner she would eat would be at home. She resisted cooperating in any way with the program and could not "incorporate" what we had to offer. True to her word, she ate only peanuts while everyone else feasted.

Most patients are uneasy about interacting with others, especially staff members who generally are not there during mealtime. Sitting down to eat with their individual therapists is much less predictable than contact during regularly scheduled therapy hours. Sibling rivalry is often evoked by the issue of where the therapist will sit. Many patients are also especially uncomfortable about "even teachers" coming. Indeed, the teachers spend less time on the unit than other staff, and their coming to the dinner is "different." The patients are not alone in their concern about possible blurring of boundaries at the dinner, and many staff, new staff in particular, wonder about how their roles change when engaging in a social situation with the patients. These questions must be addressed in staff meetings. When such feelings and concerns are aired and worked through, the staff can more effectively meet the needs of each patient.

As the dinner nears, patients talk about dressing up and whether or not to say grace, and if so, what kind. At times, a moment of silence is chosen; at others, patients thank each other and the staff for their work together. Other traditions develop as well. The chief and assistant chief of the unit carve the turkeys. The patients recognize this as an important event, and there is usually considerable discussion around the "big bosses" assuming this parental function. Once, the patients made aprons for the occasion and had written "Price" on one and

"Pride" on the other, two grocers depicted in the television advertising of a chain of supermarkets. More recently, they made chef's hats for the event. Through the committees the patients have the opportunity to work with healthy role models in a planned and organized fashion. They can achieve gratification from the problem-solving necessary to carry on the committee's work, from the results of their efforts, and from the integration of their committee's work with that of other committees.

The dinner itself is invariably a huge success with white tablecloths, candlelight, fresh flowers, and creative centerpieces and decorations. Although there are varying degrees of discomfort, everyone has the opportunity to participate in and partake of a sumptuous meal in a social setting with about 35 other people. For many patients, it becomes the best Thanksgiving dinner of their lives; for others, it is their only Thanksgiving dinner.

These many activities all represent specialized forms of therapeutic intervention whose complexities transcend the parameters of person, space, time, and things, whose analysis and application can be understood and taught, and whose efficacy supports and integrates with the work of the milieu and the psychotherapy.

10

Perspective

Our work is founded on a psychological understanding of adolescence, adolescent behavior, and the psychodynamics of delinquency. We focus on psychopathology as it shows itself in the transference relationship, we seek to establish and maintain a therapeutic alliance, and we insist that all behavior has meaning and can be understood psychologically. The adolescent's relationship to time, space, and things, his definition and appreciation of himself as a person, and his relationship to others are parameters which help us define our diagnostic understanding and help us plan our therapeutic interventions. We work toward a hospital treatment program in which individual psychotherapy and milieu therapy are integrated, rather than split off.

In order to demonstrate some of these ideas, we have chosen to talk about Nancy, a teenager who was treated on our unit for two years and a few months. Nancy is not necessarily representative of those delinquents who are "success" cases; her outcome is still in question and at time of discharge she showed persisting limitations and deficits. However, she does exemplify how we understand and work with our patients. Her story serves to underline the reality that staff gratification cannot come necessarily from "cures" but rather from the realization that we have learned, understood well, and attempted to do our best.

Nancy was 13 when admitted to our program. She is the second child in a sibship of four, having a sister two years older than she, a brother two years younger, and another sister four years younger. Her mother and father had lived together for only five years. He died toward the latter phase of Nancy's hospitalization and was never involved in the treatment program, having left home when the patient was four years of age.

Nancy's mother and father never married, but lived in common law because they "never got around" to marrying. This is a family secret and unknown to other family members, as is also the fact that the youngest child was fathered by a different man. Her mother, a waitress, and father, a truck driver, met and began living together shortly after she had moved out of her parents' home, lived together briefly in another state, but returned to Chicago where they lived together for five years.

Nancy's was a normal pregnancy with an easy, short delivery. She was bottle fed and there were no feeding or sleeping problems. Nancy walked and talked at ten months, and was toilet trained at age two with no problems, at which time she was also weaned. She began running high fevers of 102 to 103 degrees on and off for several months about the same time that her father left the family. It was around this time that mother begins to be able to distinguish Nancy from the other children in the family when she discusses those years with an interviewer. Mother had gone to work when Nancy was about one year of age, and around her second birthday, when the relationship with father began to deteriorate, she became pregnant with the brother.

At this time father lived from day to day, spending money recklessly, even giving it away, bringing strangers home, acting like Santa Claus to his children, bringing presents but providing no nurturance or limits. He would attack mother repeatedly, but spent less and less time at home, often being there only two or three days every other week. He impregnated a babysitter, and this caused mother to end the relationship. He returned to a distant state about which the patient had repeated fantasies of visiting. After the brother was born, the mother returned to work. When the mother would leave for work, the patient would fall over backwards and cry, not stopping until mother left the house; this behavior lasted about a year, but after this the patient was described as a sweet child, yet stubborn and having a mean temper. She would often fight and refuse to obey until her mother hit her.

After father's departure, a maternal aunt and her husband moved in and raised the children while mother worked. There was a great deal of conflict between mother and uncle because of his strictness which the mother opposed, often undoing his limits. This relationship went on for nine years. Around age four the patient had measles; at age four and a half her brother set fire to her bed, but she was unharmed. She started school at age five with no problems, although she was a loner and did not appear to be interested in people outside the family. When Nancy was six and a half, her mother began working two jobs and was gone from 9 a.m. till 2 a.m. every day. Around age seven, Nancy stole from her mother, and began shoplifting candy and cheap jewelry; this behavior has never stopped. Around the same time she had chicken pox. Also, around this time the family lived temporarily in another city because the mother was having minor surgery, after which they returned to Chicago and mother worked only one job.

When Nancy was eight, the older sister began having serious physical problems, and mother needed to spend more and more time with her, which caused the patient to become very jealous of her sister who was relieved of any household chores and spent a great deal of time with mother. Nancy began mimicking these symptoms, and sometimes this would result in hospitalization which was always negative diagnostically. Around the same time she began having problems in school, was bossy and demanding, would talk back to teachers and would get into fights. The school recommended she see a therapist, but this was not done. Around age ten, the mother noticed that whenever she would try to discipline Nancy, a tantrum would result; Nancy would hit mother back, and once threatened to kill her with a butter knife. She was hospitalized at a private hospital for 20 days where she was treated with Thorazine. Several months later she was again rehospitalized there for 20 days after she had a tantrum when mother refused to give her a key to the front door and she screamed obscenities about mother out of the window. Several months later, she was hospitalized at a state hospital for six months, apparently being provided opportunities to ventilate her anger including throwing things.

The mother says she was told not to set limits on the patient, and one week after the patient's discharge, mother was hospitalized for 20 days with a "nervous breakdown." Mother's therapist recommended that mother and daughter not be in the same house together. Subsequently, the patient was again hospitalized at the same private hospital for 20 days around which time the aunt and uncle moved out which made the patient very angry because of her closeness to her uncle. After discharge the patient attended public school and did well in an art competition, but because of her behavioral problems, her art work was never shown at an exhibit about which both patient and mother are still bitter.

The patient was at home for six months following the last hospitalization, and was about 12 years of age at this time. While in school, she hit a teacher who refused to change her seat in the classroom, tried to drown a cat which her mother would not let her keep, and complained of headaches. She was hospitalized for a neurological evaluation after which she received medication for two months with no relief. After the cat drowning attempt, she ran away, was apprehended by the police, was again rehospitalized at the private hospital for five months. After discharge she was in a state group home for seven months and attended school there while using drugs and alcohol to excess. She returned home, now age 13, but ran away with a boy several times for as long as a week. She threw a chair at her uncle, and was then placed in a series of foster homes where she would run away after one or two nights. She ran away with the same boyfriend, and was apprehended in a stolen car whereupon she was taken to the detention home for two weeks and placed in another state hospital, where she stayed for five months prior to referral to our program. While she was there, she assaulted both staff and patients and led a riot on the unit in which two staff members were hurt; she threw a chair at the television set and tore up the recreation room. She ran away from that facility several times, and repeatedly threatened to hurt herself and others.

Nancy was admitted in the morning and cried a great deal, clinging to the staff member from the other state hospital who brought her, saying that the staff of our program were rude and mean, and that she wanted to go back to the other hospital. She calmed down almost immediately as soon as the staff from the other hospital left. She was cooperative when the staff searched through her belongings for dangerous implements or contraband. When she was told the rules of the unit, she thought that she might have some trouble bumping into people because she often does not watch where she is going; she felt that she would have no difficulty controlling her violent tendencies despite her long history of assault. She was angry that smoking would not be permitted, did not like the idea of spending time alone in her room, and felt that she should be able to keep secrets from staff. She denied that she had any problems to discuss. Initially, she refused a physical examination because she assumed that she would not be permitted to wear a robe, but agreed when this was clarified. She spent much of her first day arranging her room and spent some time with her therapist.

On admission she weighed 127 pounds, was 5'4", and was noted to have blue eyes and long brown hair. She was described as alert, but very hostile and defensive and quickly angered. Her affect appeared very volatile and labile, her speech was loud, and she was argumentative and verbally abusive. She demonstrated poor impulse control, had a low frustration tolerance, and seemed to be quite explosive. She would have fits of temper and crying spells which seemed to be precipitated by no apparent cause. There was no evidence of a thought disorder, loosening of associations, delusions or hallucinations. Yet at times her temper tantrums appeared to be of psychotic proportion in the sense that she seemed to be completely unaware of her environment and the reality of the situation around her. When asked about her violent explosions, she did not seem to be conflicted about them, but instead many times that she liked the way she was an would resist any attempt to change. She showed virtually no remorse about any of her aggressive acts prior to hospitalization or as they occurred in the first few weeks of her hospitalization. Physical and neurological examinations were within normal limits.

On her second day of hospitalization she visited with her mother, and cried because it appeared that she would graduate from eighth grade while she was a patient in a mental hospital. The next day she was very upset, screaming and yelling during her therapy session, and crying afterwards, telling the staff that she wanted to go back to the other state hospital. Eventually she calmed down, and asked to spend some time with staff members. These episodes of volatile outbursts and then periods of calm persisted for sometime.

Diagnostic psychological testing demonstrated Nancy to be in the average intelligence range. Intense feelings overwhelmed and confused her, and at moments like that she was capable of being explosive, running away, or somatizing, though she was able to make a fairly quick recovery. She had some awareness of her vulnerabilities and her difficulty in controlling herself and maintaining self-discipline. She seemed to be aware of her intense emotional hunger with fantasies about uncontrolled indulgence and cannibalism, often projected onto others. She was cynical and distrustful of adults, yet yearned for a home-like setting and protection by adults, and there were intense rivalrous feelings with siblings with whom she must fight to define what belongs to her, both things and people. Testing suggested that transference responses to the unit and to her therapist would be strong and readily stimulated, and that her treatment relationship would be stormy, yet of great importance to her because of her wish for contact and her strong motivation to repair and change herself.

Nancy had not attended a public school for about a year and a half when she had been enrolled in the seventh grade; she then attended school for a brief time at the state operated group home and at the state hospital. In testing prior to her entry into our school program, her grade scores varied all the way from early fourth grade in language to early sixth grade in spelling, from the fourth percentile to the 34th percentile in her standing among peers. These scores would show a dramatic increase some 26 months later.

In order to observe this progress and other changes, we will now describe Nancy's course in treatment. We will not do this chronologically, however, but rather along the lines of the treatment philosophy and principles that we have already presented.

ADOLESCENCE AND BEHAVIOR

Adolescence, far from being simply a recapitulation of the psychological conflicts and solutions of childhood, is a unique maturational and developmental phase. It is characterized by the genitalization of psychosexual development, the mastery and integration of genital urges, and the investment in heterosexual relationships. Nancy had not yet progressed to this point, but, indeed, though she gave every indication of having been involved in sexual experimentation on one of her runaways from our unit, her questions about herself as a sexual being seemed to have more to do with a feeling that her body was deformed; that is, that her legs were ugly or her breasts too large.

Discussions about sexuality invariably led to talk about eating and a wish to fill herself up. At the same time, she saw sexual activity as an intrusion into her boundaries, and feared a sexual assault by staff as had happened, she said, in other hospital programs. As she approached discharge from the hospital, it was unclear whether she had yet arrived at a point where she was attempting to master and integrate genital urges. Warm and affectionate feelings which had to do with soothing and comforting seemed to be her primary focus, and not a wished for genital experience. Nonetheless, because she is attractive, she was continually confronted with the attention of boys and particularly older men, and found that many of them came on "too fast" and she was unable to deal with the flood of feelings that she experienced, largely of a pregenital nature. In the termination of her stay in the hospital, it became clear that one problem the staff had to confront was the failure to realize that she was still a young adolescent, and though she appeared to be physically mature, she was still struggling with more primitive psychosexual issues. To educate her about her sexual matters was a novel and premature experience for her, and her ability to integrate the information was severely limited by serious developmental lags.

Adolescence is also a period of psychological experimentation and progression, as new defense mechanisms are utilized to achieve psychological separation from the attachments of childhood and as the character structure is crystallized. It is a major period of separation and individuation, building on earlier such efforts and resulting in individuality and identity.

In therapy sessions, Nancy would talk about the disappointing realization that she was not going to be able to derive the kind of nurturing and support she longed for from her mother. In a sense, this is the struggle of the adolescent, but for Nancy it was intensified because of her mother's severe limitations and the narcissistic nature of the mother/daughter relationship. Nancy's failure to meet her mother's needs, particularly as she attempted to individuate, only resulted in a precipitous loss of any emotional contact with mother whatsoever. She saw her home as an unsuitable environment: "I can't grow up there." She came to realize that she was psychologically more competent than her mother and indeed more capable of parenting her sibling than her mother. To move through adolescence and become an adult is to become healthy; this is experienced as growing up and cutting oneself off from important nurturing and caring relationships. It is a mistake, however, to view Nancy's difficulty as a family problem; rather, it has become an internal conflict and an intrapsychic construct—in any relationship she fully expected to be utilized by and for the other person and fully expected that in an attempt to assert her own individuality she would become totally isolated. As a counterpart, she could not tolerate a therapist having an existence separate from hers. This is an exaggeration of the growth struggle of the adolescent, transformed into serious pathology, experiencing autonomy as deprivation.

Adolescence is also a major waystation in the transformation of primitive narcissism into its more mature forms—ambition, self-esteem, commitment to ideals, respect and admiration for others, a capacity to empathize, and a sense of humor. Nancy's grandiosity and her expectations of self-perfection with the accompanying severe depression and profound loss of self-esteem were quite evident from the very beginning. In the course of her lengthy hospitalization, failure in class or criticism by teachers became a less devastating experience; she had passed through phases of disillusionment and no longer expected an all-nurturing relationship with mother and no longer hoped that the therapist would read her mind. On a few occasions, towards the end of her hospitalization, she expressed genuine concern about the therapist's needs and could, for the first time, in some group discussions, laugh or joke about herself and not be devastated by self-depreciation.

Adolescents develop cognitively and achieve formal (abstract) thinking. Nancy has not, and requires concrete and specific instructions in, for example, planning her day outside the hospital, planning how to deal with an anticipated job interview, or assessing her progress in school. Nancy's progress in school during her hospitalization was remarkable. Her grade scores improved anywhere from one year seven months to six years, moving as high as the 60th percentile in some subjects. However, Nancy's progress in school was uneven, and oftentimes her work would be interrupted by strong emotional responses. For example, in about the third month of participation in the school program, she received a graded math test from the teacher, and began to correct her errors, but had some difficulty and asked for the teacher's help. She had to wait while the teacher was working with another student, and when help was available she became agitated, which increased as she began to understand and master the material, insisting defensively that the teacher had never explained it properly in the first place. She was unable to settle down, which was unlike her, and as her agitation increased, she looked around the room and said that she could not do the work and that she would have to see the crisis teacher. The tone in which she expressed this was not as if she could get help from the crisis teacher, but that somehow she would have to be sent out of the room before something happened. When she went to meet with the crisis teacher, she was loud, and called the teacher a liar. She continued to have difficulty settling down, attacking the crisis teacher verbally, and insisting that it was the school staff's problem, not her own. When the decision was made that Nancy would go back to the unit, and that the teacher would meet with her later, Nancy said that "She better not." She reminded the crisis teacher that in the past she had hit staff and "even jumped" them, and when the crisis teacher explained the problem to the staff member from the unit, she, too, was called a liar. As she pursued this further with her psychotherapist and with the milieu staff, it became clear that the prospect of attending a unit cookout that day was more than she could handle; nonetheless, she experienced this restriction as a blow to her self-esteem, and responded with tears and anger at the staff and the teachers. Nancy had to begin dealing with the fact that she experienced correction and making mistakes as a significant injury. Given these kinds of psychological deficits, it is difficult to assess in a neutral manner the cognitive abilities of our adolescents. Our work in school involves helping them develop the capacity to separate out cognitive and intellectual pursuits from the more emotionally difficult tasks of personal understanding.

We know, finally, that adolescence is characterized by action and activity. In many delinquents this is exaggerated in their propensity for violent behavior. Our own work has demonstrated that violent behavior in the hospital is not necessarily the result of angry or hostile feelings. Some adolescents find themselves overstimulated, particularly by affectionate longing and wishes for intense closeness. In working with these kinds of patients, it, therefore, becomes important to maintain a certain amount of distance and not increase their burden by providing intimate relationships not only in individual psychotherapy, but also in the hospital milieu.

The ward staff learned very quickly to be careful in dealing with Nancy because she seemed to become excited whenever a ward staff member showed any kind of emotion whatsoever, and they soon found that short sentences and small words and very concrete expectations of what to do, and in what order it should be done, were most helpful for her, particularly in the beginning of her hospitalization. Later, when she would find that certain interactions with the ward staff made her feel that personal boundaries were getting to be very hazy and very confused, she would become angry, not only because she had difficulty expressing what she was feeling, but also because she needed to distance and differentiate herself from the other person.

Sometimes she might become violent because of the frustration and narcissistic rage she experienced when wishes and expectations were not fulfilled. After a few months of hospitalization, Nancy was confused about some peer interactions, went to her room to be alone, and later requested that one of her favorite female staff members spend some time with her to clarify these issues. She became enraged when the staff member delayed. The staff member felt it would be important to provide Nancy with some distance, but Nancy experienced this as a rejection and she burst out of her room and attacked the staff member, hitting and kicking her. After being restrained, she complained bitterly that she had been misunderstood and that she wanted the staff member to be with her.

With her therapist, too, Nancy described very violent feelings and said she felt like a Hitler whose wishes and urges were murderous and out of proportion. Before she talked openly in therapy sessions about these wishes, she talked to the ward staff to help her organize some of these feelings and determine whether or not it was appropriate to discuss these things in therapy. Again the ward staff were being used as supportive relationships or self-objects. On many occasions, as Nancy began to feel herself becoming enraged and on the verge of expressing it verbally, she would begin to feel numb. Numbness seemed to be a way of ridding herself of all intense affect, particularly rageful feelings. It was not uncommon for her to rage at her therapist in sessions; she would scream at her therapist and her speech would become garbled. She told her therapist that she wanted not simply to hurt her, but to kill her—to strangle her. When she was told that it seemed as though she felt that the therapist would not let her grow up and therefore she needed to kill the therapist in order to mature, she regained her composure and agreed that in order to grow, one had to kill the other person, that there was no way to be able to have relationships continue once one begins to grow, that people simply won't let one do that. The therapist's ability to withstand these verbal onslaughts without retaliating or disintegrating was very reassuring to Nancy. Verbal onslaughts and threats of violence are the starting point of an escalation of violence which may result ultimately, after damage to property, to violence to another person. Verbal violence and damage to property must be confronted immediately and affectively. The therapist's affective response to Nancy's verbal onslaughts provided her with a structure for experiencing and working on her violent feelings.

But adolescent development is varied, and in its variance, we often find ourselves both fascinated and perplexed when we confront questions of normality and psychopathology. Deviant adolescent behavior, disturbed adolescent behavior, and delinquency may represent aberrations of normal adolescent development or they may represent serious psychopathology. Nonetheless, at any point along this spectrum we must emphasize that adolescent behavior can be understood psychodynamically. This is an important lesson we learned from working with Nancy: by insisting on the validity of our psychological focus, we could eventually begin to dissect the meaning and implications of her behavior.

Our own work points towards four psychologically meaningful parameters of delinquent behavior: the impulsive delinquent, the narcissistic delinquent, the depressed borderline delinquent, and the empty borderline delinquent (Offer, Marohn, and Ostrov, 1979; Marohn, Offer, Ostrov, and Trujillo, 1979).

The *impulsive* delinquent shows more violent and nonviolent antisocial behavior. He is considered quite disturbed by his therapists, socially insensitive by his teachers, and unlikeable and quick to action by most staff members. Yet, he seems to have some awareness of a need for help. His delinquency derives from a propensity for action and immediate discharge.

The *narcissistic* delinquent sees himself as well-adjusted and nondelinquent. However, parents and staff recognize his difficulties in adapting and characterize him as resistant, cunning, manipulative, and superficial. He denies problems, only appears to engage in therapy, exaggerates his own self-worth, and in his delinquency uses others for his own needs, especially to help regulate his self-esteem.

The *depressed borderline* delinquent shows school initiative, is liked by staff, and tries to engage with staff therapeutically. Relationships with parents lead to strong internalized value systems, and this delinquent shows a considerable amount of guilt and depression, from which delinquent behavior serves as a relief, but also an anaclitic need for objects to which he clings and for which he hungers.

The *empty borderline* delinquent is a passive, emotionally empty and depleted individual, who is not well-liked, is an outcast sometimes, needy and clinging at other times, and whose future seems pessimistic. This adolescent behaves delinquently to prevent psychotic disintegration or fusion and to relieve himself of internal desolation.

Though Nancy shows a good deal of impulsivity, significant narcissistic features, and recurrent episodes of depression, she is primarily an empty girl who seeks desperately to merge with other people in order to fill herself up, and who had, prior to treatment, been devoid of any capacity to look inside and understand or appreciate whatever psychological life existed. Her official diagnosis on admission was of a borderline personality disorder with explosive features. A major concern was whether or not we could design a total treatment program to help her learn to control her violent outbursts against herself and others and help her begin to tolerate affection and closeness with other human beings. Nancy felt desperately hungry all the time and wanted a great deal of food. She felt that she could never fill herself up, no matter how much she ate. At other times she experienced a devastating sense of internal numbness and psychological emptiness when her feelings were hurt or her anger stimulated.

FRAMEWORK

An adolescent cannot engage in meaningful therapy without a supportive environment. If teenagers have an important personal relationship or supportive ties to their family, they may be able to engage in outpatient therapy (Easson, 1969), but most of the delinquents that we see are unable to establish a therapeutic alliance and would be unable to experience and tolerate the stresses of a clinical transference without the support of the hospital. This, too, of course, becomes an issue when we approach discharge. Nancy, confronted with discharge from the hospital, and despite her avowed wish to be discharged, immediately experienced a structural regression when she was told of her discharge date. She confused her discharge date with a change in her therapist's work schedule. She talked in terms of needing the therapist's physical presence and immediately began thinking in terms of getting a dog to be a companion outside of the hospital. While on home visits, if she began to feel confused, she would picture herself sitting in a therapy session and talking with her therapist; she had been able to internalize something of the supportive therapeutic alliance. Yet, if she were angry with her therapist, or began to be enmeshed in a merger relationship with her mother while on a pass, this experience would be interfered with and was not available to her.

As Nancy was approaching discharge, she was reminiscing with a ward staff member about some of the early days of her stay on the unit. She remembered how she used to have to be escorted to the bathroom as she was to all activities when she would leave her room. She began to feel frightened that she might still need that kind of support outside of the hospital, even though her behavior seemed to indicate that such external support was no longer necessary. In a subsequent treatment session, she understood that she had begun to develop for herself a degree of regulation, but recognized that such a level of adjustment was still somewhat tenuous, indicating that her newly developed psychological structure was fragile (Kohut, 1971) and under serious stress, including the temporary stress of discharge, might fail.

The hospital environment supports but also assists further observation and assessment. The basic structure of the program, the daily schedule, the expectable activities, and the core experiences of being a patient on the adolescent unit provide external psychological support, but also provide the staff a backdrop or screen against which the patient's behavior, feelings, and transferences can be viewed. This was most dramatically demonstrated early in Nancy's hospitalization when she was told by the Adolescent Progress Review Committee, after she had threatened to hit her therapist, that despite her difficulties, we felt she could continue to work in treatment and that we could continue to work with her. She became disturbed and ran from the room, rushing to the other end of the building, sobbing and asking to be left alone. At this point, several of us, in attempting to determine what precipitated her explosive behavior, began speculating about a biological cycle and the hopelessness of ever determining what it was that stimulated her to explode. Yet, we stuck to the basic structure, confronting her with the daily schedule, our expectations, and a philosophy which said that behavior was explainable, provided psychological deficits were compensated for by empathic staff intervention. After weeks of uncertainty and ambiguity, the determinants of her behavior began to emerge in an outline. This is comparable to the position of the psychoanalyst who waits and listens to his patients' free associations with an even-hovering attention, listening also to his own associations, but not expecting that in any given segment of treatment solutions can be readily found.

It is against this basic structure that intrapsychic conflicts and psychological deficits are spotlighted. From this an individualized treatment plan emerges, pointing towards structuring or restructuring the adolescent personality. As Nancy revealed to the ward staff that she had many confused and conflictual feelings, it was important that the staff remain as consistent as possible and consistently define their position. Similarly in psychotherapy as she expressed confused and conflictual feelings, especially the anxiety of changing, the therapist's calm and persistent attitude conveyed that all conflicts, deficits, and behavior are understandable and manageable. This stance, like the unchangeable framework of the unit, permits a patient to internalize a therapeutic attitude toward the self, an acceptance of, tolerance for, and understanding of problems and painful feelings. Nancy's first separation from her therapist, after several months of hospitalization, was painful and increased her feelings of hopelessness; yet, our stance had become hers when she showed her therapist three signs she had put up in her room: "Stop and Think," "Look at Both Sides," and "Don't Get Angry," early indications that a therapeutic attitude was beginning to be internalized.

THE EXPERIENCE OF PSYCHOTHERAPY

Internal change occurs only in the transference relationship, in which there are both meaningful experiences and self-observations of those experiences. Nancy demonstrated this capacity for a therapeutic split after about a half year of hospitalization when after a runaway she told her therapist that she had decided to run because she did not feel that she could tolerate the intensity of relating in therapy and that in the past such relationships had been very painful to her and she had always spoiled them in some way or other. She seemed to recognize that although she wanted a nurturing relationship, she also had the need to interfere with it. Later, while she continued to talk about other people's unfairness to her, she began to recognize that feelings of hatred and the need to get revenge existed in her and not in other people. And after about a year and a half of hospitalization, she began to be able to distinguish between the therapist and her mother, that they were not the same person and that they did not behave the same ways towards her even though on many occasions she felt the same way toward both of them.

The limit-setting, confrontation, feedback, empathic support, and external soothing performed by the ward staff in the hospital milieu precede and facilitate the process of introspection hoped for in individual psychotherapy. The adolescent is taught to identify affect and is helped to think about her behavior. Any behavior that occurs in the hospital, whether it is directly verbalized by the patient to her psychotherapist or split off from the treatment session is being "brought" to the therapist. Any bit of "acting out" which occurs in the hospital is the adolescent's way of bringing to the therapist's attention her deficiencies, problems, conflicts, or specific transference issues, many times displaced from the individual psychotherapy situation, to be focused on and eventually verbalized and hopefully understood. For example, at one point in her treatment, Nancy became silent in sessions. She seemed to be frustrated with her therapist and disappointed, and as the silence continued, she began to look more and more depressed. On the unit, however, Nancy would go from one staff member to another discussing issues that were troubling her. She diffused the transference relationship, presenting many issues to different staff members at different times in an inconsistent manner, and bringing them into her therapy sessions less and less. The ward staff continually insisted that she take her problems into therapy at the same time as the therapist interpreted to her that she may be experiencing some frustration and disappointment. Eventually she brought her diary into sessions and wrote in it: she then struggled with the question of sharing her diary with her therapist and eventually she did. She told the therapist that what she was experiencing in therapy was a recapitulation of how little she felt she got from her family. She noted then that in order to compensate for the frustration she felt in sessions, she had tried to get things from the ward staff and realized that she would ask them questions that really belonged in psychotherapy. Gradually, she was able to differentiate what kinds of discussions belonged in therapy and what kinds of discussions belonged in the milieu.

At another point in her treatment she was found one night sleeping between her bed and the wall, lying on the floor. The ward staff questioned this, and she attempted to rationalize it by saying that she felt warmer there. The staff felt there was more to this, and she was encouraged to discuss it further in therapy. Eventually she was able to talk about how she feared being assaulted by other patients on the unit and being assaulted by her therapist who would attack her because of the kinds of angry feelings she was experiencing. She had nightmares and found that sleeping where she did, holding herself between the bed and the wall, seemed to lessen her terror.

A firm and consistent attitude by the ward staff encourages the patient to bring meaningful behavior and issues into the psychotherapy, and it is only with this kind of preparation that the patient is helped to understand that behavior has meaning, is taught how to introspect, and is provided with an environment supportive to the psychotherapy process.

In parallel fashion, the psychotherapist must take all behavior seriously, just as the adolescent is expected to "own" her behavior, accept the responsibility for it, for understanding it, and for attempting to modify it.

Our expectation is that certain core issues and transferences will be reexperienced, and that with each successive and successful resolution, or re-solution, more sophisticated and more adaptive processes result. As Nancy approached discharge, old behaviors reappeared, and she had three sessions of intense and cooperative work, and a fourth in which she screamed at the therapist how she hated her. She began questioning whether it was possible for her to carry the therapist in her head and she began demonstrating again the need for demonstrable external psychological support. At discharge, she demonstrated that the work of therapy was not finished and that specific conflicts and deficits would reappear time and time again.

The experience of psychotherapy for the adolescent does not end with discharge, and termination is not a terminus. Rather, it is the beginning of a new way of relating to the self, coming as it does in the midst of a developmental phase. As such, the experience of psychotherapy is a process rather than an event; its effects are not to structure or restructure the personality in stone, but rather to influence perceptibly the direction of future maturation.

PERSON

The hospitalized delinquent shows primitive transferences and marked deficiencies of psychic structure. Nancy demonstrated primitive narcissistic transferences. In her very first session, a stormy one, she stated that she felt she was being treated like "a piece of paper" as the therapist took her history. Later, she expected that her therapist would read her mind and complained that no one had been able to do so or had recognized that she was feeling physically ill. Her tolerance for change in the treatment relationship was minimal; in one session she raged that her therapist's chair had been moved about two inches and she experienced this as a rejection and felt no longer cared for by the therapist. It was only after awhile that she could accept the idea that she needed the therapist to be the same to her day in and day out.

After discharge, Nancy described to her therapist how she had begun to feel that her boyfriend was out of touch with her when she noticed that another girl was flirting with him. She recognized then that she was the one who was feeling out of touch because of her anger, and noted that she felt the same way often with her therapist when she felt that the therapist was not caring for her or thinking about her. She recognized this as a common pattern and, in talking with her girlfriend, was able to correct the distortion, and reestablish a cordial relationship with her boyfriend. She realized that the problem was inside of her and she needed to discuss it further in therapy. She and the therapist were able to clarify further that this feeling often occurs with mothering figures from whom she wants a good deal, and whom she needs in order to help her feel complete.

A particularly enlightening aspect of Nancy's narcissistic transference unfolded when the therapist seemed obviously pleased with Nancy's progress. This prompted Nancy to try to destroy her gains. She felt herself merged with a mothering person who would use her for her own emotional gratification. She found that the only way to disengage herself, as she had so often done with her mother, was to do something self-destructive so that the good feelings could no longer be shared by the other person. If, indeed, she did anything that gratified someone else, she felt robbed of these feelings and empty. "I love you" meant "I want to use you." Of course the counterpart was that Nancy expected people to read her mind and know exactly what she wanted and needed to prevent her from feeling empty. And if that did not occur, she became enraged and struck out. When on one occassion she had run from the hospital to distance herself from her wishes to merge, she hid in the bushes near the hospital and would occasionally stick her head out to see if her therapist was looking for her. She felt as though her therapist were calling her name. She feared that her therapist would fragment and have a nervous breakdown because of her run-away, and she would call the hospital to reassure herself that her thera-pist was all right.

Nancy was unable to calm or soothe herself and required a good deal of staff contact and attention in order to provide this function. When-ever she appeared anxious about any situation, she behaved impul-sively, and so when she went to a nearby medical hospital for tests, the trip had to be planned in great detail. She could tolerate and work with the structuring of this trip only up to a point, and later in therapy re-cognized that it was impossible for her to predict her behavior because after awhile her controls would fail her. We know that many delin-quents find their futures very pessimistic, largely because they, them-selves, are so unpredictable, and they know they cannot plan or an-ticipate what the next hour will bring.

Nancy also had great difficulty experiencing intense affect, particu-larly angry feelings, and would find her "brain going numb" as feel-ings began to intensify. She remembered that her first experience of numbness was when she was five and her mother yelled at her for something she had not done. She knew that when she was angry and hated people, she felt very bad. And when she felt bad, she felt cut off from others and then would begin to feel numb and empty. But it was not only intense affect that was disorganizing, but any change or inconsistency in her environment. For example, if there was a change in her treatment plan, even the addition of something she had talked about and seemed to want, like a new privilege, such changes would immediately become exaggerated in a most grandiose manner. She would flush, get "goose bumps," giggle, and appear to be overstim-ulated, and at points like this needed a great deal of staff limitation and control in order to help her through the transition. At other times she not only felt numb, but did not feel alive, let alone stimulated. And she found that being angry and threatening and swearing at people was invigorating, not because it released tension, but because it made her feel real and alive, and the other person's response facilitated that.

Nancy demonstrated a need to have certain psychological functions provided externally by staff members, who served as self-objects, and she showed a capacity to utilize staff in this manner, something that not every delinquent demonstrates. The staff would help her fall asleep at night, the staff would help her organize her study hour, the staff would help her by supervising visits with her mother, the staff would provide limits for her when she confided that she felt like running or was on the verge of losing control. But, at the same time, if the staff misperceived what she was experiencing, she felt abandoned and isolated. She would begin to appear flat and feel numb. At these times, she was incapable of realizing how fast she was moving or what she was touching, a marked disturbance in proprioception. Yet, as Nancy progressed in treatment, she did not require the constant physical presence of an external support or self-object. The reminder that staff would be checking on her was adequate. For awhile she did not feel that her therapist existed between sessions, even though cognitively she knew that her therapist was in the hospital. When her therapist was on the unit and was watching her, she felt better and performed better, receiving support and nurturance from her "spotter." This remained an important issue at discharge, even though between sessions, the patient was able to picture herself talking to her therapist and would carry on many psychotherapy sessions in her head.

Parallel to the patient's experience of herself as a person, there are many personal issues that must be confronted by the staff in their work on the unit. A research and learning atmosphere must be established which provides staff with psychological growth, opportunities for introspection, support through countertransference crises, and personal gratification. Staff gratification cannot come from therapeutic success, but rather from the professional growth and development that occur when one is challenged, questioned, and supported in one's work. Nancy has proven for us to be a "special patient," not because she represents a therapeutic success, but rather because she has exemplified rather well problems we encounter in treatment and forced us to sharply conceptualize our methodology.

TIME

The perception of time and internalization of a sense of time are basic psychological skills, parts of the neutralizing and organizing fabric built up and elaborated during psychological development and manifesting themselves in relationship to both the impersonal and personal environment. The disturbed adolescent sees time as an adversary. Nancy had great difficulty moving from one interview or experience to another during the initial screening process, so much so that toward the end of the evaluation she became violent and had to be forcibly restrained. As a result, after she had been admitted to the unit, she was provided as much predictability as possible, particularly in terms of letting her know the schedules of her program and providing her time to prepare herself for changes. During her trip to the nearby hospital for medical testing, when the staff car did not arrive on time to pick her up, she became disorganized, was not able to contain herself, and ran away. Because time was a challenge to her and waiting was overstimulating, staff interactions initially were kept to no longer than five minutes in order not to overtax her capacities.

The disturbed teenager experiences time as an enemy, feeling adrift, unable to delay, without a schedule, and having no continuity with the past or anticipation of an existence in the future. Also, she is bored. Nancy complained that her treatment plan was changing too slowly. She expected that as changes were made in her treatment, she would feel better suddenly. She could not wait for good feelings to replace bad feelings. Whenever her therapist was not working on the unit, she felt bored, and wondered what she could do to fill the time. Yet, after awhile, she began to feel alive without contact with her therapist and experienced the therapist as existing even between sessions. This kind of experience indicated that Nancy was beginning to anticipate that she, too, could project herself into a future.

For many of our delinquents, there is no internal clock, and staff adhering to schedules and making announcements about times and changes in times serve as external pacemakers which someday become internal mechanisms. Certain times are particularly fraught with difficulty, like awakening or bedtime. After the death of her father, Nancy became particularly disturbed at night and needed a light on in her room for awhile because she feared being haunted by the spirit of her dead father. This is an unusually well-demarcated problem, but we have found that most teenagers need considerable help in de-escalating and beginning to calm and soothe themselves in anticipation of going to sleep. For many of them giving up the contact with reality that sleep entails is most frightening and disorganizing, and evening bedtime stories, hot chocolate, and a general lessening of activities on the unit in anticipation of bedtime are ways in which the evening staff can structure time comfortably.

SPACE

The disturbed delinquent's appreciation of space, internal and external, has been one of a diffuse void, with ill-defined boundaries, little if any definition of purpose, and repeated episodes of inappropriate use. After a few months of Nancy's hospitalization, her therapist left on vacation, and during this time a cookout on the hospital grounds was planned. The challenge to Nancy to master the extended space of this activity overwhelmed her and her school work began to deteriorate. She threatened teachers and failed to do her work. After it was decided that she would not participate in the cookout and she was helped to refocus back on the space of the unit and the school, she was not only able to return to school, but also deal with her therapist about the interruption in sessions.

Because of these deficiencies in the appreciation of and use of space, all space on the hospital treatment unit is defined very clearly at a level the adolescent can understand and tolerate. We believe strongly in the importance of private space for the individual adolescent, and work hard to help her appreciate the importance of her own room. To this end there is no unsupervised public or interpersonal space on our unit; space is either private or supervised. Such supervision, however, does not mean staff simply monitoring or watching; it implies the active participation by staff members with patients in the utilization of that space.

We try to teach our adolescents how they can use their rooms to withdraw from stimulating experiences and begin to calm themselves. There would be many times when a staff member would take Nancy to her room or encourage her to go to her room to calm down and to begin to think about what had just happened. After awhile she described how she felt that her room was a nursery and that she recognized that in many ways she was a baby who had yet to learn how to walk. On home visits, as she approached discharge, she prepared and decorated her room at home to her liking.

Only in a defined and structured space, a therapeutic milieu, can individual psychotherapy succeed.

THINGS

The adolescent brings to the hospital her patterns of relating to the material world, her possessions, tools, the things she uses or comes in contact with everyday, which are often laden with inner turmoil and chronic disorganization.

On one occasion Nancy had tried to kill herself on the unit, and as a precaution all dangerous objects and, indeed, much of her furniture were removed from her room. After awhile she began to talk in terms of the important role her furniture played in calming her and organizing her life for her. It seemed, at times, that her furniture was interchangeable with people and that when some of her furniture was gone, it was as if parts of her were missing. The delinquent's use of material objects reflects her attitudes about herself and her relationships with other people but more importantly it reflects something of her own psychopathology, explicitly focused on the nonhuman environment. When Nancy experienced numbness, she would slam her records or books down on the table, not only because she had lost proprioception and was not able to gauge how hard to put something down, but also because she was trying to use things most forcibly to regain some sense of feeling. If she could hit something or butt up against something, maybe she could once again feel like a person.

Nancy's inability to plan and organize would become particularly obvious in the Occupational Therapy shop. Late in her hospitalization, she said she planned, while home on a pass, to make a bookcase, and in the shop proceeded both to reach for the wood and to ask for the saw at the same time. When the occupational therapist stopped her and asked her what size bookcase she wanted to make and had she figured out the dimensions, she stopped and became enraged. She screamed that she knew what she wanted to do, but the staff member was getting in her way. She threw down the wood and stood rigidly, but then began to cry. Subsequently she talked about her intense desire to do things "by myself," and her fear that she wouldn't be able to do so.

Assessing this fear and other problems and intervening in the non-human environment, through leisure time activities, games and camping, all facilitate the development of psychological structure.

WORK WITH FAMILIES

Our work with families is designed to identify the genesis of the adolescent's structural pathology, to support the treatment process, and to facilitate a reentry into the family. It usually involves not formal family therapy sessions, except for the diagnostic phase and the reentry process, but rather individual casework, parents' group, and participatory visiting. Nancy's mother received a considerable amount of support through the weekly parents' group sessions; her relationship with Nancy had always been tempestuous and Nancy would frequently threaten and confront mother with screaming, sobbing, and demanding that she never return. The group would help her rehearse her dialog for her next visit with her daughter and support her in insisting that Nancy remain in the hospital treatment program despite her constant demands to be taken home. After awhile her mother became the program booster and would reassure new parents entering the group how fortunate they were to have their child hospitalized here. Her positive institutional alliance helped maintain her daughter in treatment. During visits, the ward staff tried to support the mother's resistance to Nancy's threats and demands to be discharged. This work also enabled mother to realize her narcissistic investment in her daughter, work she also did in individual casework. She did not comply with her daughter's demands and resisted her own urges to be merged with her daughter in a blissful symbiosis. With ward staff support, she terminated a tempestuous visit and insisted that her daughter stay in treatment. Such a confrontation was extremely painful to Nancy. She sobbed as she felt impotent in no longer being able to intimidate mother and as she grieved the loss of a hoped-for idealized union.

SCHOOL

Work in school is meant to be an academic, not a therapeutic, experience. Here the adolescent is expected to separate out personal conflicts and deficits and focus on the reality of the academic task. Even a disturbed adolescent has islands of conflict-free functioning, not imbricated with transference or psychological deficits. It is these areas of personality that are fostered in the "work" the adolescent does in school and in study hour. As already mentioned, one day early in her hospitalization, Nancy was having difficulty in math class. She asked the teacher for help but had to wait because the teacher was working with another student. When the teacher turned to help her, she became agitated and insisted that the teacher had never explained the material properly in the first place. She became more and more agitated, she said she would do no more work, and insisted on seeing the crisis teacher. She interrupted the crisis teacher several times, called the classroom teacher a liar, threatened to hit the staff, and was eventually returned to the unit. She had not been able to separate out her own hurt feelings from the classroom work at hand. But about five months later, despite the fact that she was moving into the throes of intense transference experiences in her psychotherapy, she could keep such work separate from her classroom activities. On one occasion, again in math, she was told of her errors on a test and asked to correct them. She made the same mistakes again, and informed the teacher that she couldn't see how she had really made an error. When the teacher

looked at the material in greater detail and found that the answer key
had been wrong, Nancy accepted her triumph calmly. At no point did
it appear that her feelings were hurt, and at no point did she become
enraged and threatening; she simply continued her work. These experiences in school help Nancy and others learn that despite overwhelming
stress and personal problems, including the stress of intensive psychotherapy, they can function in certain spheres without disruption, and
personal problems and emotional crises can be worked on in the appropriate situations.

AUTHORITY IN TREATMENT

There are many examples of charismatic individuals working successfully with disturbed adolescents. The adolescent needs an authority
to accept treatment and needs to idealize the therapist and the chief
of the unit. Such idealized authority supports the self system; it permits the unfolding of a narcissistic transference, and fosters the respect
and admiration necessary to a therapeutic alliance. Nancy was reassured that she could not plan her own therapy and that this would be
done by the team and the management committee. Throughout her
hospitalization she would show a wished-for special relationship with
the chief of the unit whose direction and confrontation also served to
keep her nose to the therapeutic grindstone. At termination, she wondered who would perform this function for her and only later will we
know whether or not this idealized authority has been replaced by
internal standards and values.

INTEGRATING MILIEU AND INDIVIDUAL
PSYCHOTHERAPY

Most hospital treatment programs that deal with adolescent behavior attempt to convert behavior or "acting out" into some kind of
internalized conflict. One assumes that the behavior is symbolic of
underlying psychic conflict or that it represents a discharge defense
against the experiencing of such psychic conflict. In Freud's sense this
is true "acting out," behaving instead of remembering.

Others would take the position that the delinquent or antisocial "acting out" behavior is not necessarily expressive symbolically of a conflict, because, in fact, there exist deficiencies of psychic structure. In fact, some patients may have regressed to a stage of psychological functioning in which they are not capable of distinguishing between inside and outside, between thought or feeling and action. So the task of the hospital program is either to convert true neurotic acting out behavior into internalized neurotic symptomatology, or to provide externally sufficient psychic structure so that psychological deficits are compensated for and the person can achieve in the hospital setting a homeostasis without using alloplastic behavior to reestablish his psychological equilibrium.

In either event, the primary task in treating the delinquent adolescent is to help him develop a capacity for self-observation and introspection. In many instances, the adolescent defends against this process because introspection leads to psychological pain, the sadness and grief of the depressed delinquent, the empty devastation of the borderline delinquent, or the hurt feelings of the narcissistic delinquent. Other adolescents have no capacity to experience affect or think and fantasize, but move immediately from stimulus to behavioral response; they need to learn to delay and concurrently to think about their internal psychological world. This task characteristically confronts the impulsive delinquent whose cognitive style and way of experiencing the world are devoid of introspection, not defensively, but rather developmentally.

And so it is that staff members serve as external egos or self-objects, providing externally those psychological functions which the delinquent lacks internally, and helping to set limits on his behavior, to delay, to plan, to anticipate, to soothe himself, to modulate the intensity of his experiences, to look inside himself, to identify affect, to assuage hurt feelings, to organize fragments, and to clear up confusion.

Virtually any adolescent, regardless of socioeconomic status or race, is capable of participating in meaningful insight oriented psychotherapy. He may need to be taught how to introspect, how to identify affect, he may need help in focusing on those behaviors which are indicative of psychological conflict or psychological deficiencies, and may need help in tolerating, modulating, and mastering the intensity of a transference experience—but he can gain insight. It may not be insight into the roots of his oedipal competition, though that, indeed, is possible, but it may be insight into the fact that when he tries to hit someone, it is because he is angry. When he is angry, it is because his feelings have been hurt, and frequently his feelings are hurt because he anticipates that other people will view him and treat him the same way as he views himself—worthless.

To take the position that certain delinquents, because of their cultural backgrounds, cannot participate in this kind of psychotherapy, which is erroneously labeled "white middle class," is to deprive many adolescents of the very help they need, and is indeed a subtle, or perhaps not so subtle, form of racism and class discrimination.

Ultimately the kind of psychological structure building and personality restructuring that we hope to achieve in our program is accomplished in the individual psychotherapy relationship. However, initially delinquents are not ready for psychotherapy, and need a period of preparation.

In our own program the ward staff is trained to identify those deviant behaviors which indicate that the delinquent, as he relates to the basic structure of the hospital program, is experiencing some kind of psychological breakdown or conflict. Such behaviors are then targeted and the staff member attempts to work with the adolescent, insofar as the adolescent is psychologically capable, to try to understand the meaning of the behavior. With some, that may represent simply the recognition or acceptance of the idea that something went wrong. With others it may be considerably more complex and involve the understanding that something of the clinical transference is being displaced into the hospital milieu. In any event, the ward staff performs extremely important preliminary and preparatory functions in helping the adolescent begin to recognize that all behavior has meaning and can be understood psychologically.

This is similar to Winnicott's (1958) statement that in the treatment of the antisocial tendency, child care and placement must precede psychoanalysis. At the same time, the therapist is advised of certain occurrences on the unit, and both patient and therapist are expected to spend some time together talking about these issues. Traditionally, of course, the psychoanalyst holds that he is to deal with the material brought to him by his patient. In our experience, teenagers rarely bring their concerns into the office verbally and, indeed, frequently express their problems behaviorally. Our delinquents also express their problems behaviorally on the unit, viewing the unit as an extension of the office and the therapy session, and fully intending that the omnipotent, omniscient, or merged therapist be aware of and deal with all behavior. Now, on the one hand, one could view this as an unrealistic, narcissistic transference expectation not to be gratified. But on the other hand, we are dealing with structurally deficient adolescents who have little capacity to contain their psychological work within the confines of a treatment hour.

Were they able to do so, these adolescents would not be inpatients, but would be capable of engaging in outpatient psychotherapy. As a result, we do expect patient and therapist to deal with certain kinds of targeted behavior in the treatment setting. This is reinforced by interventions by the ward staff, by therapists' focusing on significant behaviors, and in the weekly team meetings which attempt to integrate data from other observational points of view with the data of the individual psychotherapy sessions. In a weekly progress review each teenager's behavior is reviewed with him in the presence of the therapist, and he is reminded in the presence of the therapist of the psychological work that needs to be accomplished.

The therapist needs to have a certain amount of administrative control in working with the delinquent, but we have found that giving the therapist absolute control over the patient's treatment is unrealistic and fraught with considerable difficulty. Consequently, our therapists are part of a team, subject to the direction of the chief of the unit, who plan and administer the hospital management of the adolescent delinquent. The therapist is viewed as part of the administrative decision-making process who, like the parent, is capable of exerting some control over the adolescent's life. At the same time, the adolescent is not presented with the myth that all treatment occurs in the individual therapy session. Now we could expect, of course, that as treatment progresses, the individual therapy becomes more and more important.

But initially the kinds of interchanges and confrontations, limit-setting, and feedback, and attempts to help the adolescent introspect which occur daily in the living unit, shop, the gymnasium, or school, lay the groundwork for a meaningful individual psychotherapy experience.

The philosophy and process of treatment with delinquent adolescents are complex. One must be creative and flexible in understanding the delinquent act. One must work diligently to establish a therapeutic alliance with an adolescent, capitalizing on those psychological functions which the adolescent so desperately craves in the treatment relationship and not being embarrassed by the adolescent's idealization or frustrated by his negativism. One must understand the nature of the adolescent's grandiosity and tendencies to idealize or deidealize the significant adults in his life. And one must provide a supportive, safe, and therapeutic milieu in which individual therapy is sown, nurtured, and allowed to bear fruit.

The task is arduous, but the harvest, in those good seasons when it occurs, can be bountiful.

References

AICHHORN, A. (1925). *Wayward Youth*. New York: Viking Press, 1935.
———. (1964). *Delinquency and Child Guidance—Selected Papers*. New York: International Universities Press.
ALEXANDER, F., and STAUB, H. (1931). *The Criminal, the Judge and the Public: A Psychological Analysis*. New York: Collier Books, 1956.
ALLPORT, G. W. (1960). "The Open System in Personality Theory." *J. Abnorm. Soc. Psychol.*, 61:301-311.
BAITTLE, B., and KOBRIN, S. (1964). "On the Relationship of a Characterological Type of Delinquent to the Milieu," *Psychiatry*, 27:6-16.
BALINT, M. (1955). "Friendly Expanses—Horrid Empty Spaces," *International Journal Psychoanalysis*, 36:225-241.
BECKETT, P. G. S. (1965). *Adolescents Out of Step*. Detroit: Wayne State University Press.
BERGLER, E., and ROHEIM, G. (1946). "Psychology of Time Perception," *Psychoanalytic Quarterly*, 15:190-206.
BETTELHEIM, B. (1974). *A Home for the Heart*. New York: Alfred A. Knopf.
BIRD, B. (1957). "A Specific Peculiarity of Acting Out," *Journal American Psychoanalytic Association*, 5:630-647.
BLOCH, D. A. (1952). "The Delinquent Integration," *Psychiatry*, 15:297-303.
BLOS, P. (1962). *On Adolescence*. New York: Free Press.
———. (1966). "The Concept of Acting Out in Relation to the Adolescent Process," in *A Developmental Approach to Problems of Acting Out*, (ed.) E. N. Rexford, New York: International Universities Press, Inc., pp. 118-136.
———. (1967). "The Second Individuation Process of Adolescence," *Psychoanalytic Study of the Child*, 22:162-186.
———. (1972). "The Function of the Ego Ideal in Adolescence," *Psychoanalytic Study of the Child*, 27:93-97.
BONAPARTE, M. (1940). "Time and the Unconscious," *International Journal Psychoanalysis*, 21:427-468.
DULIT, E. (1972). "Adolescent Thinking à la Piaget: The Formal Stage," *Journal of Youth and Adolescence*, 1:281-301.
EASSON, W. M. (1969). *The Severely Disturbed Adolescent*. New York: International Universities Press.

283

ERIKSON, E. H. (1950). *Childhood and Society.* New York: W. W. Norton and Co. (Second Edition, 1963).

———. (1959). *Identity and the Life Cycle, Psychological Issues, #1.* New York: International Universities Press.

FLAVELL, J. H. (1963). *The Developmental Psychology of Jean Piaget.* Princeton: Van Nostrand.

FREUD, A. (1946). *The Ego and the Mechanisms of Defense.* New York: International Uiiversities Press, Inc.

———. (1958). "Adolescence," *Psychoanalytic Study of the Child,* 13:255-278.

———. (1965). *Normality and Pathology in Childhood: Assessment of Development.* New York: International Universities Press, Inc.

FREUD, S. (1905). *Three Essays on the Theory of Sexuality. Standard Edition* (ed.) J. Strachey. Vol. 7. London: The Hogarth Press, 1958.

———. (1921). *Group Psychology and the Analysis of the Ego. Standard Edition.* (ed.) J. Strachey. Vol. 18. London: The Hogarth Press, 1958.

FRIEDLANDER, K. (1960). *The Psycho-Analytical Approach to Juvenile Delinquency: Theory, Case Studies, Treatment.* New York: International Universities Press.

FROMM-REICHMANN, F. (1959). "Problems of Therapeutic Management in a Psychoanalytic Hospital," in *Psychoanalysis and Psychotherapy.* Chicago: University of Chicago Press.

GLOVER, E. (1950). "On the Desirability of Isolating a 'Functional' (Psychosomatic) Group of Delinquent Disorders," *British Journal of Delinquency,* 1:104-112.

———. (1960). *The Roots of Crime. Selected Papers on Psychoanalysis.* Vol. II. New York: International Universities Press.

GOLDBERG, A. (1971). "On Waiting," *International Journal of Psychoanalysis,* 52:413-421.

———, and RUBIN, B. (1970). "A Method of Pacification of the Psychotic Excited State: The Use of the Hospital as a Transitional Object," *Comprehensive Psychiatry,* 2:450-456.

HAMADY, B., and SWAN, D. (1973). "The Therapeutic Use of the Room," unpublished manuscript, presented at the 1973 Illinois State Psychiatric Institute Nursing Conference, Chicago, Illinois.

HOLMES, D. J. (1964). *The Adolescent in Psychotherapy.* Boston: Little, Brown, and Company.

HOLMES, M. J., and WERNER, J. A. (1966). *Psychiatric Nursing in a Therapeutic Community.* New York: Collier MacMillan.

JOHNSON, A. M., and SZUREK, S. A. (1952). "The Genesis of Antisocial Acting Out in Children and Adults," *Psychoanalytic Quarterly,* 21:323-343.

KAYTON, L. (1972). "The Relationship of the Vampire Legend to Schizophrenia," *J. Youth and Adolescence,* 1:303-314.

KERNBERG, O. (1975). *Borderline Conditions and Psychological Narcissism.* New York: Jason Aronson, Inc.

KOHUT, H. (1971). *The Analysis of the Self.* New York: International Universities Press.

———. (1976). "Creativeness, Charisma, Group-Psychology. Reflections on Freud's Self Analysis," in *Freud: Fusion of Science and Humanism* (ed.) J. Gedo and G. H. Pollock, *Psychological Issues,* #34/35. New York: International Universities Press, pp. 379-425.

———. (1978). "Discussion of 'On the Adolescent Process as a Transformation of the Self' (Wolf, Gedo, and Terman)" in *The Search for the Self*, (ed.) P. H. Ornstein, Vol. 2, pp. 659-662, New York: International Universities Press, Inc.

LION, J. R., LEVENBERG, L. P., and STRANGE, R. E. (1972). "Restraining the Violent Patient," *Journal of Psychiatric Nursing and Mental Health Services*, March-April, pp. 9-11.

LYMAN, S. M. and SCOTT, M. V. (1967). "Territoriality: A Neglected Sociological Dimension." *Social Problems*, XV.

MAHLER, M. S., PINE, F., and BERGMAN, A. (1975). *The Psychological Birth of the Human Infant*. New York: Basic Books, Inc.

MANN, D. (1976). *Intervening with Convicted Serious Juvenile Offenders*. Santa Monica, Calif.: Rand Corp.

MARCUSE, D. J. (1967). "The 'Army' Incident: The Psychology of Uniforms and Their Abolition on an Adolescent Ward." *Psychiatry*, 30:350-375.

MAROHN, J. K. (1977). "Integrating Psychotherapy and Academic Functioning —Use of the Crisis Teacher in a Hospital School," unpublished manuscript, presented at the Annual Meeting of the American Society for Adolescent Psychiatry, Toronto, Canada.

MAROHN, R. C. (1969). "The Similarity of Therapy and Supervisory Themes," *Int. J. Group Psychother.*, 19:176-184.

———. (1970). "The Therapeutic Milieu as an Open System," *Archives General Psychiatry*, 22:360-364.

———. (1974). "Trauma and the Delinquent," *Adolescent Psychiatry*, 3:354-361.

———. (1977). "The 'Juvenile Imposter': Some Thoughts on Narcissism and the Delinquent," *Adolescent Psychiatry*, 5:186-212.

———, OFFER, D., and OSTROV, E. (1971). "Juvenile Delinquents View Their Impulsivity," *American Journal of Psychiatry*, 128:418-423.

———, DALLE-MOLLE, D., OFFER, D., and OSTROV, E. (1973). "A Hospital Riot: Its Determinants and Implications for Treatment," *American Journal of Psychiatry*, 130:631-636.

———, OFFER, D., OSTROV, E., and TRUJILLO, J. (1979). "Four Psychodynamic Types of Hospitalized Juvenile Delinquents," *Adolescent Psychiatry*, 7:466-483.

MASTERSON, J. (1967). *The Psychiatric Dilemma of Adolescence*. Boston: Little, Brown and Company.

———. (1972). *Treatment of the Borderline Adolescent: A Developmental Approach*. New York: John Wiley and Sons.

———, and RINSLEY, D. B. (1975). "The Borderline Syndrome: The Role of the Mother in the Genesis and Psychic Structure of the Borderline Personality," *International Journal of Psychoanalysis*, 56:163-177.

MEEKS, J. (1971). *The Fragile Alliance*. Baltimore: Williams and Wilkins, Co.

MORSE, W. C. (1965). "The Crisis Teacher," in *Conflict in the Classroom*, (ed.) N. J. Long, W. C. Morse, and R. G. Newman. Belmont, California: Wadsworth Publishing Co., pp. 251-254.

OFFER, D. (1969). *The Psychological World of the Teenager*. New York: Basic Books, Inc.

———, and OFFER, J. B. (1975). *From Teenage to Young Manhood: A Psychological Study*. New York: Basic Books, Inc.

———, MAROHN, R. C., and OSTROV, E. (1979). *The Psychological World of the Juvenile Delinquent*. New York: Basic Books, Inc.

PEARSON, G. (1958). *Adolescence and the Conflict of Generations*. New York: W. W. Norton and Co.

PIAGET, J. (1969). "The Intellectual Development of the Adolescent," in *Adolescence, Psychosocial Perspectives*, (ed.) G. Caplan and S. Lebovici. New York: Basic Books, pp. 22-26.

REDL, F. (1966). *When We Deal With Children*. New York: Free Press.

————. (1972). "Impact of Game Ingredients" in *Children Away from Home*, (ed.) J. K. Whittaker and A. E. Trieschman, New York: Aldine Atherton, pp. 321-364.

————, and WINEMAN, D. (1957). *The Aggressive Child*. Glencoe, Ill: The Free Press.

RINSLEY, D. (1971). "Theory and Practice of Intensive Residential Treatment of Adolescents," *Adolescent Psychiatry*, 1:479-509.

SABONIS, L. S. (1974). "The Progression of Interventions into Violent Behavior in the In-Patient Setting," unpublished manuscript, presented at the Illinois State Psychiatric Institute Nursing Conference, Chicago, Illinois.

SCHWARTZ, G. and PUNTIL, J. E. (1972). *Summary and Policy Implications of the Youth and Society in Illinois Reports*. Chicago: Institute for Juvenile Research.

SEARLES, H. (1960). *The Non-Human Environment in Normal Development and Schizophrenia*. New York: International Universities Press, Inc.

SKLANSKY, M. A., SILVERMAN, S. W., and RABICHOW, H. W. (1969). *The High School Adolescent*. New York: Association Press.

SLAVSON, S. R. (1965). *Reclaiming the Delinquent*. New York: The Free Press.

STANTON, A. H. and SCHWARTZ, M. S. (1954). *The Mental Hospital*. New York: Basic Books, Inc.

Time Magazine. (1977). "Youth Crime Plague," July 11, 1977, pp. 18-28.

TRIESCHMAN, A. E., WHITTAKER, J. K., and BRENDTRO, L. K. (1969). *The Other 23 Hours*. Chicago: Aldine Press.

VON BERTALANFFY, L. (1962). "General System Theory: A Critical Review," *General Systems*, 7:1-20.

WEXLER, M. (1951). "Structural Problem in Schizophrenia," *International Journal of Psychoanalysis*, 32:157-166.

WINNICOTT, D. W. (1958). "The Antisocial Tendency," in *Collected Papers*. New York: Basic Books, Inc.

————. (1973). "Delinquency as a Sign of Hope," *Adolescent Psychiatry*, 2:364-371.

WOLF, E. S., GEDO, J. E., and TERMAN, D. M. (1972). "On the Adolescent Process as a Transformation of the Self," *Journal of Youth and Adolescence*, 1:257-272.

Index

Abstract thinking, 9, 260
Acting out, viii, 13, 71, 268, 278
  aggressive/sexual, 132
  antisocial, 58
  and depression, 113-14
  and group dynamics, 42
  and treatment, 11, 22, 41
Adolescent Progress Review (APR),
    38, 39, 96, 192, 200, 208-209,
    211-12, 215-17, 266
Age:
  appropriate tasks for, 218
  and crime, xiv
Aggravated assault, xiv
Aggression, xiii, 28-29, 106-107
  acting out of, 132
  denial of, 56
  phallic, 83
  and play, 80, 234, 236
  verbal/physical, 210-11
Aichhorn, A., 11, 12, 13, 26, 283n.
Alcohol use, 72, 169-70, 256
Alexander, F., 12, 283n.
Alloplastic behavior, 85, 279
Allport, G. W., 40, 283n.
Ambition, 260
American Society for Adolescent Psy-
    chiatry, 217n.
Antisocial behavior, 58, 81, 278-79
Anxiety, 25, 48, 278-79
  of fusion, 71
  in hospital schedule, 34
  intolerance of, 73
  and living space, 145-46
  minimization of, 15

and object world, 160
  in occupational therapy, 231-32
  and psychotherapy, 19
  and self-object relations, 81-83
  and separation, 115-16, 159
  and transference, 70
  about treatment, 44
  and violence, 205
Approach-avoidance behavior, 131-32
Arrests, incidence of, xiv
Arson, xiv, 17
Asceticism, 5
Assault, 17
Authority in treatment, 278
Autonomy as deprivation, 260

Baittle, B., 14, 283n.
Balint, B., 117, 283n.
Beckett, P. G. S., 40, 283n.
Bedtime routine in hospitals, 139-41
Behavioral model, 28
Behavior modification, 206
Bergler, E., 112, 283n.
Bettelheim, B., 119, 283n.
Biological patterns, 29-30
Bird, B., 13, 283n.
Bloch, D. A., 15, 283n.
Blos, P., 6-9, 14, 78, 283n.
Body territories in hospitals, 126. *See
    also* Space
Bonaparte, M., 113, 283n.
Borderlines, xix, 6, 7, 9, 23. *See also*
    Empty borderline behavior; De-
    pressed borderline behavior
Boundaries, personal:

287